SOVEREIGNTY
FOR
SURVIVAL

SOVEREIGNTY
FOR
SURVIVAL

AMERICAN ENERGY DEVELOPMENT

AND INDIAN SELF-DETERMINATION

JAMES ROBERT ALLISON III

Yale UNIVERSITY PRESS
New Haven and London

Published with assistance from the foundation established in memory of Philip Hamilton McMillan of the Class of 1894, Yale College.

Yale University Press books may be purchased in quantity for educational, business, or promotional use. For information, please e-mail sales.press@yale.edu (U.S. office) or sales@yaleup.co.uk (U.K. office).

Set in Sabon type by Newgen North America.
Printed in the United States of America.

Library of Congress Control Number: 2015933806
ISBN: 978-0-300-20669-2

A catalogue record for this book is available from the British Library.

This paper meets the requirements of ANSI/NISO Z39.48-1992 (Permanence of Paper).

10 9 8 7 6 5 4 3 2 1

Contents

Acknowledgments

I have never understood why authors wait until the end to thank the most important people. I vowed not to make that mistake. Nothing I do would be possible without Julie. She married a promising lawyer and ended up with a struggling academic. Most would rank that a downgrade; she has not. Julie remains incredibly supportive of my passions and has patiently provided perspective when I needed it most. This project is dedicated to her and our amazing young sons, Aidan and Axel. Thanks, too, to all our family members for sticking with us. Our decisions may not have always made the most sense, but they have made us happy. Thank you for understanding.

I have been fortunate to have a diverse array of advisers who have met my every intellectual, professional, and social need. Sara Pritchard at Montana State University (and now Cornell) graciously introduced me to the world of academia and patiently guided me through the thicket of environmental historiography. Edmund Russell at the University of Virginia (and now Kansas) is the best adviser in the business. Not only does Ed rigorously poke and prod the intellectual content of his students' work, but he dedicates enormous energy to ensuring we know the professional rules of the road. From conference talks, to job cover letters, to book proposals, and more, he has demystified one of the most arcane professions known to man. I am very lucky to have him on my side. Christian McMillen at the University of Virginia is quite simply the academic I want to be. His scholarship is unassailable; its rigor matched only by the thoughtful and creative narratives Christian constructs. He has pored over this manuscript more times than is fair to ask of anyone, and any improvements are largely to his credit. Most important, Christian's priorities are always where they should be, a lesson I will not forget. I consider them all great friends and giants in their fields.

As for future academic greats, I have met, socialized with, and studied with many of them. My graduate student cohort provided inspiration and support throughout this long and winding process. It started with the "Gang of Four" in Bozeman, Montana—Jerry Jessee, Megan Raby, Mike Wise, and myself—but certainly included Bob Gardner and Brad Snow as well. In Virginia, the list is long thanks to Ed Russell's community-building efforts. Our "Russell Lab" was a supportive rock in an otherwise isolating ABD world. Many thanks go to Bart Elmore, Thomas Finger, Leif Frederickson, Philip Herrington, Laura Kolar, Andrew McGee, Katy Shively Meier, Eric Stoykovich, and Stephen Macekura. In particular, Stephen and Brent Cebul provided great friendship and desperately needed non-academic banter. Thanks for keeping me sane.

Many supporting institutions made this project possible. Montana State University's Research Enhancement Award funded my initial journeys to the reservations of southeastern Montana. At the University of Virginia, numerous grants from the History Department, the Raven Society, and the Bankard Fund for Political Economy allowed me to return to the American West, to spend summers in both dingy archives and vibrant tribal communities. A fellowship from the Cody Institute for Western American Studies supported oral history interviews on the Crow and Northern Cheyenne Reservations, and funds from the Charles Redd Center for Western Studies carried me to archives across the Southwest. A residential fellowship at the Hagley Museum and Library in Wilmington, Delaware, provided key insights into the murky world of global energy development, particularly the coal business, and the American Society for Legal History's Cromwell Fellowship helped me discern the legal implications of the energy tribes' struggle to control their resources. Finally, my year as the Sara Shallenberger

Brown Fellow in Environmental Writing at the University of Virginia's Brown Residential College provided an incredible space to bring it all together. The final chapters of this book were drafted on the grounds of James Monroe's law office and family farm. Although my current digs at Christopher Newport University cannot match the grandeur of the former president's residence, neither can the warmth of my new colleagues be surpassed. It is a welcoming community to call home, and I am grateful for their support during the revisions.

Of course, along the way there were dozens of archivists, librarians, and generally helpful folks who assisted me. A few stand out. Bill Bryan was instrumental in getting me "inside" the Northern Cheyenne revolt that is at the center of this book. He introduced me to Marie Sanchez, who patiently walked me through the concerns of her community and the brave actions she and her fellow Northern Cheyenne took decades ago. On the Crow Reservation, dozens of people opened up to me about past coal debates and current mining concerns. More than any other, though, Faith Bad Bear Bartlett, the former archivist at Little Bighorn College on the Crow Reservation, made this study possible. Faith was an imposing woman. She once told me she played high school football with the boys in southeastern Montana and I believed her. But over the course of numerous visits to her tiny archive in Crow Agency, this intimidating figure gradually welcomed me into her records, her community, and even her home. This story could not be told without her. She is missed and greatly appreciated.

Introduction

IN THE SPRING of 1973, in the heart of the same Powder River Country of Montana where George Armstrong Custer met his death a century earlier, a modern-day Indian revolution erupted. Much like the nineteenth-century conflict sparked by white prospectors seeking gold in the sacred Black Hills of Dakota, the twentieth-century version featured an impassioned revolt against the incessant intrusions of non-Indians hoping to extract precious minerals. Also as in the earlier conflict, Indian resistance was fueled by fear that losing control over an indigenous land base would produce the end of the People, erasing the unique social customs and cultural values that distinguished their group from others. Survival once again hung in the balance. And as in the earlier conflict, this revolt would fundamentally alter the relationship between the federal government and Native American tribes.

There were, of course, important differences. For one, rather than seeking yellow gold in the Black Hills, white prospectors during the 1970s desired the "black gold" of the Yellowstone Country known as low-sulfur, subbituminous coal. Changing patterns in world energy production and domestic consumption following World War II had combined with new environmental legislation during the early 1970s to transform this once overlooked energy source into a highly valuable commodity. And vast quantities of this desirable resource happened to lie tantalizingly close to the surface of the Northern Cheyenne and Crow Reservations in southeastern Montana. To access this coal, non-Indians once again worked through and with the federal government. But rather than employing military force, as was done during the nineteenth century, multinational companies exploited a broken and outdated legal regime that sought to promote the development of western resources at the expense of tribal sovereignty, ecological health, and simple equity.

Although the tactics differed, the initial results of this late twentieth-century grab for Indian resources were comparable to nineteenth-century efforts. By 1973, energy firms had gained control of hundreds of thousands of acres of Indian land and millions more were threatened. On the Northern Cheyenne and Crow Reservations alone, the combined acreage opened for mining exceeded 600,000 acres, allowing energy companies to prospect over half the Northern Cheyenne's total land mass. It is no surprise, then, that Indian leaders such as the Northern Cheyenne's John Woodenlegs drew parallels to their tribes' nineteenth-century battles. As Woodenlegs explained, "Our Cheyenne people fought hard to be allowed to live in Montana. Our whole history has been a struggle for survival. The impact of uncontrolled coal development could finish us off."[1]

But unlike the tragic, if also heroic, nineteenth-century battles that relegated Northern Plains tribes to small parcels of their once vast homelands, circumscribing their control over daily activities and all but eliminating the tribes' political sovereignty, the postwar contest ultimately expanded tribal powers. It left Indians better positioned to capitalize on their abundant natural resources, if they chose to do so. This story, then, is not another romantic account celebrating valiant but largely unsuccessful fights for freedom on the Northern Plains. It is, instead, a powerful tale of tribes becoming skilled negotiators, sophisticated energy developers, expert land managers, and more effective governing bodies. In this story, Indians worked meticulously to increase their understanding of the complicated legal, political, and economic mechanisms governing their lands and created a sovereign space where tribes decide the fate of their resources. These tribal governments asserted control over reservation resources to ensure their communities' survival. And the story begins in the same remote corner of southeastern Montana where a century earlier the Northern Cheyenne and Sioux dealt the United States military its most crushing Indian defeat.

At its most essential, what happened on the Northern Plains in the 1970s was that energy tribes—those American Indian groups possessing substantial energy resources—expanded their governments' *capacity* to manage reservation land, and as a result, there came a belated recognition of the tribes' legal *authority* to govern communal resources. Indian people seized the skills necessary to protect their sovereignty because sovereignty was crucial to protecting tribal lifeways and land. To accomplish this, energy tribes had to first dismantle a century-old legal regime built on the premise of inherent tribal sovereignty but corrupted with an ideology of Indian inferiority. As far back as the 1830s, the Supreme Court had articulated a seemingly expansive view of tribal sovereignty that should have afforded Indian groups control over their own affairs. In *Worcester v. Georgia* (1832), for instance, Chief Justice John Marshall explained, "The Indian nations had always been considered as distinct, independent, political communities, retaining their original natural rights, as the undisputed possessors of the soil, from time immemorial." President Andrew Jackson's infamous retort, however, that "the decision of the Supreme Court has fell still born" set the tone for how local, state, and federal authorities would respect this and other early holdings favorable to Indian rights. With few exceptions, nineteenth-century government officials and non-state actors ignored federal case law, enacted statutes overriding judicial decisions, or reinterpreted Marshall's opinions to eviscerate their holdings. Whites desired Indian land and resources, and they'd be damned if an impotent federal judiciary would stop them.[2]

To justify this taking of indigenous lands, nineteenth-century Americans constructed complicated and evolving ideas about Indians' inferior capacity to manage their own affairs. Early, ambivalent views of Native Americans as either noble savages or ignoble beasts rendered eastern tribes beyond the pale of Euro-American civilization, supporting an Indian removal policy thinly veiled as a humanitarian mission to protect unprepared Indians from encroaching American settlers. These efforts to separate a supposedly inferior people gradually gave way by midcentury to more benevolent, if misguided, assimilation policies designed to indoctrinate Indians with the civilizing values of settled agriculture and Protestantism. By the end of the century, however, the dominant conception had changed once again, as pseudo-scientific racial theories emerged to challenge the efficacy of this cultural uplift program, claiming race permanently relegated Indians to the periphery of American society. Discouraged by the persistence of Indian culture, eastern policy makers gladly handed over responsibility for "the Indian problem" to western politicians, who employed more "realistic" views of Indians' inability to evolve in order to justify an imperial land policy. Recast as people doomed by their race, Indians now became "assimilated" through industrial education, federal wardship, partial citizenship, and the loss of more land and resources.[3]

The "Indian New Deal" of the 1930s supposedly changed all this. Orchestrated by the social crusader John Collier, whom Franklin Roosevelt appointed commissioner of Indian Affairs in 1933, the federal government set about reversing its Indian policy of the past 150 years. Collier ended the disastrous program of allotting tribal lands to individual Indians—which had also opened "surplus" areas to white settlers—and sought to empower tribal governments to protect communal holdings. As we will see, however, Collier himself was not immune to paternalistic assumptions of Indian inferiority. The scion of a prominent southern family, Collier turned from his capitalist roots to fight for the preservation of Indian culture because he believed it offered vital lessons in communal living to a spiritually bankrupt, individualistic America. Still, Collier's Progressive faith often overrode his benevolent intentions. Under his tenure, the Office of Indian Affairs constructed a legal regime that gave tribal governments some tools to protect their land base yet also ensured that decisions over how to manage reservation assets remained largely in the hands of federal experts.[4]

Nowhere was this Progressive, paternalistic impulse more evident than in the laws governing Indian minerals. Prior to the 1930s, a hodgepodge of narrow and often conflicting statutes left the development of these resources in disarray. Collier and his colleagues within the Department of the Interior sought to provide a uniform system for Indian mineral development, but they differed in approaches. In particular, a young assistant solicitor named Felix Cohen resurrected John Marshall's early nineteenth-century opinions on inherent tribal sovereignty to advocate for tribal governments making their own development decisions, free of federal influence. For Collier, however, the risk of allowing unprepared tribal leaders to develop reservation resources by engaging in the cutthroat world of industrial capitalism proved too much. Instead, the Office of Indian Affairs adopted an approach used for public minerals: federal officials would survey reservation lands, judiciously select tracts for development, and then require competitive bidding to determine which mining companies could prospect and lease Indian minerals. Tribes had to consent to the extraction of their minerals, but federal law gave them no specific authority to develop these resources themselves. The regime fit Collier's twin goals perfectly. Federal officials would help tribes develop reservation economies to support their communities, and in doing so they would insulate indigenous lifeways from capitalism's divisive influence.[5]

It was within this legal context that most tribes first encountered multinational energy companies seeking to extract reservation minerals to feed America's post–World War II energy demands. Driven by stubborn ideologies that cast doubt upon Indian capacity for managing tribal resources, statutory law failed to provide explicit authority for tribes to develop their own resources. Instead, Native Americans were forced to rely on their federal trustees, who had been tasked with surveying reservation land and selecting appropriate tracts for development. These officials, however, were completely unequipped to do so. The results were predictable. Energy firms, not federal agents, surveyed Indian reservations, proposed which areas to open for development, and then secured permits to prospect and mine. They also accomplished this under a veil of secrecy, careful not to attract competition from other developers that would drive up the price of Indian minerals. By 1973, energy companies had opened millions of acres of Indian land to prospecting and mining, yet tribal governments had collected miniscule payments for this privilege.

That is, until the Northern Cheyenne took action to ensure the survival of the tribe. Located at the epicenter of a booming new trade in western, low-sulfur coal, Cheyenne tribal members saw the grandiose scale of mining proposed for their reservation and envisioned hordes of non-Indian coal miners descending on their lands, disrupting the social customs and cultural norms that sustained their unique indigenous community. Many Cheyenne lamented the potential environmental impacts of massive strip mines, but far more feared becoming minorities on their own reservation. Tribal members of all stripes thus mobilized to fight for what they believed to be their tribe's survival, organizing a grassroots campaign to protest potential mining that prompted tribal leaders to take legal actions to protect the reservation. Here, the tide of energy companies exploiting Indian minerals turned.

What follows is a "movement history" that explains how this small group of American Indians organized to halt a specific mining project they viewed as a threat to their indigenous community and then mobilized similarly situated energy tribes into a national coalition to educate tribal leaders and demand changes to federal law. The tale begins in Lame Deer, Montana, but travels quickly to the adjacent Crow Reservation, then to reservations and courtrooms across the West, corporate boardrooms in the East, federal agency headquarters in Washington, D.C., and ultimately, the United States Congress. The Northern Cheyenne and the Crow tribes are featured prominently, but this is not a tribal history. These two groups were the first to successfully challenge reservation energy projects, thus a tribal-level investigation is warranted into the reasons why these communities, and not others, were able to halt mining until their governments controlled reservation resources. Such an analysis is provided, as is an explanation of how heated intratribal fights over mining wrought important changes within the Northern Cheyenne and Crow communities. But what happened after these tribes asserted control over reservation mining had a far greater impact on tribal sovereignty nationwide. The explanation for that sea change in federal Indian law is the true burden of this book. By organizing disparate energy tribes into a national coalition focused on increasing tribal capacity to govern reservation land, the efforts begun in southeast Montana ultimately delivered a new legal regime—anchored by the 1982 Indian Mineral Development Act—that recognized tribal, not federal, control over reservation development.

Scholars of Native America should have little trouble fitting this remarkable tale into the broader trajectory of federal Indian policy at the close of the twentieth century. After all, the 1970s began with President Richard Nixon publicly rebuking the existing Indian policy of "Termination," which sought to end the government's special trust relationship with Indian tribes, and proclaiming "a new era in which the Indian future is determined by Indian acts and Indian decisions" rather than federal agencies. Labeling this new policy "Indian Self-Determination," the president affirmed his goal was not to assimilate Indian people into the larger American mass, but to empower tribal governments so that they may "strengthen the Indian's sense of autonomy without threatening his sense of community." The move fit clearly within Nixon's burgeoning New Federalism philosophy to transfer responsibility and power for social welfare from federal to local governments. With respect to Native Americans, Nixon also sought to end what many viewed as an unhealthy dependence on the federal government. For American Indians who had been clamoring for more control over their lives and land since the reservation system began in the mid-nineteenth century, the message could hardly have been more welcomed. These people had never stopped working to determine their own fate, but now the president provided rhetorical cover for their actions. A policy window to effectuate real change had opened.[6]

Yet despite the lavish attention paid to Nixon's message by both contemporary observers and historians, the self-determination policy was not self-executing. There was no sudden transfer to tribal governments of authority and responsibility over reservation land, people, and programs. Simply put, no white man could grant Indian sovereignty; tribal governments themselves would have to fill in the contours of the self-determination policy. Even Nixon's legislative proposals to hand over federally funded programs required tribal governments to first request such authority and demonstrate their capacity to run these programs effectively. Many tribes seized this opportunity to take over programs related to reservation housing and education, as authorized by the 1975 Indian Self-Determination and Education Act, but Indians also pursued self-determination through other measures not anticipated by federal policy makers, most famously Indian gaming.[7]

In pursuing these paths to power, then, tribal actors worked within the political and legal structure crafted by non-Indians, but they also took extralegal actions to shape that structure to address the issues most important to them. And no issue was more important than control over reservation land and resources. Yet there are no histories explaining how tribes reclaimed authority over these items. This book tackles this crucial, and as yet unexplained, transition, demonstrating how energy tribes worked beyond the existing legal structure to transform the promise of sovereignty contained in the self-determination policy into actual control over reservation development. In doing so, tribes greatly enlarged a third area of sovereignty within the federal system where tribal, not federal or state, governments now hold primary authority over reservation land and resources.[8]

There are also important lessons here that transcend interests in American Indian history and policy, and none is more important than demonstrating how control over *energy* confers *power*. To state as much sounds axiomatic, but this book reveals the complicated, underlying material and social forces that make such a statement appear self-evident. On the material side, we know that energy underlies power. Physicists have long told us that energy is the life force of all activity, that it exists in all matter, and every organism uses energy, mostly derived from the sun, to accomplish tasks. Energy is the capacity to do work. In converting energy into useful motion, scientists describe organisms as exhibiting power. Power is thus energy put to work, and all beings exercise some form of it. Of course, one of the greatest conversions of energy into power has come with the ability to burn fossil fuels to produce electrical and mechanical power.[9]

But energy also produces power in the social realm. Older sociological conceptions of power, dating back to Max Weber, defined the term as a function of social position or status. More recently, sociologists of science and technology, environmental historians, and historians of technology have come to recognize that "social power" has a material, energetic basis as well. The ability of humans to effectuate their desires, often by shaping the actions of others, derives not from their position in society but is produced through their increasing ability to control material inputs, mostly by exhibiting mastery over social structures governing those inputs. As Bruno Latour explains, "This shift *from principle to practice* allows us to treat the vague notion of power not as a cause of people's behavior but as the consequence of an intense activity of enrolling, convincing, and enlisting." Power, in other words, is not the result of status and does not explain how people achieve their ends. Instead, it is created though the process of acquiring capacity to control matter—and thus energy—and must itself be explained.[10]

Throughout the 1970s, American Indians increased their capacity to control energy and thus grew more powerful. They secured energy experts to review potential mining projects, educated tribal leaders so they could negotiate better mineral contracts, and passed tribal ordinances to shape how energy resources would be extracted. They improved their mastery over those social structures governing access to energy. Ultimately, as we will see, this increased capacity produced changes in federal law that recognized tribes' legal authority over reservation resources. Again, increasing capacity to control energy expanded tribal power within the federal structure. Lawyers call such power "sovereignty."

Precisely because control over energy produces power, this book also demonstrates the far-reaching impacts of local conflicts over natural resources. Environmental historians, in particular, have spent years explaining how the pursuit of valuable resources structures relations between developed cores and distant peripheries. The incorporation of outlying commodities into global markets, we are told, renders faraway places dependent on urban regions, while producing untold environmental destruction and social dislocation at the point of extraction. Influenced by anthropologists, the best of these studies complicate the story by recognizing how local actors shape the implementation of seemingly "universal" forces like global capitalism or the high modernist ideology of nation building. Instead of an easy, top-down application of these forces to extract resources, peripheral elites, peasants, wage workers, indigenous communities and their laws, customs, and norms all influence development. In the creative space where universals and local influence meet—what Anna Tsing calls "friction"—resources often get extracted, but on compromised terms.[11]

These nuanced investigations into global resource development, however, still tend not to follow the trajectory of impacts outward, from local to regional, national, or global implications. Environmental and social effects are felt in the periphery, and perhaps local actors influence the method of extraction, but their actions rarely alter the larger structures shaping development. This book demonstrates the opposite, that local efforts to control how development unfolds in particular places produces power at the periphery, which can radiate beyond those locales. Certainly, changes in the global energy industry and antiquated federal laws created pressures to develop energy minerals on Native American reservations, where energy firms were forced to negotiate with increasingly knowledgeable tribal leaders to get deals done. But local concerns over tribal survival not only informed the types of development Indians would allow, they also shaped the overriding economic and legal structures that first brought energy firms to their reservations. To ensure survival, energy tribes increased their control over tribal resources and authorized only mining projects in which their governments could control the pace and scale. This then affected regional development schemes from the American Southwest to the Northern Plains. But when federal law seemed to prohibit even this type of tribal control over reservation mining, energy tribes set out to change the national legal structure governing their resources. Ultimately, the tribes succeeded in securing new legislation granting tribal authority over reservation minerals, and in doing so they encoded local concerns over tribal survival into federal laws governing energy development nationwide. The local emanated outward to shape regional mining projects, national laws, and global energy flows.[12]

The final lesson drawn from this book involves the intimate connections between a group's physical and social landscape, its approach to governance, and how the community defines itself. Arthur McEvoy stresses the mutability of a society's legal and political structures, explaining how they "evolv[e] in response to their social and natural environments even as they mediate the interaction between the two." For McEvoy, the manner in which a group decides how to govern itself reflects cultural choices made over the best method for mediating social relations and managing the surrounding nonhuman environment. Groups value certain behavior between their members and toward their land and thus establish political institutions and pass laws to achieve those desired results. But these social structures are not all-controlling. Physical and social environments change due to external or internal forces, and when they do, the people often change their governments to better align with the altered conditions. Laws and political institutions are simply culture manifested, with roots in both the physical and social environment.[13]

To McEvoy's apt description of the basis of governance, I would add that once group members establish their governing principles and procedures, they then partly define their community based on these decisions. They might say, for example, "We are Crow, thus we manage the environment this way"; or, "As Northern Cheyenne, we believe this is the best manner to police ourselves." Changing governing structures, such as ratifying new constitutions or placing power over natural resources in new government bodies, is thus an incredibly disruptive event for the community because it fundamentally alters how the group has previously defined itself. Some members may support the move as a reasonable extension of the community's belief system, but for others the change is a threat to the group identity they subscribe to. These members ask the fair question: "Are we still Crow if we no longer govern ourselves and our resources the way the Crow used to?"

For many American Indian communities wrestling with the prospect of reservation energy development, these contentious internal struggles over natural resource governance and identity left the most lasting legacies. Groups like the Crow and Navajo altered their governments to take advantage of development opportunities and better control mining's impacts, but these changes deeply divided their communities. These divisions, in turn, often made it difficult to form the consensus necessary to capitalize on their abundant resources. Tribal factionalism is, of course, nothing new, and scholars have sometimes explained these conflicts in terms of internal groups vying for control over valuable resources. But few studies explain the ferocity of these debates in terms of changes to the legal structures governing natural resources. Under the auspices of "modernizing" or improving the "efficiency" of their tribal governments, energy tribes altered their governments and increased their capacity to manage reservation land. For some, however, these changes signified much more than improvements to governance. They represented a revaluing of an essential component of tribal culture (how the group manages its environment) and thus a redefining of tribal identity. Governance, the environment, and culture were inextricably entwined. As the cultural geographer Don Mitchell explains, "Moments of intense political and economic restructuring . . . are also moments of intense cultural restructuring."[14]

The remarkable tale of Indian agency that follows, then, not only explains how energy tribes reconfigured the legal relationship between tribal and federal governments, it also demonstrates how this process wrought fundamental changes within tribal communities. Considering the intimate relationships between the environment, law, and culture, how could it be any other way?

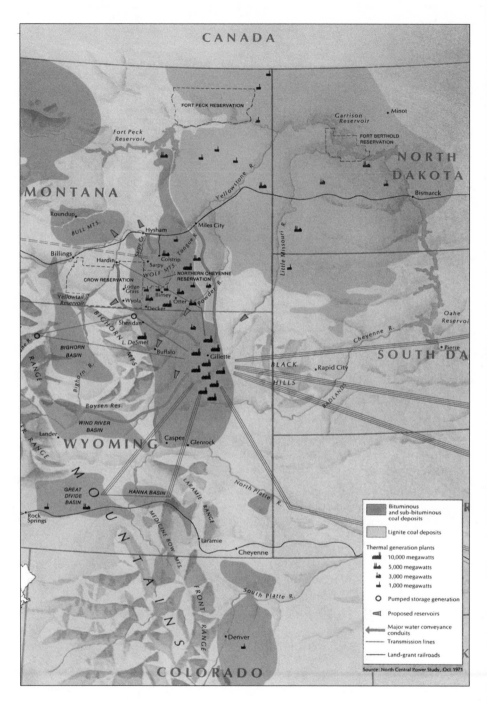

Map 1. Projects proposed by the *North Central Power Study.* Map detail,
adapted, reproduced with permission from Alvin M. Josephy, Jr., "Agony on the
Northern Plains," *Audubon* 75, no. 4 (July 1973), 76–77.

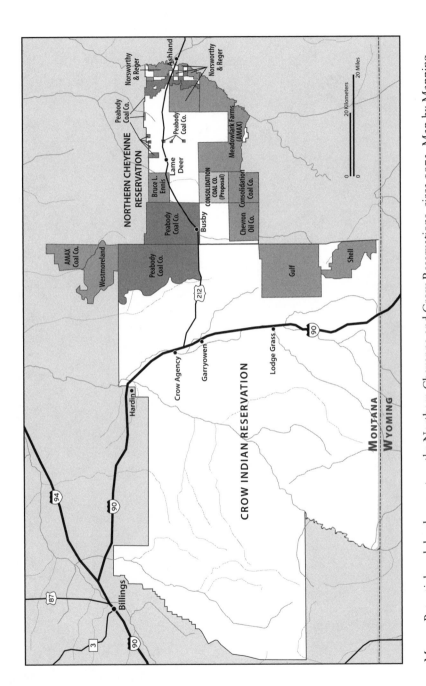

Map 2. Potential coal development on the Northern Cheyenne and Crow Reservations, circa 1972. Map by Mapping Specialists, Ltd.

I

CONSTRUCTING BAD DEALS

Prologue

ON JULY 6, 1972, in the small reservation town of Lame Deer, located forty-two miles east of the Custer battlefield in southeastern Montana, a handful of Northern Cheyenne leaders received a proposal that would forever alter their community. Representatives of the behemoth Consolidation Coal Company, a subsidiary of the Continental Oil Company (CONOCO) and the second largest coal producer in America, presented these leaders and Bureau of Indian Affairs (BIA) officials with a lucrative offer to build a $1.2-billion coal gasification complex on the Cheyenne's small, 440,000-acre reservation. The proposal included plans for a 70,000-acre coal mine that would feed four on-reservation gasification plants, which would convert Cheyenne coal into natural gas to be transported via pipeline to population centers throughout the country. Annually, the complex would consume thirty million tons of coal over thirty-five years of operation and required a dedicated reserve of one billion tons. The project was so large that, by Consolidation's own admission, a new reservation town of thirty thousand people would be needed just to fill the required jobs. To place these figures in perspective, in the previous year the surrounding states of Montana, Wyoming, and North Dakota collectively produced only twenty-one million tons of coal, and the Northern Cheyenne population hovered around three thousand. The Consolidation Coal Company planned for a project of enormous dimensions.[1]

For their trouble, the coal company promised the impoverished Northern Cheyenne prosperity for generations to come. The day after the July 6 meeting, Consolidation's vice president for western operations, Dell Adams, wrote to the tribe that his company would pay royalties of 25 cents per ton of coal mined plus "bonus payments" of $35 an acre for each of the 70,000 acres the mine would cover. The Northern Cheyenne thus would receive an immediate $2.5 million and could expect another $250 million in royalties over the life of the project. To sweeten the pot further and to appeal to one of the tribe's most pressing needs, Adams committed an additional $1.5 million for the construction of a local health care center, hoping to erect a tangible reminder of the important relationship between his coal company and the community. These benefits, Adams understated, would "solve the unemployment problem" and ensure that the "standard of living should rise dramatically." On a reservation where the 1969 average per capita income was just $988, these figures resonated loudly.[2]

Yet despite the seemingly sudden promise of fortune, Consolidation's proposal did not shock tribal leaders or federal officials. If anything, the offer represented a culmination of the hard work these groups had put forth over the previous years to land a lucrative mining deal. Ever since mining companies began expressing interest in Cheyenne coal in the mid-1960s, tribal representatives and regional BIA staff had consistently touted energy development as the answer to reservation poverty. In taking this position, the Northern Cheyenne and their local trustees were far from alone. Across the American West in the years following World War II, multinational energy firms targeted cheap Indian energy to fuel the nation's booming economy, and tribal leaders and federal officials warmly welcomed mining as the ticket to prosperity. More than being passive witnesses to the appropriation of their resources, Northern Cheyenne and other tribal leaders, in fact, worked actively to promote reservation development. And why would they not? Suffocating poverty threatened their people, and these leaders' primary mission was to save the community.[3]

With Consolidation Coal Company's proposal, Northern Cheyenne leaders believed they would guarantee their tribe's survival. This was the deal they had been working for, one that could lift their community out of generations of poverty. But the massive proposal also poised the tiny tribe at the intersection of several perilous paths. Down one road was Consolidation's promise of wealth, though the experiences of other tribes were starting to reveal the adverse consequences this choice might have on the Cheyenne community and landscape. A large mining project would mean an influx of outsiders and massive land distur-bances that could change the way tribal members interacted with one another and their land. In a community with strong memories of their ancestors' nineteenth-century sacrifices to secure a tribal homeland, the thought of opening up the reservation to non-Indian coal miners con-jured up painful emotions. The counter-option was to simply close the reservation to all mining. Rampant poverty, however, hardly made this a choice at all. Desperate conditions are what spurred tribal leaders to pursue deals like Consolidation's in the first place.

Yet another approach meant rejecting mines operated by outside firms and developing tribal resources themselves. Theoretically, this strategy could secure modest revenues while positioning the tribal gov-ernment to ensure that the pace and scale of mining did not upset exist-ing norms, customs, and natural environments. But this last path had not yet been traveled by any tribe. To successfully navigate it would require a monumental effort to develop the institutional capacity to market tribal resources while also controlling unwanted mining im-pacts. It would also necessitate wholesale revisions of federal Indian law to recognize tribal authority to pursue such development.

As it turns out, Northern Cheyenne leaders did not make the choice; ordinary tribal members did. Catching wind of Consolidation's massive mining project, a grassroots opposition movement emerged that con-nected this proposal to even larger, regional development schemes that clearly threatened the tribal community. Faced with resistance from below, the tribal government not only rejected Consolidation's pro-posal but moved to develop their own resources. These actions spurred a national, pan-tribal movement to prepare other tribes to do the same and spearheaded a campaign to change federal law to recognize Indian rights to develop tribal resources.

The summer of 1972 was thus a turning point. For decades, Indian energy resources had been developed with little input from Indian people. An outdated and paternalistic legal regime—a holdover from the 1930s—insured that Indian sovereignty was in practice meaningless. Energy firms developed tribal resources for an insatiable western market, yet tribal members remained mired in poverty. This situation began to change, however, when the Northern Cheyenne, suspicious of Consolidation's plans and militant in defense of their homeland, decided to go it alone.

1 The Tribal Leasing Regime

TRUE COMMERCIAL INTEREST in Northern Cheyenne coal began in December 1965, when a geologist from Laramie, Wyoming,
named Max Krueger submitted the first formal proposal to develop
the reservation. A consultant for the Big Horn Coal Company, Krueger
sought an exclusive two-year prospecting permit to explore the entire
440,000-acre reservation. At the coal company's discretion, the permit
could be renewed for an additional two years, during which time the
parties could negotiate the specific terms of a lease to extract any coal
found. Krueger suggested 10 cents per ton as a fair royalty to mine
Cheyenne coal. Big Horn was very clear, however, that it did not intend
to develop the reservation immediately. According to Bureau of Indian
Affairs (BIA) staff who followed up on the proposal with company
officials, they were given the distinct "impression that [Big Horn was]
interested in holding reservation coal in reserve for development some-
time in the future." In these early days of coal prospecting along the
Northern Plains, the coal company planned to sit on Cheyenne mineral
rights until market conditions improved.[1]

Despite the vague terms and uncertainty of future development, federal officials could barely conceal their excitement. Immediately upon
receiving Krueger's offer, the BIA's superintendent of the Northern
Cheyenne Reservation, John Artichoker, wrote to his Billings, Montana,

supervisor, gushing that "the prospect of developing the coal resource on this reservation is an exciting one as this for some time has appeared to be the reservation's 'white elephant.'" Artichoker's boss, BIA Area Director James Canan, and his staff were equally delighted, although they proceeded with more caution. Questioning the sufficiency of Krueger's proposal to mine the entire reservation for a mere 10 cents per ton royalty, these officials noted other interest being generated for similar coal in the region and feared selling Northern Cheyenne minerals for less than market value. The issue, they surmised, was not whether to develop Cheyenne coal—that was a given considering the dire reservation poverty. The only question was how to determine a fair price in the unproven western coal market. Working without sufficient geological or market data, Billings officials concluded that to determine a truly equitable value they must conduct a competitive auction for the right to prospect Cheyenne coal.[2]

INDIAN (IN)CAPACITY

Relying on market forces to establish a fair coal price sprang from two unique provisions of federal Indian law—one a broad principle, the other a specific statute. The first was the federal government's general trustee duty, which the Supreme Court has affirmed repeatedly as "one of the cornerstones of Indian law." This duty requires federal officials to manage American Indian land and resources as any private fiduciary would, ensuring responsible development in order to meet Indian, not private or public, needs. First articulated by Chief Justice John Marshall in a series of early nineteenth-century cases, the trust doctrine developed as a way to balance the United States' superior title to Indian lands with the acknowledgment that Indians possessed some property rights to territory they had possessed since "time immemorial." Marshall resolved this tension by reasoning that tribes' status as "domestic dependent nation[s] . . . in a state of pupilage" placed this special trust responsibility upon the United States. The federal government interpreted the duty liberally during the nineteenth and early twentieth centuries to justify the broad disposition of Indian property into non-Indian hands, but over the course of the twentieth century courts had become increasingly willing to hold executive agencies to "the most exacting fiduciary standards" when managing tribal resources.[3]

Securing the highest possible return for reservation resources was the key to fulfilling the BIA's trustee duty to the Northern Cheyenne. Economic development was the agency's singular concern, but in pursuing this goal federal officials faced the challenge of appropriately pricing Northern Cheyenne minerals. They needed to make the terms of any reservation coal sale attractive enough to draw developers but not short-sell the tribe and fail to meet their trustee obligations. With little information about the geology of the Northern Cheyenne Reservation or contemporary western coal prices, federal agents determined to let market forces establish coal values. As BIA Area Director Canan would later recall, "Everything we did was based on a competitive assumption."[4] With the market setting a price, federal officials felt assured their trustee duty would be met.

The second aspect of federal Indian law guiding BIA actions was the 1938 Indian Mineral Leasing Act, which gave federal officials the authority to decide the fate of Indian minerals. Dating back to the 1790 Non-Intercourse Act, Congress had prohibited tribes from transferring interests in real property without its express consent. This meant, in theory, that the only way Indian property—including resource rights—could legally change hands was through a congressionally created process overseen by federal officials. Under the guise of protecting unsophisticated "savages" from encroaching white settlers, early nineteenth-century laws had authorized unilateral transfers of Indian lands to non-Indians, facilitating the removal of tribal communities west of the Mississippi. By the 1870s, the justification for appropriating Indian land had shifted toward assimilating Native Americans into the national mainstream, but the result was much the same. Working in tandem with a liberal reading of the trustee duty, federal officials continued to dispose of Indian property without tribal input.[5]

The "Indian New Deal" of the 1930s, however, substantially altered this practice. Crafted by John Collier, Franklin Roosevelt's commissioner of Indian Affairs, the new approach halted disastrous federal land policies, such as allotting communal land to individual tribal members, and helped establish tribal governments to provide tribal control over tribal property. The centerpiece of Collier's new regime was the 1934 Indian Reorganization Act, though the lesser known 1938 Indian Mineral Leasing Act governed the disposition of tribal minerals. Both statutes promised indigenous control over communal property, but, as we will see, that promise was never kept. Well into the 1960s, the BIA, not the Northern Cheyenne, was still deciding what to do with the tribe's coal.[6]

*

Only during the heady, experimental days of the New Deal could a man like John Collier preside over federal Indian policy. The son of a former Atlanta mayor and grandson of one of the city's founders, this Progressive crusader spent his early adulthood as a community organizer in New York's immigrant communities before following a twisted path to Taos, New Mexico. There he encountered the elaborate rituals of the Pueblo Indians and saw in them a "Red Atlantis" that needed protection from the outside world's corrupting influence. His desire to save what he believed to be a communalistic, gemeinschaft mode of living, however, stemmed not simply out of concern for the Pueblos, though he certainly feared for their future. More than that, Collier believed the Pueblos and other tribal communities could offer vital lessons in living to an American society spiritually bankrupted by the profit-driven, individualistic pursuit of prosperity. Animated by this idealistic crusade, Collier spent much of the 1920s expanding his mission to other tribes, forming the American Indian Defense Association and carrying with him a monolithic understanding of Indian culture forged through his Pueblo experience. When Franklin Delano Roosevelt assumed the presidency in 1933, Collier was tapped to head Indian Affairs. In one of the more stunning reversals in the history of the federal bureaucracy, the preeminent critic of federal Indian policy over the previous decade was now in charge of the shop.[7]

Collier, the crusader, assumed his position determined to overhaul federal Indian policy and protect Native communities. By the end of his first year in office, he began work on a major piece of legislation to renounce the federal policy of assimilation and end the practice of allotting communal reservations. These radical redirections of federal policy, however, would be the easy, first steps. The new commissioner understood that tribes could not survive without healthy reservation economies, and therein lay his largest dilemma. It was one thing to eliminate threats to indigenous culture and the tribal land base; it was quite another to figure out how Indians could engage with the surrounding economy to provide revenue without threatening the communal values Collier so valued.

Ever the Progressive, Collier intended to use the expertise of the federal government to help tribes negotiate this difficult balance. He envisioned a process whereby indigenous groups would establish formal governing bodies to collectively manage communal land, while government officials remained active to guide tribes through the process of self-government and ensure that these groups exercised their powers appropriately. Moreover, because Collier believed, as most did, that Native Americans were unprepared to engage in the cutthroat world of industrial capitalism, BIA staff would continue to provide "technical assistance" to the new tribal bodies, essentially acting as intermediaries between tribes and commercial interests. Such a system would provide Indians with a tribal mechanism to capitalize on their resources and, in theory, check the previously unlimited power of federal officials to dispense with tribal property. It also positioned federal trustees to ensure reservations would not be opened to the nefarious practices that had exploited these lands in the past. Collier called the approach "indirect administration." It was an altruistic yet ultimately paternalistic project.[8]

John Collier had the drive and vision to reformulate federal Indian policy, but the process of transforming his ideas into actual legislation revealed deep tensions within the Department of the Interior over the appropriate level of tribal autonomy. The fault line in this debate ran between Collier and a young lawyer from the department's Solicitor's Office named Felix Cohen, who had been conscripted to help write the Indian New Deal's cornerstone legislation, the Indian Reorganization Act. The son of Morris Cohen, the renowned philosopher and advocate of multiculturalism, the younger Cohen complimented his Columbia law degree with a PhD in philosophy from Harvard, bringing to his legal work a clear vision for how laws should be structured to protect and empower minority groups. According to his biographer, Felix Cohen espoused a strand of legal realism known as "legal pluralism," which argued that America should be organized not as a nation of individuals in pursuit of their own self-interests, but as a collection of independent groups through which individuals attach their identity and pursue collective goals. This normative vision for how society should operate supported Cohen's affinity for laws that decentralized state power and increased group autonomy so that these organizations could regulate their own internal affairs. Only by structuring society as a collection of special interest groups did Cohen believe "disparities of power, particularly economic power, could be minimized if not eliminated." To neutralize any relativistic implications of this group-based, egalitarian legal structure, the young philosopher-attorney also preserved a governmental role to ensure "group power should be exercised to benefit the society at large." As applied to American Indian law, legal pluralism meant the federal government was needed to ensure tribes did not infringe upon the rights of other groups and that their collective pursuit was for the common good. But within tribal communities, the state must respect tribal sovereignty.[9]

John Collier and his staff at the Bureau of Indian Affairs, however, pursued a more limited agenda. Collier envisioned a much closer federal-tribal relationship, at least initially, with the BIA carefully guiding the tribes toward self-government. In this role, federal agents would remain involved in tribal affairs to help draft constitutions, issue tribal business charters that outlined the extent of tribal powers, and negotiate with non-Indian developers to provide a material basis for survival without sacrificing cultural values.

The Department of the Interior's legislative proposal for the Indian Reorganization Act reflected this tug-of-war between Collier's and Cohen's visions of tribal sovereignty. The cumbersome and contradictory forty-eight-page bill authorized tribes "to organize for the purpose of local self-government and economic enterprise," listing dozens of possible government powers the tribes could wield. It retained for the federal government, however, the authority to define the scope of these powers through the issuance of corporate charters. The bill also ended the policy of assimilation through land allotments, but it imposed severe restrictions on what tribes could do with their remaining lands without federal approval. In short, Interior's proposal was Janus-faced, recognizing the need for Indian control over a self-sufficient land base in one breath yet retaining federal authority to meddle in Indian affairs with the next. It represented a process of conflict avoidance within the department, rather than one of compromise.[10]

Ultimately, Congress settled this internal agency dispute, but in doing so it opened a window for Cohen's expansive reading of tribal authority to take hold. After months of deliberations, hearings, and numerous tribal conferences held to elicit Indian input, Congress slashed Interior's forty-eight-page proposal to a mere five pages. The final Indian Reorganization Act replaced the laundry list of possible tribal powers with three specific grants: the authority to hire attorneys; the ability to prevent the disposal of communal land without tribal consent; and the right to negotiate with federal, state, and local governments. In addition to these enumerated powers, Congress included boilerplate language recognizing that tribes organized under the statute retained "all powers vested . . . by existing law." This phrase, which was most certainly intended to ensure only that the act did not unwittingly extinguish any well-established rights, provided Felix Cohen with the opportunity to redefine the nature of tribal sovereignty. In a Solicitor's Opinion entitled "Powers of the Indian Tribes" issued four months after the Indian Reorganization Act became law, Cohen made the radical argument that those tribal powers vested by existing law *"are not, in general, delegated powers granted by express acts of Congress, but rather inherent powers of a limited sovereignty which has never been extinguished."* Although not a novel theory—Chief Justice John Marshall had articulated a similar principle a century earlier—Cohen's explanation of the source of tribal power was revolutionary for its time. Because tribal powers did not originate in grants from Congress but were inherent in the tribes' status as aboriginal sovereigns, Cohen reasoned that tribes retained all powers normally vested in sovereigns, unless they had been explicitly extinguished by the federal government. These powers included the right to choose their own form of government, to determine tribal membership, to regulate all internal relations, and most important, to determine the use and disposition of tribal property. As Vine Deloria, Jr., and Clifford Lytle point out, since Congress had probably never considered that tribes possessed powers not expressly granted to them, the list of those powers not specifically limited could be fairly long.[11]

*

This principle of inherent tribal sovereignty laid the foundation for the rest of Cohen's work at the Department of the Interior and would continue to animate debates between Cohen and his allies in the Solicitor's Office and Collier's Bureau of Indian Affairs.[12] These conflicts were particularly fierce over the issue of reservation mineral development, which both camps saw as a potential base of prosperity if only the confusing and conflicting laws governing these resources could be clarified. Beginning in the summer of 1933, the Bureau of Indian Affairs thus began work on a uniform, systematic process for developing these resources. Consistent with Collier's cautious views of tribal capacity, this paternalistic plan proposed a system whereby the federal government would issue mineral leases on behalf of the tribes, subject to tribal consent only on the final terms. These leases would authorize outside companies to mine reservation resources, but they would not empower tribes to mine and sell the minerals themselves. Moreover, the BIA would retain authority to unilaterally grant prospecting permits, renew leases, and release lessees from their contractual obligations should conditions warrant it.[13]

Landing on Felix Cohen's desk in January 1935, the BIA's proposal was dead on arrival. In a fiery retort to Collier, drafted for Solicitor General Nathan Margold's signature, Cohen blasted the bureau for "contemplat[ing] a very serious diminution of the existing rights of those tribes that still have some mineral resources" and admonished the agency for failing to include "any basis for this sudden change of legislative policy." Cohen's draft rebuke was so emphatic that it launched a debate within the Solicitor's Office over that institution's role in the legislative drafting process. Assistant Secretary Rufus Poole intervened with a strongly worded memo to Margold questioning Cohen's tone and arguing that the proper response should have been merely to point out the proposed bill's effects on existing law, not to suggest policy. Picking his fights carefully, Cohen relented. But while he graciously softened the tone of his memo to Collier, the new draft retained all the substantive criticisms.[14]

Soon after Cohen's revised memo reached Collier's desk, the young attorney and BIA staff began cooperating on new legislation. The amended bill retained the lease form as the singular method of reservation mineral development but placed authority to issue leases with the tribes, not the federal government. This proposal, transmitted to Congress on April 15, 1935, also expressly reaffirmed all tribal powers recognized by the Indian Reorganization Act—as elucidated in Cohen's Solicitor's Opinion—and repealed any previous statutes inconsistent with this expansive view of tribal sovereignty. It included, however, language allowing the secretary of the Interior to veto any lease deemed inconsistent with the tribes' best interest. On one hand, then, the revised bill reflected Cohen's insistence that authority to issue mineral leases rested with the tribes, but, on the other, it included Collier's desire to carefully monitor tribal relations with outside developers so as to protect indigenous communities. Moreover, the proposal said nothing of methods other than leases to dispense with Indian minerals, including the possibility of tribes developing their resources themselves. This omission would prove costly for tribal governments in the 1960s and 1970s. As Native Americans learned the value of their vast mineral deposits and sought to control their development, federal officials claimed reservation resources could be extracted only through leases issued to outside mining firms, pursuant to the 1938 Indian Mineral Leasing Act.[15]

Although Cohen and Collier may have reached a compromise that met Cohen's demand for tribes to decide the fate of their own minerals while preserving Collier's desire for government oversight, lawmakers clearly mistook the proposed legislation as an expansion of federal authority alone. The bill's sponsor, Senator Elmer Thomas (D-Okla.), explained to his colleagues on the Senate floor that the law was needed to "give the Secretary of the Interior power to lease unallotted Indian lands for different purposes," which, of course, was the exact opposite of Cohen's intent to give this authority to the tribes. In the House, the bill was equally misconstrued as a noncontroversial enlargement of Interior's powers, and it passed on that body's consent calendar without debate. Such a misinterpretation was understandable considering senior officials within the Interior Department continued to push legislation that, in the words of Assistant Secretary Frederick Wiener, would "protect the Indians against themselves, in view of their marked incompetence in money matters." In fact, granting tribes unsupervised government powers, such as the authority to dispense with real property, Wiener argued, amounted to a flawed policy "representing a triumph of hope over experience." With a confused Congress and a divided Department of the Interior, on May 11, 1938, President Roosevelt signed into law the Indian Mineral Leasing Act.[16]

On its face, the 1938 act recognized tribes' inherent right to issue mineral leases but then circumscribed that power with federal veto authority. As we will see, federal officials charged with ensuring that leases conformed to tribal interests would fail to construct a tribal-led leasing process whereby tribal governments could cultivate skills and knowledge to make their own development decisions. Instead, the BIA would model the leasing program on a flawed regulatory regime designed for public minerals, where federal, not tribal, officials solic-ited bids for Indian resource development, evaluated those bids, and made recommendations to tribal governments. Unfortunately, federal officials were completely unprepared to carry out these tasks, and un-informed and impoverished tribes were in no position to critically eval-uate BIA recommendations. Flawed federal oversight, not expanded tribal sovereignty, would become the tribal leasing program's primary characteristic.

A BROKEN TEMPLATE

At the turn of the twentieth century, mineral development on federal lands was lightly regulated and characterized by wasteful production practices, and it succeeded mostly in transforming public resources into private wealth. Mid-nineteenth-century gold and silver strikes in newly acquired western territories had spurred some federal legislation, but these early laws generally encoded mining camp practices that regarded public lands as "free and open to exploration and occupation by all citizens." Both the 1866 and 1872 General Mining Acts established the principle, adopted from Spanish colonial law, that the first to locate and make a valid claim on public minerals obtained ownership over them. Recognizing the importance of coal to the nation's industrial economy, Congress attempted to limit the practice of free public entry for lands containing this valuable fuel source, but these restrictions were easily bypassed, and no limitations were placed on other energy minerals. By 1912, private developers operating on public lands were produc-ing annually 58 million tons of coal and 141 million barrels of oil, all without paying for the right to do so. In the words of historian Samuel Hays, the entire regime was premised on "promot[ing] rapid disposal to private individuals rather than to aid in systematic development" of the nation's resources.[17]

Beginning with Theodore Roosevelt's presidency, however, federal officials began to question the wisdom of the existing regulatory re-gime, especially with respect to fuel minerals. This reexamination of federal mining laws was part of a larger Progressive critique of nineteenth-century land policies that encouraged the quick but ineffi-cient development of public resources to benefit large companies rather than common citizens. In 1904, following a report by the Public Lands Commission, President Roosevelt proposed a new mineral develop-ment regime whereby the federal government would retain ownership over fuel minerals and lease the rights to developers for a per-ton roy-alty. Such an arrangement would maintain federal regulatory authority over minerals, allowing officials to ensure that development proceeded in a manner consistent with the public interest. Although endorsed by a growing cadre of scientific conservationists within the federal bu-reaucracy, led by Gifford Pinchot, Roosevelt's leasing plan faced stiff opposition from western mining interests. It was not until after World War I, as the country turned again to developing its public resources, that Congress passed the 1920 Mineral Leasing Act. The law required federal officials to first survey and catalog lands containing valuable fuel and fertilizer minerals before deciding whether it was in the pub-lic's interest to lease additional resources.[18]

Apparently, federal officials believed that what was good for public minerals could apply equally well to tribal resources. When drafting the bill that would become the Indian Mineral Leasing Act, the BIA simply adopted this public minerals leasing template and shared their legislative drafts with the U.S. Geological Survey to ensure consistency. In fact, in passing along the BIA's earliest draft, the assistant solicitor of the Interior, Charles Lahy, explained his agency's desire that "the procedure suggested by the Indian Office should as nearly as possi-ble conform to the policy of the Department [of the Interior] relating to public land." Lahy requested a memorandum from the Geological Survey highlighting any potential conflicts between the public leas-ing program and the proposed tribal leasing legislation and then un-equivocally reemphasized his point: "It is desired that any policy now adopted or continued with reference to leases on Indian lands have in mind the policy governing permits and leases on the public lands." Once this leasing framework was adopted for tribal resources, it never changed throughout the drafting process. Cohen and Collier may have battled over who should have the authority to issue leases, but no one questioned the leasing approach. After passage of the Indian Mineral Leasing Act, federal officials charged with implementing it then simply followed the procedures used for public minerals, determining to open Indian reservations to mining when they believed it to be in the tribes' best interests.[19]

In theory, the new regulatory regime governing both public and tribal minerals would provide federal oversight to protect against wasteful overproduction and the unfair transfer of wealth from public or tribal hands into corporate coffers. Federal agencies would survey public and Indian lands, judiciously select tracts for development, require competitive bidding to set prices, and ultimately determine which companies received prospecting permits and mining leases. Bidding was necessary to rectify the previous regime's failure to secure a fair return for federal and Indian resources, but as historian Richard White argues, "revenue was . . . not the main goal of the legislation." Instead, the true intent of these laws was to ensure the "government could curtail wasteful overproduction by holding back on leases and prospecting permits."[20] Under the new systematic leasing program, federal officials could also ensure that no one company gained monopolistic controls over a particular resource in a specific area.

Or so the theory went. The reality was that the Department of the Interior and its bureaus—the Geological Survey, the Bureau of Land Management, and the Bureau of Indian Affairs—lacked resources to properly determine which lands to open to coal development and to evaluate potential bids. Again, legislators intended these executive agencies to first analyze geological data, assess potential environmental and social costs for mining in a given area, and evaluate the potential market for coal so as to maximize returns and minimize adverse consequences. Instead, after World War II multinational energy firms with ample resources and a desire to diversify their energy holdings performed the legwork to evaluate particular tracts of land and then recommended to Interior which sections should be opened for bidding. As was the case with the Northern Cheyenne, government officials often had no independent information with which to evaluate the appropriateness of a lease offering but typically opened suggested lands to leasing nonetheless, citing either the nation's interest in developing domestic energy sources or tribal needs for revenue. For their part, tribal governments, which the Indian Mineral Leasing Act had empowered to formally issue the leases, were unprepared to critically evaluate BIA-recommended leases and deferred to their federal trustees. Thus, by retaining federal veto authority and adopting the public mineral leasing template, the legal regime that had intended for tribes to control reservation development had reversed the roles of tribal and federal governments. Federal officials controlled the process, and tribal leaders awaited their recommendations. As with many Progressive plans, implementation failed to match altruistic designs.[21]

COLLABORATION

This was the regulatory regime facing Northern Cheyenne leaders and federal officials when Max Krueger submitted his December 1965 coal mining proposal. Despite the promises of the Indian New Deal, initial responsibility for evaluating Krueger's offer fell to the BIA, not the tribal council. Regional staff, cognizant of their trustee duty and pointing to the 1938 Indian Mineral Leasing Act's implementing regulations, made the determination that a federally run competitive auction was the best way to secure a fair price in this unproven area.

Clearly, BIA officials followed the correct protocol, as the controlling regulations authorized such a bidding process for Indian minerals. The actual 1938 act, however, said nothing of requiring such a procedure for Indian *coal*. Instead, the act mandated public bidding only for oil and gas rights on Indian lands, which in the 1930s were in greater demand. When the Department of the Interior promulgated regulations to implement the statute, the rules for coal simply followed the process Congress laid out for Indian oil and gas—and all public minerals— noting that reservation resources "shall be advertised for bids." Perhaps cognizant the statute did not require an auction for minerals other than oil and gas, Interior's regulations included an exception to competitive bidding for coal if "the Commissioner grants the Indian owners written permission to negotiate for a lease." In other words, the law did not demand a public auction for Indian coal, and private negotiations between tribes and developers were allowed, but the auction was the default process and the BIA had the authority to determine which process to use. In the case of the Northern Cheyenne, where the extent of reservation minerals was unknown and no mature market existed to provide a benchmark the BIA could use to evaluate a negotiated price, federal officials concluded the competitive lease sale was the safest method for fulfilling their duties.[22]

Eager to establish a revenue stream, the Northern Cheyenne offered no resistance to the BIA's plan for a competitive auction. In February 1966, the tribal council passed a resolution acknowledging that "[Krueger's] basic proposal as presented has merit" but that it was "in the best interest of the Tribe to Advertise [*sic*] for Exclusive Coal Prospecting Permits." Once the tribal resolution reached BIA officials, Acting Area Director Ned Thompson solicited advice from his Washington, D.C., superiors for structuring the auction to attract major coal developers. Thompson explained he would like to "make the offer [to coal companies] as attractive, and with as few obstacles or determents, as possible." He also noted that time was of the essence as "there is a lot of [coal mining] activity on state lands in these areas, and both [the Northern Cheyenne and Crow] tribes are anxious to get something going." Again, both local BIA and tribal officials were eager to initiate coal development.[23]

Fortunately for anxious tribal leaders and regional BIA staff, the agency's central office shared their optimism that coal mining could alleviate reservation poverty. Washington officials began enthusiastically recommending auction terms to attract major energy developers, including a provision granting the winning bidder a prospecting permit with the exclusive option to lease at *pre-fixed* royalty rates. This move contravened the process laid out in federal regulations, which envisioned future royalty negotiations when the mining company sought to transform its prospecting permit into a lease. But the BIA wanted to remove the uncertainty of such negotiations from the concerns of prospective mining companies. Thus the agency set this term at 17.5 cents per ton, eliminating the tribe's primary financial benefit from competitive bidding despite the fact that the inability to set a fair royalty price was the main reason for holding a public auction in the first place. Moreover, this pre-fixed royalty figure was taken directly from royalty rates contained in nearby public coal leases. We will see how, by the early 1970s, the federal leasing system that established this figure was so dysfunctional that the Department of the Interior imposed a moratorium on all federal coal leasing. Nevertheless, in 1966 federal officials were more than happy to borrow from this broken system to establish a fixed royalty rate for Cheyenne coal. With this number set, the only substantial financial term left to bid on was the onetime "bonus" payments paid for each acre of land opened to prospecting. For an agency intent on promoting competition, the BIA was quick to eliminate such competition if it would help attract major developers.[24]

In addition to promising the winning bidder an exclusive contract to mine Cheyenne coal at low rates, BIA officials suggested other changes to lure major mining firms to the reservation. Deputy Assistant Commissioner Charles Corke waived the regulation limiting coal leases on Indian reservations to 2,560 acres, recognizing that to make mining profitable in this desolate region coal companies would need to construct "mine-mouth facilities" that generated electricity at the reservation mine and then distributed it through regional power grids. Only large firms had the capacity to construct such facilities and the BIA knew this. The agency sought out these types of bidders, hoping that electricity produced on the reservation would spur additional, local industrial activity. To further encourage it, BIA officials provided for a 2.5-cent royalty reduction for coal burned on the reservation.[25]

Clearly, then, federal officials intended to bring major energy developers to the reservation, but if Northern Cheyenne leaders were wary of such development, their words and actions indicated no such concern. Instead, the opportunity to develop reservation minerals to generate badly needed revenue was a source of pride for many leaders, most specifically tribal president John Woodenlegs. The grandson of famed Cheyenne warrior Wooden Leg, who fought Custer at the Battle of the Little Bighorn, John Woodenlegs consistently touted his administration's efforts to develop reservation resources for the good of his people. When a February 1966 editorial in the *Lincoln (Nebraska) Star* lamented the Northern Cheyenne's state of affairs, for instance, Woodenlegs shot back that his reservation was "almost totally underlain by sub-bituminous coal" and that his government was negotiating to develop these lucrative deposits. The tribal president was so outraged by the paper's inaccurate portrayal of his community as hopelessly destitute that he had Montana's Senator Lee Metcalf introduce his letter of retort on the Senate floor to correct the historical record. Woodenlegs also met personally with BIA Area Director Canan to make the case for coal development, expressing his frustration that agency personnel were not moving fast enough to publicize his tribe's coal auction. These complaints spurred BIA official Ned Thompson to again harass his superiors in Washington for immediate authorization for the coal auction, explaining "the Northern Cheyenne Tribe and the

Superintendent are very anxious to have the advertisement published as soon as possible." With federal officials orchestrating the auction, and the Northern Cheyenne providing the impetus, the BIA finally distributed the notice of sale for a Cheyenne coal auction to more than fifty mining companies in late May 1966.[26]

What happened next was typical of American energy development during the murky days of the 1960s, when energy companies quietly acquired vast amounts of western resources at incredibly discounted prices. Despite the generous terms offered and the widespread dissemination of notice, the Cheyenne's July 13, 1966, coal auction attracted only one bidder, the Sentry Royalty Company. A known prospecting agent of the world's largest coal producer, Peabody Coal Company, Sentry "won" the right to prospect almost 100,000 acres of the Northern Cheyenne Reservation for a mere 12-cents-per-acre bonus. The figure represented a whopping 2-cent improvement over the original deal Max Krueger offered a year earlier. Unlike Krueger's proposal, however, the amended auction terms meant Sentry also secured the exclusive option to mine this area for a fixed royalty of 17.5 cents per ton, or 15 cents if the company decided to burn coal on the reservation. With BIA assistance, the Northern Cheyenne auctioned away rights to millions of dollars of highly desirable low-sulfur coal for less than $12,000 in bonuses and a promise to pay miniscule future royalties.[27]

How had this happened? And how was it that tribal and federal officials were ecstatic to receive such a low offer to develop Cheyenne coal? The answer to these questions rests mainly with the antiquated legal regime governing Indian minerals. Driven by an ideology of Indian inferiority and built on a broken template designed for extracting public minerals, the law tasked federal, not tribal, officials with developing reservation resources. The government then failed to equip BIA agents with the tools necessary to carry out their mandate. Without the requisite expertise and resources, the legal regime rendered both federal and tribal officials ignorant about the extent of reservation minerals and their value in global energy markets. When interest emerged to mine Cheyenne coal, federal officials pushed to maximize revenue by attracting large-scale developers. They got just one. Without the hoped-for competition, the world's largest coal company secured Cheyenne minerals on the cheap.

2 Postwar Energy Demands and the Southwestern Experience

SADLY, THE NORTHERN Cheyenne's initial experience with coal development was not unique. The opening of this small, southeastern Montana reservation was part of a much broader, post–World War II movement to develop energy resources across the American West. In fact, long before the 1973 Arab oil embargo called attention to the importance of domestic energy production, private firms had been quietly, but fervently, locking up western minerals to meet America's incessant postwar energy demands. These multinational corporations understood potential instabilities in global oil supplies, possessed capabilities to prospect and evaluate western energy deposits, and had a firm grasp of the complicated regulatory structure for accessing domestic minerals. In other words, they had the knowledge, skills, and resources that federal and tribal officials did not. Employing these advantages, mining firms pursued energy resources of all kinds on both public and tribal lands. But unquestionably, their efforts centered on the West's most abundant resource: low-sulfur coal.

THE QUIET CREEP

Ironically, the great push for western coal began during the period of, and was partly triggered by, America's infatuation with consuming foreign oil. As has been well documented, American use of petroleum skyrocketed in the years following World War II, tripling from 5.8 million barrels a day in 1948 to 16.4 million barrels by 1972. Common understandings link this sharp rise in oil use to increasing levels of postwar American prosperity, thus increasing demand. But changes in global oil production were as important as rising consumption to explaining oil's emergence as America's dominant fuel choice. Quite simply, the Texas oil fields that fueled American might during World War II were not expansive enough to power the country's postwar economic boom. For that, foreign oil was needed.[1]

In the immediate aftermath of World War II, the United States, Great Britain, and other western states worked feverishly with multinational oil firms and Middle Eastern royals to unlock the vast petroleum reserves underlying the Arab and Persian worlds. The complicated deals they constructed flooded America and the world with cheap oil, making the United States a net importer of petroleum for the first time in 1948. Just two years later, oil supplanted coal as the United States' primary energy source, and this unyielding flow of petroleum worked important changes in American patterns of consumption, which is where most scholars pick up the story. Cheap oil made cheap gasoline and electricity possible, which in turn fueled the dramatic suburbanization of postwar America. On this foundation of cheap imported petroleum, the country returned to its earlier infatuation with the automobile, producing an extensive car culture with all its accompanying accoutrements, including expanded highway systems, motels, fast-food restaurants, suburban shopping malls, and even drive-in churches. As American tastes and values shifted to accommodate the abundance of cheap fuel, the rising demand provided the market to justify further production. It was this dialectic process between foreign oil production and incessant American consumption that produced the incredibly wealthy and powerful global oil companies that dominate world energy production today.[2]

These conditions also set the stage for a new era in the American energy industry: the entry of multinational oil and gas companies into the coal mining business. During the postwar period of rapid American growth and cheap Middle Eastern oil, coal production dropped to its lowest levels since the Depression and prices remained remarkably stable and low. Large oil and gas firms flush with cash from Middle

Eastern production took advantage of these low barriers to entry and began quietly buying devalued coal companies by the dozens. Such giants as Gulf Oil, Continental Oil, Occidental Petroleum, and Standard Oil of Ohio gobbled up the longstanding coal concerns Pittsburgh and Midway Coal Mining Company, Consolidation Coal Company, Island Creek Coal, and Old Ben Coal, respectively. By the mid-1960s, energy industry observers were noting a dominant trend of conglomerated "energy entities" replacing individual corporations focused on the production of a single energy source, which had been the traditional approach. Bracing for a drawn-out battle with the emerging nuclear power industry and concerned about rising instability in the Middle East, oil companies understood the need to diversify their holdings with cheap, domestic sources of energy, and coal was by far the most abundant.[3]

Much of this corporate consolidation took place with an eye toward the American West. Explosive postwar western growth ignited energy companies' interest in the region, and by locating fuel sources and constructing power plants near this expanding demand, they could reduce transmission costs. Changes in mining technology also made western coal easier and less expensive to mine. Engineering firms developed larger and more powerful drag lines to remove overburden covering western coal, which was generally younger and thus located closer to the surface than its eastern counterpart. The cost advantages of surface mining with massive equipment, rather than employing an army of underground miners, became especially clear after passage of the 1969 Federal Coal Mine Health and Safety Act, which imposed costly new regulations on deep-shaft mining. Moreover, the lack of entrenched western labor unions—particularly John L. Lewis's United Mine Workers—removed one of the larger impediments to efficient and profitable mining. Widespread eastern coal strikes in 1971 and 1974 further reinforced this advantage for western coal.[4]

Beyond these production advantages for western coal, America's emerging concerns over air pollution provided mining companies with yet another reason to invest in this emerging energy source. Due to one of those ancient geological processes that now shapes much of today's geopolitics, western coal generally formed in freshwater swamps, not in brackish or saltwater swamps as in the East. This meant that as millions of years of geologic heat and pressure transformed decaying plant matter into carbon-rich material, western coal often contained significantly less sulfur than its eastern counterpart. Historically this distinction mattered little, for coal companies generally avoided low-sulfur, subbituminous western coal because it contained less thermal heat than eastern bituminous or anthracite coal. Beginning in the mid-1960s, however, in response to public pressure, the federal government began to address the nation's declining air quality by authorizing research into methods for monitoring and controlling air pollutants. These initial efforts focused on limiting sulfur emissions from coal-burning utilities and industrial manufacturers, which sent mining firms scrambling to secure low-sulfur alternatives. Imported low-sulfur oil provided an obvious solution, but by the late 1960s, such critics as the editor of *Coal Age* were warning that America's dependence on foreign oil created "a serious deficit in our balance of trade and our security could be threatened." The half-hearted 1967 Arab oil embargo confirmed suspicions regarding instability in global oil supplies, and the 1970 Clean Air Act made clear that sulfur emissions would be highly regulated. Both events greatly enhanced western coal's transformation into a highly desirable, "clean" fuel and further accelerated the movement of coal production west.[5]

*

As energy firms reoriented their perspective westward, they encountered a regulatory system well attuned to their needs. Eighty percent of coal west of the Mississippi was found on public or Indian lands rather than on private property, meaning federal law, not private contracts, governed its procurement and development. These existing laws replaced a previous, nineteenth-century legal regime that had encouraged the wasteful overproduction of western resources with a leasing system reflecting Progressive desires to rationalize and control development. The goal was to inject federal oversight, but in practice, the new system looked very similar to the old. Federal agencies without the resources to carry out their legislative mandates simply abdicated responsibility to multinational mining companies with the manpower and expertise to do the job. These firms, of course, were all too happy to survey and propose which public and tribal lands should be opened to development, and they hoped to do so without attracting competitors that could drive up prices in subsequent auctions.[6]

For energy companies looking to secure potentially valuable coal at cut-rate prices with little to no competition, the mid-twentieth-century legal regime worked beautifully. In fact, *every* coal lease issued by the Department of the Interior prior to the mid-1970s was done at the request of an energy company rather than because the agency determined that a strong market existed for the particular resource. As Gary Bennethum, a mining engineer with the Bureau of Land Management, confirmed in 1974, despite the fifty-year existence of the competitive bidding process, "there has never been a Bureau[-initiated] lease sale." Moreover, of the 247 leases issued at competitive lease sales, only 76 attracted more than one bidder. The average royalty established through this "competitive" process was merely 12.5 cents a ton for federal coal and 15.8 cents for Indian coal. Compare these royalties to the fact that in 1920, when the government switched to this leasing regime, the average price of coal on the open market was $3.75 a ton, while by 1972 it had more than doubled to $7.66. Public and tribal mineral owners, however, enjoyed only a fraction of coal's increasing value. By 1974, the federal government and Indian owners had collected barely $30 million from the production of almost 250 million tons of coal.[7]

Beyond establishing incredibly low royalties through this distinctly noncompetitive process, the Department of the Interior further undercut the intent of the mining laws by failing to enforce production requirements contained in the leases issued. This lack of enforcement allowed energy companies to lock up coal reserves in long-term leases, which they kept in their portfolios to be developed should global oil prices rise. Despite this obvious advantage, federal regulators did not require firms to allocate capital to the development of these coal leases or pay the public or Indian owners for the privilege of monopolizing their resources.[8]

In the 1960s, sophisticated, multinational energy corporations with the ability to evaluate potential coal lands, the necessary familiarity with federal laws for developing domestic sources, and a firm understanding of the increasing instability of the global oil market took full advantage of this opportunity to secure valuable energy sources with minimal investment. Coal leasing exploded in the 1960s (figure 1).

No. of Leases

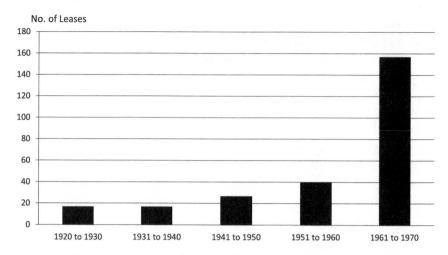

Figure 1. Number of public and Indian coal leases, 1920–70. Author-generated graph. Data from James S. Cannon and Mary Jean Haley, *Leased and Lost: A Study of Public and Indian Coal Leasing in the West* (New York: Council on Economic Priorities, 1974), 6.

During the decade, the Department of the Interior issued 67 percent of all leases ever granted. These new leases covered 939,000 acres of public and Indian lands—nearly four times the amount of acreage under lease prior to 1960—and close to 20 billion tons of recoverable coal. Only 11 percent of these leases, however, actually produced coal before the 1973 Arab oil embargo. In fact, in the entire history of the leasing program to that point, leased federal or Indian coal mines contributed less than 1 percent to the nation's coal production, despite the fact that these lands contained 45 percent of recoverable domestic reserves. Further, these nonproducing lands were controlled by a small number of large companies. By 1974, the largest fifteen leaseholders, which included major oil firms like Continental Oil (CONOCO), Shell Oil, Sun Oil (SUNOCO), and Gulf Oil, held 70 percent of the nation's coal leases. Of these leases, only 7 percent were producing coal. Energy firms had successfully tied up Indian and public coal, but they paid very little for the privilege.[9]

By the early 1970s, numerous government and private entities began decrying the structural flaws preventing the equitable development of the country's vast coal reserves. Tasked with reviewing the effectiveness of the program, the General Accounting Office condemned the competitive leasing process in 1972, explaining that "the mere leasing of federal land is not accomplishing the objective of the leasing program," which was to efficiently develop domestic energy sources and return fair profits to taxpayers and Indian owners. One year later, the National Academies of Sciences and Engineering noted that the mining laws were "conceptually and operationally outmoded" and declared that energy firms had so manipulated the leasing process that "the situation has become nearly chaotic." Assessing the program in 1974, the Council for Economic Priorities was even more direct in its criticism, stating, "In practice, the [Department of the Interior] has abdicated all responsibility for land use planning to corporate interests and has mismanaged the competitive leasing program so badly, it makes a mockery of the word competition."[10]

Recognizing the utter failure of the system to meet the original intent of the leasing legislation, the Department of the Interior halted further federal coal leasing in 1971. Two years later, after numerous reviews condemned the program, the agency announced an official moratorium, allowing limited mining to maintain existing operations but suspending prospecting permits "to allow the preparation of a program for the more orderly development of coal resources upon the public lands." This moratorium continued until 1976—right through the 1973 Arab oil embargo—until Interior officials devised new policies and procedures to ensure that public coal was developed in a responsible manner that returned revenue to the nation and reclaimed disturbed land.[11]

*

But the moratorium did not extend to tribal lands. Despite the fact that the Indian mineral development program was built on the same leasing template used for public minerals, and thus suffered the same problems, tribal leasing continued apace. In the eyes of many, it simply had to. Federal officials, energy executives, and even tribal leaders portrayed the tribes' vast energy reserves as the answer to crippling reservation poverty. Ceasing to lease would stymie development deemed essential to Indian survival.

Such enthusiasm for tribal energy development was understandable given the depth of Indian poverty. In 1960, at the beginning of the decade of intense leasing activity, the median income for all Indians was just $1,348, with Indian males claiming $1,792 compared to $4,300 for their white male counterparts. By the end of the decade, Indian income had risen to $4,347 but still was one-third the average 1970 American income of $13,188. This discrepancy in Indian wealth and the associated conditions of such poverty were particularly pronounced on rural reservations, where approximately 70 percent of Indians lived. In 1967, 76 percent of reservation families earned less than the poverty threshold of $3,000. Unemployment hovered at an astonishing 40 percent. The median years of schooling for Indian males was 8.4 years, two years less than the national average, and 22.4 percent had less than five years of school all together. In 1961, the Bureau of Indian Affairs could count only sixty-six Indians graduating from four-year colleges; in 1968, the number was still under two hundred. Infant mortality rates on rural reservations were nearly four times the national average, and the median life expectancy for reservation Indians was merely sixty-three years old, seven years below the average American.[12]

By the mid-1970s, these depressing statistics moved Congress to create the American Indian Policy Review Commission to make the first full accounting of Indian policy since the 1920s. Among its many tasks, the commission catalogued the substantial natural resources contained on Indian reservations and investigated how these assets were being used. The results confounded the commissioners. According to the BIA's head of Trust Services, in 1975 Indian reservations contained 50 of the nation's 434 billion tons of recoverable coal. That same year, the U.S. Geological Survey estimated tribes held 100 to 200 billion tons of the nation's 1,581 billion tons of known coal reserves. Under either measurement, at least 10 percent of the country's demonstrated coal resources were found on Indian reservations. In the West, where the locus of coal production had shifted and where the majority of Indian reservations were located, this meant tribes controlled a full 30 percent of the highly desirable, low-sulfur coal.[13]

In addition to coal, Indians possessed other energy resources in abundance. The Geological Survey conservatively estimated Indian oil and gas reserves to be 4.2 billion barrels of oil and 17.5 trillion cubic feet of gas, representing 3 percent of the nation's capacity. Many thought the tribal cache to be much higher. The Navajo tribe itself claimed to possess 100 billion barrels of oil and 25 trillion cubic feet of gas. Uranium numbers were also in dispute, but by 1979 the Department of Energy and national Indian groups agreed that tribes most likely possessed 37 percent of the nation's recoverable stash. While the specific figures could be contested, there was no doubt that American Indians stood to be major players in the energy industry. As LaDonna Harris, founder of Americans for Indian Opportunity, put it, "Collectively, they're the biggest private owners of energy in the country."[14]

Considering the extent of tribal resources, of which energy minerals were just a subset, the American Indian Policy Review Commission struggled to explain the pervasiveness of reservation poverty. Its 1977 final report noted:

> From the standpoint of personal well-being the Indian of America ranks at the bottom of virtually every social statistical indicator. On the average he has the highest infant mortality rate, the lowest longevity rate, the lowest level of educational attainment, the lowest per capita income and the poorest housing and transportation in the land. How is this disparity between potential wealth and actual poverty to be explained?

More baffling was the fact that these abundant tribal resources included the same energy sources that multinational energy firms were now seeking to develop with increasing vigor. The commission drew the only conclusion it could, stating that "at least one explanation [for the discrepancy] lies in the fact that a very significant part of this natural abundance is not controlled by Indians at all."[15]

For years, American Indians and their allies, including Felix Cohen during the 1930s, had argued this same point. In order to maximize benefits, tribal governments should control tribal resources. But federal law denied tribes this right. It paid lip service to sovereignty, efficient management, competitive bidding, pollution reduction, and other public goods. Yet in practice, the law left the control of energy resource development in the hands of government agencies not up to the task. The result was predictable. With Indians shut out and flaccid federal oversight, private energy firms well-versed in the intricacies of mining law and with abundant capital to invest in cheap coal stepped in and took over.

THE PREQUEL: NAVAJO AND HOPI ENERGY DEVELOPMENT

The Navajo and Hopi nations of the American Southwest would come to understand this wrecked system better than any other group.

For generations, the tribes' desert landscape had been deemed too remote and inhospitable for industrial development, but by the early twentieth century, tribal members, federal officials, and mining firms were learning of the region's ample mineral deposits. In 1923, federal agents orchestrated the formation of the Navajo Tribal Council specifically to manage such resources. In 1955, the Hopi Tribal Council was reconstituted for the same purpose. It was not, however, until the Southwest's post–World War II transformation into the centerpiece of the nation's new military-industrial complex that energy firms began targeting these resources in a sustained manner. During the war, area boosters had touted the region's strategic location and its vast, open land to secure numerous military bases, and after 1945, massive infusions of federal dollars spurred unprecedented growth in associated defense industries. Midwesterners flocked to fill these jobs, area farmers subdivided their struggling farms to meet the ensuing housing demand, and federal subsidies generated enough affluence to confirm most residents' faith in the American Dream.[16]

But to keep the dream afloat, enormous amounts of cheap energy were needed. New Deal dams had generated enough hydroelectricity to run wartime factories, but after World War II, southwestern energy demand increased exponentially. In 1940, the peak electricity consumption for New Mexico, Arizona, and Southern California, collectively, was only 1,329 megawatts on the most demanding summer day. By 1960, peak demand for Southern California alone was 5,467 megawatts. This explosion in demand sent regional leaders, utility executives, and federal officials scrambling to locate additional energy sources. L. M. Alexander, a senior official with Arizona's Salt River Project—originally a federally subsidized irrigation project that was now transforming into one of the region's largest utilities—summed up his and other energy companies' driving commitment: "[We] make certain there is enough electricity to operate every air conditioner, heater, and other type of electrical appliance our customers may want to use. They [the consumers] dictate—it is up to us to respond."[17]

And respond they did. To meet surging energy needs, mining firms and utilities began working with the federal government to access minerals locked away on public and Indian lands. In particular, early efforts focused on Navajo oil; energy executives obtained leases that increased reservation oil production by more than 300 percent during the 1950s. Oil drilling not only unlocked desperately needed energy for the region but also resulted in substantial tribal revenues. In 1959 alone, the Navajo netted close to $10 million in oil royalties. Combine these royalties with rents and bonuses paid for accessing reservation lands, and by 1962, the tribe had secured close to $76.5 million in oil proceeds. One wonders what the tribe could have received had the BIA been demanding fair market value.

Oil was not the only Navajo energy source in high demand. In 1951, the discovery of uranium on the Navajo Reservation triggered another frenzy of activity over this newly valuable resource. Timothy Benally, director of the Navajo Uranium Workers office, recalled, "Right after World War II, when the government found out what uranium could do, they decided to mine some of those areas and a lot of it was found on the reservation. People just went crazy looking for uranium, prospecting all over the reservation." Uranium development produced millions more, though as many have documented, the adverse environmental and health legacies of this mining remained long after the tribe dispensed all royalty revenue.[18]

Considering mining's monetary benefits, Navajo leaders warmly welcomed these early energy deals and collaborated with federal officials whom they trusted were working on the tribe's behalf. Explaining the relationship between his government and their federal trustee in 1956, Tribal Chairman Paul Jones noted:

> Basically we are determined to work cooperatively with Federal and State agencies in the development and execution of programs in which Navajos have such a heavy stake. . . . We do not approach this cooperative relationship with a defensive attitude based on the conviction that outside agencies are primarily designed to exploit us. Rather, we believe they and most of their personnel are sincerely devoted to the solution of problems.

Three years later, as oil and uranium royalties mounted, Jones continued to celebrate reservation resource development, publicly thanking "Divine Providence" for bringing his community "unexpected wealth from . . . natural resources."[19]

In fact, Navajo leaders actually hoped to quicken the pace of development and increase the tribe's role in mining ventures. In 1959, for instance, the same year Chairman Jones counted his divine blessings, the tribal council bypassed the BIA and negotiated directly with the Delhi-Taylor Oil Company to provide drilling rights for over five million reservation acres. Importantly, this agreement was not a typical lease but a partnership that promised the Navajo a 50 percent share of the profits, if also an increased percentage of the risks. Not for the last time, however, the BIA thwarted this attempt by a tribal government to increase its role in energy development. Claiming the trustee duty compelled them to prevent such a risky arrangement, federal officials vetoed this tribal-led energy project.[20]

*

Throughout the 1950s, then, Navajo oil and uranium provided vital energy for the expanding Southwest and desperately needed revenue for the tribe. Coal, however, would be the crown jewel in the region's future development plans. Changes in electricity transmission technology made cheap Indian coal particularly attractive to civic leaders, who sought to burn this dirty energy source far away on reservations and then transmit electricity via new, high-voltage wires to their clean and booming metropolises. In the mid-1950s, a consortium of energy companies began work on the Colorado Plateau's first coal-fired power plant, to be located on the eastern edge of the Navajo Reservation. To provide coal to the Four Corners Generating Station, BIA officials facilitated negotiations between the Navajo tribe and Utah International that opened almost 25,000 reservation acres to mining, returning fixed royalties to the tribe of 15 cents per ton. Beginning operations in 1962, Utah International's Navajo Mine would grow to be the largest strip mine in the world, supplying coal to the Four Corners plant, which by most accounts became America's single largest atmospheric polluter.[21]

But the world's largest strip mine and America's dirtiest power plant were just the beginning. Seizing on the momentum of these projects, in 1964, ten private utilities formed Western Energy Supply and Transmission Associates (WEST) to construct the largest regional power grid the world had ever seen. The "Grand Plan," as it was termed by one of its visionaries, James Malloy of Los Angeles's Department of Water and Power, was conceived as an integrated network of hydroelectric dams on the Southwest's mighty but infrequent rivers, nuclear facilities on the West Coast, and most important, dozens of coal-fired power plants along the interior Colorado Plateau. In addition to producing electricity for exploding population centers in Southern California, Nevada, and Arizona, power generated from this network would also fuel the Salt River Project and, later, the Central Arizona Project, both of which pumped millions of tons of precious water uphill, through the desert, to irrigate farmlands and supply such urban centers as Las Vegas and Phoenix. Trying to capture the magnitude of the project, a WEST spokesman explained that the program would "produce more than three times as much power as TVA, seventeen times as much as the Aswan Dam project in Egypt and eight times as much as the Soviet Union's largest power project." In the intoxicating times of the postwar American Sunbelt, anything seemed possible.[22]

Like many grandiose western schemes, the project, WEST's proponents claimed, would be a purely private endeavor, but nothing of this magnitude gets done in the American West without federal aid. WEST officials quickly recognized that although their proposed coal-fired boilers could provide the region's base supply of electricity, they would need to tap into the Bureau of Reclamation's existing power grid to efficiently meet peak demand. From the federal perspective, a partnership with the private utilities also made sense. Interior Secretary Stewart Udall understood that the dated U.S. hydroelectric system could not keep up with the Southwest's exploding energy demands, and environmental challenges made the construction of more large-scale federal dams untenable. Thus, in June 1965, federal and WEST officials announced plans to connect their systems, designing a joint private-federal grid that would produce electricity in the most efficient manner possible and allow excess power to be moved wherever it was most needed. And once committed, no one became a stronger advocate for this fantastic regional scheme than Stewart Udall, who hailed the partnership as "a giant step forward in the development of a formula for joint public and private resource development in the Colorado (River) Basin that will become a model for the Nation." Addressing Arizona State University graduates the same month this private-public partnership was announced, Udall beamed, "If we can perfect this new and unique partnership to produce low-cost electrical power for all, it will be the best region in the nation both to live in and work in." Arizona's native son intended to make his home a model of planned regional development for the rest of the country.[23]

By the time Udall began promoting his desert paradise, the ground-work for acquiring Indian coal to fuel the Grand Plan had already been laid. In 1961, the Sentry Royalty Company—the same prospecting arm of the Peabody Coal Company that would later secure Northern Chey-enne coal rights—began exploratory activities on Black Mesa, a mas-sive butte located within the Joint Use Area shared by the Navajo and Hopi tribes. The very next year, a subsidiary of Gulf Oil, the Pittsburg & Midway Coal Mining Company, obtained a prospecting permit for the eastern side of the Navajo Reservation. At WEST's formation in 1964, then, both Peabody and Gulf had already exercised lease options in these contracts to extract coal from over 35,000 acres on the Navajo Reservation. Just two years later, Peabody obtained more leases from the Hopi and Navajo to mine Black Mesa, and another joint venture by Consolidation Coal and the El Paso Natural Gas Company secured 40,000 more Navajo acres for coal mining. These same multinational energy firms would later become active on Northern Plains' reserva-tions, but they first exploited the broken leasing regime here on Navajo and Hopi lands. In doing so, they strategically positioned themselves to supply the many WEST-affiliated power plants scheduled to come on line in the late 1960s and early 1970s.[24]

Interestingly, with the exception of the last coal lease obtained by Consolidation Coal and El Paso, these energy firms acquired Navajo and Hopi mineral rights through negotiations with the BIA and tribal councils rather than through the competitive bidding process. Recall that federal law allowed for this possibility for Indian coal if BIA offi-cials determined it was in the tribe's best interest. Yet even a cursory re-view of the resulting lease negotiations make clear the dangers involved in negotiating complicated mineral deals with the world's largest energy firms. Simply put, tribal leaders and federal officials were not equipped to do battle. This is not to say that savvy and powerful energy execu-tives simply overwhelmed their incompetent and weak opponents, or that they used their supreme bargaining position to easily force Indians into exceptionally bad deals. Far from it. As the economist Brian Mor-ton demonstrates, Navajo and Hopi leaders actually struck deals that were either comparable to or better than federal leases issued for public coal during the same period. Still, Morton acknowledges these deals were "suboptimal"; the financial terms could have been much better, and tribes could have demanded more control over mining operations to ensure such things as better environmental protection.[25]

So why did the tribes end up with suboptimal leases? The long list of reasons should now sound familiar. To begin with, tribal leaders possessed little geological or market information for their minerals and lacked experience in negotiating long-term energy contracts, both of which left them unprepared to structure deals to return the greatest profits over the life of the contract. Anthropologist Lynn Robbins interviewed nineteen Navajo council members who "negotiated" the 1966 coal lease for Black Mesa, in the area jointly shared with the Hopi tribe, and found that most council members "knew nothing of the value of the coal, the extent of coal deposits on their own lands, alternatives to coal developments, or the possibility of raising coal prices through competitive bidding." Instead, Robbins noted that few of the councilors were proficient in English, they did not have sufficient time to review lease documents, and the interpretations of the contracts provided by the energy company and the tribe's own lawyers were insufficient to convey details of potential mining impacts. As council member Ken Smith explained, "we were asked, in effect, to say yes or no to the proposal" and not given sufficient time or information to carefully deliberate the decision.[26]

On the Hopi Reservation, tribal council members possessed a similar lack of information, especially with respect to strip mining's impact on the local ecology. As the Hopi's BIA land officer admitted to Alvin Josephy, a prominent Indian scholar active on both reservations at the time, the Hopi Tribal Council "didn't know [the energy companies] were going to pile mountains of dirt and just go off and leave it. If [the council] had known what they were going to do, you couldn't have got that lease for any amount of money." According to this official, the lease was worked out between the Hopi's attorney and BIA officials in Washington, D.C., with the tribal council never receiving advice from the local BIA office.[27]

Added to a dearth of information, reservation poverty clearly hamstrung tribal leaders' ability to evaluate the long-term benefits of energy projects. These officials understood their authority to lead rested upon their ability to return financial benefits to their desperate communities, and they narrowly focused on this result to the exclusion of all other considerations. Again, interviews with Navajo leaders who approved the 1964 and 1966 coal leases reveal how BIA and corporate promises of wealth drove their decisions. As Robbins reports, these leaders "believed [any] sacrifices to be decidedly limited," and "realiz[ing] the desperate need for a source of tribal income," they "believed tribal revenues from coal sales and new jobs created by construction, maintenance, and mining would be worth the sacrifices."[28]

Of course, if Navajo and Hopi leaders did not fully understand the deals they signed or were poorly positioned to negotiate them, the tribal populations they served were even more oblivious and powerless to shape development. During the 1966 Navajo negotiations, for instance, members of the local chapters that provided the basic political organization of the tribe were unaware negotiations were even occurring. According to Peterson Zah—at the time a young legal aid attorney assisting tribal members, but who later would become tribal chairman (1983–87) and president (1990–94)—this was not uncommon on the Navajo Reservation. Many Navajo never knew of the mineral leases until they were being evicted and given nominal consideration for their land, or given incomplete information about the environmental impacts of mining and "railroaded" into moving.[29]

The situation on the Hopi Reservation was even more distressing, as the BIA, energy companies, and the tribe's own representatives conspired to shut tribal members out of the deliberation process. For decades, the Hopi had been embroiled in an intense intratribal dispute over which governing institution formally represented the community. When energy companies came calling in the 1950s, the tribe's non-Indian attorney, John Boyden, convinced the Department of the Interior to recognize the Hopi Tribal Council as the legitimate governing body, rather than a coalition of traditional village chiefs known as the *Kikmongwis*. Despite ample evidence that the tribal majority opposed the council's authority and policies, Interior vested the tribal council with the authority to execute mineral leases. The agency then approved numerous tribal council energy deals, including the monstrous 40,000-acre coal lease, signed in 1966, to allow Peabody to mine Black Mesa. None of the details of these deals, however, were shared with tribal members. As Alvin Josephy noted in 1971, "The negotiations and the signing of the [Black Mesa] lease were conducted by the council and their lawyer in such secrecy that few other Hopis were aware of what was going on."

It gets worse. John Boyden, the lawyer leading negotiations on behalf of the Hopi, who had worked so hard to get federal officials to recognize the tribal council so that it could issue mineral leases, was secretly and simultaneously working for the Peabody Coal Company! At the same time Boyden was negotiating away Hopi coal rights underlying Black Mesa, he was representing Peabody in front of the Utah Water and Power Board. There, he quietly secured water rights for a proposed power plant designed to burn the Hopi coal he and his tribal council client granted to Peabody. The situation represented the worst of the worst for tribal members opposed to mining. Summing up the outrage shared by Hopi villagers once news of the Black Mesa lease leaked, one traditional leader condemned the council in the strongest possible terms:

> Your organization [the tribal council] was founded yesterday, "illicitly," a tool designed by the government to disrupt our cultural ways of life, rob us of our land and resources for industrial development of our land, to live like whiteman's ways, snare into financial difficulties, a scheme to claim our land by means of foreclosures. Without sufficient fact weighing you have blundered most dangerous positions, our land is in jeopardy and the generations to come.

But the deed was done. Even when knowledge of energy development created opposition, the political process for expressing such opposition was hijacked by energy companies, the Interior Department, and a few Hopi leaders.[30]

Stymied by internal tribal politics—politics adroitly exploited by outsiders—Navajo and Hopi anti-coal activists also found their federal trustee ill prepared to advocate on their behalf. Especially at the local level, BIA officials responsible for helping tribes negotiate mineral contracts were often as ignorant as their tribal clients in understanding how to construct energy leases that maximized return to Indian mineral owners. A decade after the Navajo and Hopi leases, the General Accounting Office was still noting the pervasive inadequacy of federal expertise, telling a Senate committee that the local BIA office overseeing these leases, "by its own admission, does not have adequate minerals expertise. Minerals management is, generally, carried out by staff without formal minerals training." Beyond the lack of expertise, local officials also lacked knowledge about the Indian resource base. Again, subsequent federal investigations revealed that only after energy companies nominated the particular tracts of land they wanted to prospect would federal officials conduct "a rudimentary exploration on each tract," though even "these surveys [were] rarely extensive." According to the Federal Trade Commission, the BIA's evaluation of reservation mining proposals amounted to "essentially guesswork." Faced with facilitating complicated mineral negotiations between equally inexperienced tribal leaders and the world's largest energy firms, federal officials were, at best, overmatched.[31]

At worst, the federal trustee duty was compromised by other, seemingly more pressing, obligations within the Department of the Interior. This large federal agency was charged not only with meeting its trustee duty to responsibly manage Indian resources but also with managing public resources to meet national needs. These dual mandates often brought several of Interior's bureaus—the Bureau of Reclamation, the Bureau of Land Management, the Geological Survey, and the Forest Service—into conflict with Indian interests. The risk for such conflict was especially acute with large-scale, private-public partnerships like WEST, where different resources had to be coordinated across multiple bureaucratic jurisdictions. By their very nature, these massive development projects united powerful interests within and outside the federal government, including southwestern congressmen, civic leaders, regional utilities, agribusinesses, and federal agencies that prioritized regional development over tribal well-being.

Such regional priorities became readily apparent in the mid-1960s as more tribal members questioned whether they were receiving all they should from reservation mining. As we saw with the Hopi—and will see again on the Northern Plains—Navajo mining opposition was tied closely to internal tribal politics, especially after the 1963 *Healing v. Jones* court case that designated portions of Black Mesa a Joint Use Area to be shared by the Navajo and Hopi. This decision split the Navajo over whether to partition the area, remove tribal members from their ancestral homelands, and relatedly, allow additional mining on Black Mesa. Raymond Nakai, the new tribal chairman, supported partition as well as ongoing negotiations with Peabody. Nakai's political opponents on the tribal council, however, opposed both. In December 1964, the tribal council moved to assert control by passing a resolution affirming its exclusive right to manage Navajo minerals and then revoking Peabody's Black Mesa prospecting permit, which Nakai had authorized a few months earlier. With Peabody's permit revoked, this internal tribal dispute suddenly threated one of the key coal sources for WEST's regional power grid.[32]

Peabody representatives were cautious not to intervene directly in this intratribal matter, but federal officials showed no such restraint. In June 1965, the same month the Bureau of Reclamation announced its partnership with WEST, Interior Secretary Udall called a meeting in Washington, D.C., to mediate the Navajo dispute. But to federal officials' dismay, the tribal council boycotted the gathering, forcing Udall to take his case to the press. In his July press conference, the Interior secretary publicly admonished Navajo leaders, noting:

> We have some very serious problems and some very fine opportunities in terms of economic development [on the Navajo Reservation]. I am hoping that some of them will come to a head within the next few weeks and if they do . . . most of them are going to involve not just the [Navajo] tribe; they are going to involve the state of Arizona. They are going to involve some of the large industrial concerns—this WEST electric power organization is keyed into the development of the Navajo and Hopi resources.

Udall next ratcheted up the pressure by appointing a special task force to address land management issues on the Navajo Reservation. In response, the Navajo's non-Indian attorney, Norman Littell, released his own press statement, complaining that federal officials had issued "a not-too-subtle implied threat on the Navajo Tribe that they had better do what Udall wishes" and that the secretary himself "has gone to great lengths over the past two years to force on the Navajo Tribe a lease agreement for Peabody Coal Company on his own terms." According to longtime Navajo activist John Redhouse, Littell's exposure of top-level government influence won him and the tribal council the support of most Navajo. The tribal attorney, rather than Chairman Nakai, now became the point man for coal negotiations.[33]

Despite this shift in leadership, Littell and his tribal council client understood the need for coal revenue and felt constant pressure to develop this resource. By November 1965, Udall's efforts forced the council back to the bargaining table, where Littell led months of new negotiations with Peabody. These talks ended in February 1966 with the tribal attorney returning triumphantly to the reservation and, as BIA Area Director Graham Holmes remembers, "walking up the Council aisle, waiving papers for the Council to approve, like the Savior had returned." Persuaded this was the best deal it could muster under federal pressure, the council ratified the renegotiated agreement, which was hailed as a victory for the Navajo, though it included a mere 25 cents per ton royalty. Meanwhile, Peabody secured cheap coal to fuel one of the key cogs in WEST's power-generation grid, the Mohave Generating Station.[34]

Interior officials applied similar pressures to obtain the coal and water necessary for the even larger, and aptly named, Navajo Generating Station. Located on land leased from the Navajo tribe adjacent to the recently completed Glenn Canyon Dam, this facility would supply electricity to the Central Arizona Project, a massive irrigation scheme concocted by Arizona Senators Barry Goldwater and Carl Hayden to pump water through the desert and onto nearly a million acres in central and southern Arizona. Originally the project called for dams to be constructed along the Grand Canyon, but Interior scrapped these plans under pressure from environmental groups, especially David Brower's Sierra Club. The Navajo Generating Station thus was an ingenious back-up plan to have a WEST supplier, the Peabody Coal Company, provide coal to a WEST member, the Salt River Project, which would run a power plant that sold electricity to another WEST partner, the Bureau of Reclamation, to move water uphill through the Arizona desert. And of course, this last WEST affiliate was part of a federal agency that, through another of its sub-agencies, the BIA, controlled access to the Indian coal and water needed to run the entire system. The conflict of interest was palpable.[35]

Yet despite the conflict, the Department of the Interior and WEST pushed ahead with this grandest of all plans, easily obtaining the necessary coal by expanding previously negotiated leases with the Navajo and Hopi tribes to mine Black Mesa. To meet the power plants' vast water needs, the Bureau of Reclamation—again, part of the same agency that was tasked with protecting Indian resources—convinced the Navajo to commit more than 34,000 acre-feet of water, leaving the tribe with less than 16,000 acre-feet from the Colorado River for future needs. In exchange for this concession, WEST promised to lease Navajo land for the power plant, purchase their coal, provide a limited number of jobs to Navajo laborers, and contribute $125,000 to the Navajo Community College.[36]

Not all were impressed by the equity of the exchange. Reviewing the agreement a few years later in 1971, Alvin Josephy, who by this time had served as a special consultant on Indian affairs to Interior Secretary Udall and authored a presidential report on the state of tribal communities, described the deal as an explicit "bilking of the Indians." In a blistering exposé entitled "The Murder of the Southwest," Josephy wrote:

> A conflict of interests seems to have been overlooked in the rush to get the deal settled. As trustee for the tribe's resources, the Department of the Interior was leasing the land at Page, giving away the Navajo's water, and selling the coal at Black Mesa; but, through the Bureau of Reclamation's role as purchaser of power at Page, it was also on the receiving end. It had a vested interest in the acquisition of the site and water at Page and the coal from Black Mesa. In a sense, [the Department of the Interior] was both buyer and seller.

And this condemnation came from the president's and Interior secretary's own advisor.[37]

*

By the early 1970s, Josephy's was not the only voice criticizing the use of Indian resources to meet non-Indian needs. As the infrastructure tying together WEST facilities began to take shape, many Navajo and Hopi protested the changes they witnessed to their land. Navajo tribal members organized the "Committee to Save Black Mesa" to voice complaints about energy companies' incessant road construction, the wasteful use of precious water supplies, and the potential relocation of more than six hundred Navajo families to make room for massive strip mines. Next door, Hopi anti-coal activists tied the irreparable environmental harm being done to their tribe's spiritual identity. As one group of Hopi elders explained:

> The area we call "Tukunavi" [which includes Black Mesa] is part of the heart of our Mother Earth. Within this heart, the Hopi has left his seal

by leaving religious items and clan markings and paintings and ancient burial grounds as his landmarks and shrines. . . . The land is sacred and if the land is abused, the sacredness of Hopi life will disappear and all other life as well.

Beyond these spiritual pleas, Hopi villagers also continued their fight against the tribal council. Aided by the newly formed Native American Rights Fund, members filed a 1971 lawsuit to halt reservation mining, arguing that the council lacked legal authority to issue coal leases. The court ultimately threw out the case, ruling the tribal council's sovereign immunity protected it from suit, but the publicity generated by the anti-coal backlash resulted in special, on-site Senate hearings to assess the social, economic, and environmental implications of WEST's regional plans. Anthropologist Richard Clemmer posits that these hearings may have contributed to the cancellation of even larger projects, but existing development continued unabated.[38]

And such was the fate of many Indian energy projects begun before the 1970s. The potent mix of environmental justice claims, declarations of cultural loss, and sensational accounts of corruption temporarily captured national attention, but organized opposition to reservation development in the Southwest came mostly too little too late. In 1970, *Time* magazine, the *Washington Post,* and the ABC nightly news all ran stories on the Navajo's and Hopi's travails. By 1971, however, as the *New York Times* warned that "the magnificent red buttes and virgin forests of the Navajo nation may soon . . . become a vast slag heap . . . to satisfy the need of Los Angeles and Phoenix for more electricity and smog," the majority of these reservation energy deals were done and the projects under way.[39]

Revelations regarding the unsavory conditions in which these early deals were consummated did have substantial impacts on the future direction of Indian mining. New tribal leadership emerged to offer a different model for controlling such development. In 1970, Peter MacDonald unseated Navajo Tribal Chairman Nakai by tapping into growing nationalist sentiments among younger tribal members who tied exploitative energy development to a larger critique against the objectification of Navajo culture. To these young activists, corrupt, capital-driven mining projects represented the final step in incorporating Navajo society into the national mainstream, replacing indigenous values and customs with non-Indian patterns that threatened to colonize not only the land but also tribal lifeways. Informed by third world intellectuals spurring nationalist movements abroad and contemporary minority movements within the United States, this colonial critique blamed bad energy deals on an imperialist federal government intent on "modernizing" (that is, anglicizing) the "savage" Navajo, exploitative corporations and urban consumers that sought to capitalize on Indian resources, and corrupt or incompetent tribal leaders who let it all happen. Reflecting this sentiment, the new chairman vowed to end "the colonial relationship between the Navajo Nation and the cities of the Southwest" by insisting on "Navajo control of Navajo resources."[40]

But Peter MacDonald did not seek to simply halt all reservation mining. He understood that once energy infrastructure was in place, it would be incredibly difficult to dislodge. The strip mines, power plants, and connecting roads and wires crisscrossing his reservation provided tangible reminders of how much effort and capital had been expended to extract Navajo coal. These items also indicated how strong the forces were that intended to continue production. For MacDonald, then, success lay not in attacking and shutting down ongoing operations but in shaping this development to meet Navajo needs. The new leader thus taxed and regulated those projects responsible for so much local opposition, ensuring that more revenue stayed on reservation while limiting the overall scope of development. For future projects, MacDonald explored new commercial arrangements outside the typical lease form that better positioned the tribe to control the pace and scale of mining and regulate its unwanted impacts. By exerting control over this industry, not foreclosing it, MacDonald believed his government could develop the economic base necessary to free the Navajo from their dependence on federal subsidies and regional development plans. In a theme that other tribal leaders would later pick up on, the Navajo chairman understood energy development as an opportunity to realize tribal sovereignty, not just a threat to it.[41]

Still, the early, intrusive energy projects on the Navajo and Hopi Reservations remained as testaments to the hard lessons learned. During the 1960s, tribal leaders who were theoretically positioned to negotiate and issue mineral leases were simply unequipped to do so. Locked within the same broken, bureaucratic system used to manage public minerals, the tribal leasing program shared all the same inadequacies. Tribal and federal officials lacked geological and market data to evaluate leasing bids and failed to generate competition to establish fair market mineral values. Yet the situation on tribal lands was even more dire. Suffocating reservation poverty lent an air of urgency to federal trustees' efforts to secure tribal revenue, and Navajo and Hopi leaders could hardly afford to turn away any revenue source, however meager. Their desperation made it nearly impossible to critically evaluate mining proposals from the world's largest energy firms. Encouraged by ignorant or duplicitous federal officials, Navajo and Hopi leaders thus welcomed the opportunity to develop their minerals, failing to recognize potentially harmful impacts on their communities and landscapes.

But tribal members living near energy projects understood the consequences all too well. Faced with the loss of home and community, these Navajo and Hopi launched the first wide-scale Indian opposition to industrial energy development. Sadly for them, their voices were often silenced by tribal politics orchestrated by outsiders. Moreover, competing directives within the Interior Department sometimes compromised their federal trustee, subjugating the trust duty to other, seemingly more pressing, national concerns. Whether thwarted by ignorant or corrupted representatives, these Indian anti-coal activists sounded the alarm but were unable to halt the threat.

Their resistance, however, was not without effect. Southwestern protests informed a new generation of leaders dedicated to tribal control of tribal resources. These leaders responded to their constituents' desires to reject imperialistic energy projects, but they also explored innovative ways to make development meet tribal needs. In addition, the resistance helped train consultants and attorneys to assist tribal communities. Out of the southwestern experience, for example, the Native American Rights Fund would emerge to guide the tribal response to energy development. As prequels do, these events shaped the course of future, more successful actions to control reservation mining along the Northern Plains.

3 "The Best Situation in Their History"

THE NAVAJO AND Hopi nations of the American Southwest may have had the most experience with postwar energy development, but they were not alone. Across the country, other tribes were receiving similar educations. The exploding American economy continued to demand more and more energy, and federal officials seized the opportunity to secure tribal revenue and meet national needs. From 1964 to 1974, the Bureau of Indian Affairs held hundreds of lease sales for Indian oil and gas, producing tens of thousands of individual leases. This activity was focused and sustained, with the federal government approving 13,200 oil and gas leases in 1964, 12,096 leases in 1969, and 13,619 leases in 1974. Uranium leasing was more moderate during this period, but these dangerous mining operations continued to be disproportionately located on tribal lands. In fact, by 1974, 100 percent of the nation's non-private uranium production was found on Indian reservations.[1]

Despite the importance of reservation oil, gas, and uranium to meeting the nation's growing energy needs, coal remained the key Indian contribution to America's energy plans. In the decade and a half leading up to the 1973 Arab oil embargo, the BIA approved leases authorizing the removal of low-sulfur coal from more than 250,000 reservation acres in New Mexico, Arizona, Colorado, Utah, and Montana, with millions more acres opened to prospecting. More astonishing than the amount of tribal land opened to mining was the typically massive size of each individual lease. The average coal lease on public land, for instance, authorized mining on approximately 1,470 acres. On Indian reservations, the average coal lease covered 23,523 acres, a figure that was ten times larger than acreage limits contained in the Department of the Interior's own regulations.[2]

Just as troubling as the immense size of these leases was the fact that the dysfunctional legal system that produced them continued to provide meager tribal revenues. Again, on average, tribal leases in the 1960s and early 1970s paid royalties of 15.8 cents a ton. Contrast this figure with the fact that by 1974 the state of Montana was taxing coal extracted from Indian lands at 62.5 cents a ton. In other words, Montana could expect to receive four times more tax revenue from Indian minerals than the mineral owners would receive. To make matters worse, the deals put together with the BIA's blessing contained no escalating royalty clauses to reflect changes in coal's market price. The Department of the Interior had discarded the practice of using fixed royalty terms for public coal in favor of royalties based on a percentage of the sale price, but the same approach, inexplicably, was not applied to Indian leases. As coal prices skyrocketed during the 1970s in response to disruptions in the flow of Middle Eastern oil, the injustice of these terms became all too clear. During the 1960s, Indian royalties of 15 cents a ton looked bad compared to average coal values of $4.50 a ton. When the 1974 average hit nearly $15.00 a ton, the discrepancy appeared more like out-and-out theft.[3]

EXPANDING THE FIRST COAL SALE

The efforts of the Peabody Coal Company to gain access to Northern Cheyenne coal, detailed in chapter 1, fit clearly within this broader process of multinational energy firms exploiting a broken regulatory regime to control Indian resources. Working under blind conditions with no geologic or market data, but faced with stark reservation poverty, the BIA had staged the Northern Cheyenne's first coal auction in 1966, securing exactly one bid from the prospecting arm of the world's largest coal producer. Yet federal and tribal officials were happy to have it. Charles Corke, the same federal agent who originally suggested a fixed royalty of 17.5 cents, admitted after receiving the Sentry Royalty Company's bid that "the quality and quantity of coal on Northern Cheyenne was completely unknown at the time of the bid opening"; thus he considered the low bid price appropriate considering the risk of finding little coal. Similarly, BIA regional staff member F. F. DuBray reported that his Washington superiors "were surprised that any bids were received and felt that the 12¢ per acre was very good in this unproven area, particularly from a reputable bidder."[4]

For their part, the Northern Cheyenne's reaction was not much different. The new reservation superintendent, John White, recalled that "both the Tribal Council and Bureau personnel felt at the time that it was fortunate that even one bid was received from an experienced and well-financed operator." White surmised the tribe "would benefit, at the very least, from learning definitely whether or not it had merchantable coal in the northeastern sector of the reservation." After the auction, Tribal President John Woodenlegs took it upon himself to meet with BIA Commissioner Robert Bennett to thank his agency for being "instrumental in promoting this phase of resource development" and reported that "the Cheyenne people today find themselves in the best situation in their history." With no information as to how much coal underlay the reservation nor a firm sense of its market value, all were simply anxious to get any mining project started.[5]

This eagerness to realize an immediate return for reservation resources showed in the swift actions taken to begin production. Exactly one week after the lackluster auction, the Northern Cheyenne Tribal Council accepted Sentry's offer, clearing the way for the BIA to authorize prospecting to begin before the end of summer. Sentry wasted no time, drilling several exploratory wells within the first month of authorization. The prospecting proceeded so quickly, in fact, and the geological data proved so encouraging, that by the end of 1966 Peabody had already stepped in to take over Sentry's interests in the coal contract. By the following summer of 1967, Peabody sought to expand the permit and again requested a waiver of the acreage limitation so that it could construct a massive, mine-mouth facility on the reservation. Things were going according to plan. Reservation Superintendent John White assured Peabody that the acreage limitation "should present no problem," and by the end of October 1967, the tribe approved the permit expansion under the same terms of the original permit (12 cents per acre bonus, with potential royalties of 17.5 cents per ton of coal mined). Again, the tribe was just as eager as any other party to begin mining to generate revenue.[6]

But by the time the Northern Cheyenne granted Peabody's 1967 extension, some federal officials had collected enough data to question the financial terms contained in the original contract. On November 9, 1967, BIA Area Director James Canan wrote to the commissioner of Indian Affairs agreeing in principle with Peabody's permit expansion but inquiring whether the bonus was still sufficient. Canan suggested that instead of incorporating the terms of the original permit, the tribe should be given the authority to negotiate directly with Peabody for better returns. Charles Corke agreed, claiming the original bonus "was merely a token bid and should never be used as a basis for negotiations for additional acreage." Noting that recent coal sales in the region produced better financial terms, officials from both the BIA and Geological Survey recommended that the Northern Cheyenne now demand a higher price. In the rapidly changing world of western energy development, the same federal officials that were delighted to receive any offer for Cheyenne coal one year prior were now pushing the tribe to demand more.[7]

Armed with new market information, the Northern Cheyenne went back to Peabody to renegotiate the extension. Prepared to accept bonuses of two to three dollars an acre, tribal leaders were astounded when Peabody responded with a February 1968 offer of over thirty dollars an acre to expand the permit. Superintendent John White recalled council members expressing "general, if somewhat concealed, pleasant surprise" at the counterproposal, which represented the highest price Peabody had ever paid for western coal. Obviously, the world's largest coal company saw something in Cheyenne coal. The tribe quickly accepted the offer "without haggling," according to White, giving "the Tribal Council its first 'big money' from the coal resource."[8]

THE SECOND COAL SALE

Emboldened by their successful renegotiations over Peabody's permit extension, the Northern Cheyenne leadership now pressed their advantage. On its own accord, the tribal council passed a resolution directing the BIA to offer the entire remaining reservation for coal development. Interestingly, the Northern Cheyenne council member spearheading this resolution was Allen Rowland, the man who would later lead the fight against reservation mining. As tribal president in the 1970s, Rowland would epitomize the hard education many tribal leaders received, belatedly turning against coal development after it became clear such activity threatened his government's control of the reservation. As a council member during the early heyday of prospective mining, however, he demanded that the council's initial resolution offering only the "western portion" of the reservation to mining be amended to include all reservation lands not already under contract. The rest of the Cheyenne leadership agreed. Noting "the proper time for permitting, leasing and developing coal has arrived," the tribal council resolved that the BIA advertise the entire reservation at a second coal auction, urging that "such advertising for leasing and permitting be done without further delay."[9]

This time, however, federal officials resisted. BIA Assistant Area Director Reinholt Brust wrote to Superintendent John White that the area office had "no objection to offering some lands, [but] we feel that offering the entire reservation at this time may not be very successful since there has not been a specific request from the [coal] companies." Officials from the Geological Survey agreed. Suddenly concerned about the low demand reflected in the first coal auction and the low bid price it garnered, Regional Mining Supervisor Albert Czarnowsky proposed a staggered plan of development, first offering a few select tracts and only opening up additional land "as market tested." These officials argued for an incremental approach that would allow all parties, including coal companies, to gradually acquire more geological data, which if promising, would produce higher bids. As the industry generated more data and word of the Cheyenne's extensive holdings circulated, the thinking went, more competition would emerge to drive the price up further.[10]

Seeking to maximize revenue over the long run, federal officials once again unilaterally altered Cheyenne coal auction terms. Without tribal input, the BIA drafted a notice of sale offering only a few tracts of land near Peabody's existing permit area and forwarded a draft tribal resolution to the tribal council, now led by newly elected President Rowland, to ratify. Deferring to the supposed expertise of federal officials, the council agreed to the incremental approach and passed the BIA-drafted resolution on February 6, 1969. When asked why his administration did not push back against BIA suggestions, Rowland later admitted, "We thought the U.S. Government wouldn't rip us off so we let it ride." The tribal president and other Cheyenne leaders desperately desired income, but they seemed content to leave the details for maximizing profits to their federal trustees.[11]

The resulting second coal auction, held on July 30, 1969, must have provided little solace that this trust was appropriately placed. As with the first coal sale, the auction attracted only one bidder, and again that bidder was the Peabody Coal Company, which offered miniscule bonuses. Although tribal and federal officials were disappointed, the federal trustees pushed forward nonetheless, recommending the tribe accept Peabody's bid. The Geological Survey's mining supervisor, Albert Czarnowsky, explained his recommendation:

> Although the bids were not as large as expected by some, I recommend that the bids be accepted and the permits issued. We have no knowledge of the extent of workable coal seams or the reserves on the lands. Peabody has demonstrated its willingness to expend large sums of money in prospecting when given the right. The information gained is valuable both to the company and the mineral owners. It must be remembered that the big monetary return to the Tribe will not be from the bonus, but from the royalty if prospecting proves up workable deposits. Since there was not competitive interest it appears that to turn down the bids at this time would probably delay any other prospecting on the lands for years to come.

The federal "experts" admitted their ignorance but were happy to let Peabody start digging on the cheap until it found coal. Once everyone had a better understanding of the extent of Cheyenne coal deposits, officials figured, the tribe could cash in on subsequent deals. As for the tens of thousands of acres promised to Peabody for low bonuses and pre-fixed royalties of 17.5 cents, apparently that was a cost of doing business.[12]

In addition to federal recommendations that the Northern Cheyenne accept the new Peabody offer, the mining company applied its own pressure by threatening to halt other coal development activities unless the Northern Cheyenne accepted the latest proposal. Sensing that the dream of mining revenues could slip by, the tribal council not only accepted Peabody's offer on the second coal sale, but it then immediately entered negotiations for a lease on the first permit and the right to construct a railroad line to the coal fields. These discussions resulted in a July 1970 agreement for Peabody to construct "transportation facilities, either railroad or pipeline or both" and an August 1970 lease to authorize the first commercial coal mine on the Northern Cheyenne Reservation.[13]

Although the tribal council granted Peabody these concessions, it would be a mistake to characterize the negotiations that produced them as completely one-sided. Certainly, it was clear that tribal leaders desired to get the deals done, but they did not simply roll over to Peabody's demands. Instead, they pushed hard to meet immediate tribal needs and shape Peabody's operations as much as their bargaining power would allow. In the negotiations over the transportation corridor, for instance, Peabody's director of land, W. H. Oestreicher, was forced to acknowledge that "the questions raised by the members of the Council were well taken, and showed that much thought has been given to this matter by the members." Likewise, when consummating the August 1970 lease, tribal leaders pushed through amended royalty terms making revenue immediately available to meet pressing needs, rather than delaying royalties until production began as the original deal stipulated. In theory, securing these advanced royalties may have cost the tribe money in the long run, but as one BIA official who assisted the tribe put it, "The Northern Cheyenne Tribe could ill afford the luxury of economic theory instead of an early return." Tribal leaders were beholden to impoverished constituents and made pragmatic decisions to address critical concerns.[14]

THE THIRD COAL SALE

Still, despite tribal and BIA efforts, by the end of the summer of 1970, the Northern Cheyenne had secured just one lease and one prospecting permit, with one coal company, to mine one portion of the reservation at incredibly low prices. Undeterred, tribal leaders pushed forward, believing Peabody's prospecting efforts would reveal the potentially enormous dimensions of the Northern Cheyenne coal deposits. Federal officials had originally deemed Peabody's drilling information confidential, but they ultimately concluded that publicly releasing data for lands outside Peabody's lease area would generate interest in the tracts Peabody chose not to mine. The tactic paid off. The tribe and the BIA began fielding numerous inquiries from multinational oil companies such as Gulf, Texaco, Shell, Mobil Oil, and Belco Petroleum; from giant coal companies like Consolidation Coal and AMAX; and even from regional prospectors and speculators like the Billings-based firm Norsworthy & Reger.[15]

Eager to capitalize on this increased interest, the Northern Cheyenne suggested innovative techniques to enhance potential returns from yet another coal sale. In October 1970, Allen Rowland wrote to BIA Superintendent White requesting again that the BIA open the entire reservation to mining and that the agency take action at "as early a date as possible to advertise such lands as apparently contain coal." Convinced substantial interest now existed for his tribe's coal, the Northern Cheyenne leader proposed the latest auction be held in two phases to drive up the price: an initial silent auction where bids were submitted in writing, followed by oral bidding between those companies that had submitted written bids. Rowland told White he was aware this tactic had been used on other reservations, and that "by proceeding in this manner, the Tribe then would be able to receive the greatest available amount of royalty and rental for the tracts of land advertised for mineral bids." As Peabody's prospecting work continued to provide more geological data, and regional mining activity intensified, Cheyenne leaders were learning how to structure coal sales to maximize revenue.[16]

This time, armed with sufficient information regarding the Cheyenne resource base and confident substantial interest existed, federal officials relented to Rowland's request for a massive, reservation-wide coal sale. On April 22, 1971, the BIA split the reservation into eighteen tracts of land and offered the remaining 367,429.03 acres to mining. Unlike the previous coal sales, this auction produced stiff competition. Twelve different firms submitted bids covering every tract of land offered. These bids diverged widely in price, but the total amount of bonuses offered exceeded $2 million. It seemed the Northern Cheyenne had finally secured the lucrative payday it and BIA officials had been working toward.[17]

Yet despite the long-awaited materialization of competition and the relatively high bid prices, federal officials now split on whether the tribe should accept these offers. The Geological Survey advised accepting all bids so the Northern Cheyenne could finally get a full accounting of its mineable reserves. BIA staff, however, recommended that only the five highest bids be accepted and that the tribe then negotiate with the highest bidders on all other tracts to reach a more acceptable price. Cheyenne leaders, buoyed by their successful Peabody talks, elected to negotiate. After first brokering deals with the highest bidders—one of which was the Consolidation Coal Company—on five selected tracts, the tribal council entered talks with other energy companies to secure better financial terms. Leaders successfully consummated contracts with some but refused to compromise with others. Ultimately, these negotiations opened a total of 243,808 acres to prospecting, representing 56 percent of the reservation. The talks also secured close to $2 million in additional bonuses.[18]

More interesting than the deals the tribal council brokered, however, were the ones they rejected. Cheyenne leaders refused additional proposals from Belco Petroleum and Consolidation Coal that would have paid hundreds of thousands, if not millions, more bonus dollars for particularly promising tracts in the central and western part of the reservation. In rejecting these deals, the tribal council left badly needed revenue on the table, but the Northern Cheyenne were beginning to grasp the immense size of their assets and held out for better terms.[19]

The actions of the Consolidation Coal Company would soon prove these leaders correct. After the heavy Montana snows melted in the spring of 1972, Consolidation began exploratory work on the single tract of land it won during the Cheyenne's third coal auction, in an area immediately adjacent to the promising tracts it and Belco had been denied. By the end of June, the company informed the BIA that its surface mapping was complete and its initial drilling nearly done. Seven days later, on July 6, 1972, Consolidation officers then walked into a closed-door meeting to present the massive mining proposal that tribal and federal officials had been working for (see prologue). This offer, which included a bonus payment of close to $2.5 million and the promise of over $250 million in future royalties, appeared to reward the Cheyenne's long and difficult efforts.

But something on the reservation had changed. As news of this grandiose plan traveled beyond tribal headquarters and into the homes of ordinary Cheyenne, the community began to mobilize against it. Suddenly, desperately needed revenue was not the singular goal. This grassroots resistance would ultimately cripple Consolidation's plans. It also would spark a national indigenous movement that both equipped tribes with the tools to develop their own minerals and restructured the legal system governing Indian resources. The decades of chicanery, incompetence, and riding roughshod over tribal sovereignty were coming to an end. A new era was beginning, and the Northern Cheyenne were at the center. Indeed, the movement would produce changes so profound that the eminent Montana historian K. Ross Toole labeled the tiny Northern Cheyenne "the most important tribe in America." It is to that remarkable tale that we now turn.[20]

2

LOCAL RESISTANCE

4 "The Most Important Tribe in America"

IN THE FALL of 1971, as Navajo Chairman Peter MacDonald began regulating reservation development and Northern Cheyenne President Allen Rowland was negotiating new deals following his tribe's successful third coal auction, the United States Department of the Interior quietly released a technical report with the innocuous title *North Central Power Study*. Produced in conjunction with thirty-five private and public energy suppliers to fourteen different states, this study outlined plans to construct forty-two power plants in the coal-rich fields of southeastern Montana, northern Wyoming, and the western Dakotas. Together, these facilities would produce annually 50,000 megawatts of electricity, encompass almost 8 percent of regional surface land, and consume more water than New York City did in half a year. Considering 80 percent of the prospective electricity was tagged for markets outside the Rocky Mountain region, the transmission line right-of-ways would encompass another 5,000 square miles—approximately the size of Connecticut. Analysts estimated a population influx of more than half a million new residents to the region and remarked that the project held the potential to generate more power than any country in the world, save the United States and the Soviet Union. Confident this astronomical undertaking could be accomplished, the *North Central Power Study* concluded that, considering the United States' extensive energy needs and the realities of constricting international oil supplies, "the further development of the vast coal fields of the North Central region of the United States is almost a certainty." In short, the technical report with the innocuous title proposed nothing less than a "national sacrifice area" to meet the nation's pressing energy needs.[1]

Situated squarely in the middle of this forsaken region, the Northern Cheyenne knew nothing of the *North Central Power Study*. Almost no one did. According to K. Ross Toole, the University of Montana historian who took up the contemporary cause of exposing the breadth of development planned for the Northern Plains, fewer than one hundred people in the entire state of Montana likely knew about the document. Even though federal officials at the Bureau of Reclamation coordinated the study, and despite the fact that Indian coal would provide a major fuel source for these regional power plants, there is no indication that the Cheyenne's federal trustees at the Bureau of Indian Affairs knew of the report. This is not to say that BIA officials and tribal leaders were unaware of the growing demand for the area's low-sulfur coal. After all, we have seen how they cultivated such interest. But they failed to connect the individual deals they negotiated with the massive plans being drawn for the surrounding region. Without this connection, Cheyenne coal proponents could not fully appreciate the impacts this scale of energy development would have on the tiny Northern Cheyenne community.[2]

This lack of recognition changed dramatically with the Consolidation Coal Company's July 1972 proposal. To Allen Rowland, his fellow council members, and BIA officials, the audacious plan to construct four gasification plants and a 70,000-acre reservation mine marked the culmination of their efforts to land a lucrative mining enterprise that would uplift the impoverished Northern Cheyenne. These folks focused on development and revenue, and they desired both immediately. Consolidation executives, who were well aware of the *North Central Power Study* and understood the impending explosion of demand for the region's low-sulfur coal, also appreciated the time-sensitive nature of the project, and their urgency showed. The day after presenting his company's lucrative offer to tribal leaders, Consolidation's vice president for western operations, Dell Adams, followed up with a letter outlining the deal's specific terms and including a not-so-subtle threat. Urging the tribe to forego the usual competitive bidding procedure so as to save time, Adams warned:

If Consol cannot conclude negotiations with the Northern Cheyenne tribe at an early date, Consol will be forced to take this project elsewhere. If it becomes necessary to do this, this project will be lost to the Northern Cheyenne, and it may be a long time before a project of this magnitude comes again, if ever.[3]

But there was more. In an apparent attempt to demonstrate the feasibility of the project, Adams made clear that Consolidation was not acting alone but for years had been "working with . . . major suppliers and transmitters of natural gas with the objective of developing a major coal-gasification complex." These partners were essential, Adams explained, to coordinating "the various aspects of the project—mining, gasification, and transportation," and thus Consolidation must be able to assign its property rights to these entities if it were deemed "essential to the sound business organization of the project." Moreover, Consolidation asked the tribal government to help obtain any and all property rights necessary for the construction of "roads, buildings, pipelines, plants, tanks, dam site locations, transmission lines, and other structures" necessary for the project. In short, Consolidation demanded that the tribe relinquish sovereign control over land-planning decisions so that the mining firm could make rational economic calculations about what parts of the reservation to develop, how to develop them, and when.[4]

Despite Consolidation's aggressive demands, tribal leaders did not initially reject the project but continued to entertain the coal company's proposal. They had put too much work into landing this lucrative energy project to let the deal dissolve. Tribal and BIA officials met again with Consolidation on July 25, and although the parties could not reach a final agreement, the Northern Cheyenne began work on a counteroffer, implicitly accepting the process of negotiation over competitive bidding. As Cheyenne leaders focused on the details of the deal, however, trouble brewed outside the tribal government's offices.[5]

STRANGE BEDFELLOWS

Bill Bryan was just one of several unfamiliar faces in the crowd that gathered in Billings, Montana, on July 25, 1972, to discuss energy development in eastern Montana. Held the same day Consolidation executives were meeting with BIA and Northern Cheyenne officials, this public meeting was organized by the coal company to assuage fears that its proposed operations would disrupt life on the Northern Plains. By summer 1972, the *North Central Power Study* was losing its anonymity, and a small but dedicated group of environmentalists and ranchers sought more information about proposed regional coal development. Fearing Consolidation's plans signaled the implementation of the *North Central Power Study*, numerous state officials, including future governor and current director of State Lands Ted Schwinden, several concerned academics, and a smattering of environmental activists attended Consolidation's meeting.

As it turns out, this small gathering represented ground zero for the nascent environmental movement in Montana, and these folks were just beginning to know one another. Bryan, a freshly minted PhD from the University of Michigan, had just completed a dissertation examining how ten individual "change agents," including David Brower, Ralph Nader, and Saul Alinsky, employed guerilla warfare tactics tinged with the principles of judo to combat powerful, entrenched corporate interests and produce social and environmental change. It was a heady time. Another of Bryan's dissertation subjects, Clancy Gordon, was a "radical botanist" at the University of Montana who was making a name suing Montana corporations whose air emissions damaged local flora. Professor Gordon also happened to be one of the few Montanans possessing a copy of the *North Central Power Study*. Encouraged by Huey Johnson of the Nature Conservancy to get some "scars on his face" in the world of environmental activism, Bryan took a $15,000 grant Johnson secured from the *Whole Earth Catalog* and arrived at Gordon's Missoula home in the summer of 1972 to fight the *North Central Power Study*.[6]

Calling himself the "Northern Rocky Mountain Environmental Advocate," Bryan was full of determination but short on direction. He came to Montana to fight the *North Central Power Study*, but by summer 1972 it was becoming difficult to find anyone to defend the project. Gatherings like the July 25 Consolidation meeting triggered fears among the plan's proponents that they had set off an environmental backlash. Now, energy executives and government officials alike rushed to distance themselves from the project. As one Montana legislator told an inquiring K. Ross Toole, "Oh hell, [the *North Central Power Study*] was just a trial balloon. It's [already] out the window." Why thirty-five power companies and the federal government would invest substantial resources into a year-long, coordinated study to float a "trial balloon" that no one knew about is unclear.[7]

With no clear picture of whether the massive, region-wide energy scheme was still viable, Bryan worked all summer organizing a general network of "advocates to build a sophisticated action center that concentrates on environmental problem solving throughout the region." This vague objective was as specific as the young activist could muster as he traveled the region looking for a wedge into the environmental fight. Even after the July 25 Consolidation meeting, which Bryan described as "a very interesting experience . . . watching both the oil and coal interests in action as well as some environmentalists," there was no clear path forward. By the end of the summer, Clancy Gordon was cautioning Bryan against "overcommitment and [the] superficial treatment of many issues," but Bryan still had no specific issue to attack or community to defend.[8]

He finally found his mission in a small apartment in Bozeman, Montana. On September 7, 1972, local attorney Jim Goetz summoned Bill Bryan to meet with a client who could use his specific skill set. An active member of the burgeoning Montana environmental movement, Goetz was litigating several environmental lawsuits across the state, but this particular client had a problem Goetz believed needed an extralegal approach. The meeting was set for a one-room apartment in Montana State University's student and faculty housing. Bryan later recalled that when he entered the dimly lit room he was unable to make out any faces but knew immediately it was packed with American Indians. Sitting down, the young activist expected to hear a detailed account of this group's specific problem and a plea for his assistance, but he got no such reception. Instead, after a few gruff introductions and some silence, a young woman named Marie Sanchez startled Bryan with the blunt question, "What can you do for us?"[9]

Descended directly on her mother's side from the nineteenth-century leader Little Wolf and on her father's side from the famous Cheyenne warrior Braided Hair (or Braided Locks), Marie Brady Sanchez was a full-blooded Northern Cheyenne. She was also part of a group of tribal members growing increasingly alarmed by their government's policies to pursue energy development at all costs. Since 1968 when the first Peabody prospecting crews arrived on the reservation to drill exploratory wells, Sanchez and other Northern Cheyenne had convened regularly at Dave Robinson's ranch near Muddy Creek to discuss the impacts of coal mining. Most of the group's members owned small allotments of land on the reservation, which they leased to Cheyenne and non-Indian ranchers for modest, but vital, revenues. On a reservation where 62 percent of the land was tribally owned, these landowners were a distinct minority, but they were directly positioned to be harmed by the tribal government's energy deals and had the numbers to lodge an effective protest. It was their land that would be disturbed and their precious ranching revenues that would be disrupted by coal mining. The landowners who met at the Robinson ranch were only a small fraction of this minority, but they were a committed bunch.[10]

They also were a fairly eclectic group. Most attendees were "breeds," the descendants of mixed-race parents who typically fared better negotiating the non-Indian economic system surrounding the reservation. Due to their relative success, these breeds were more likely to own property on the reservation, not having been forced to sell their allotments back to the tribe or outside creditors. A smaller but significant percentage of this group, however, were "bloods," like Sanchez, who typically faced greater barriers interacting with the surrounding community. A lack of fluency in English, disparate cultural values, and an incomplete understanding of non-Indian economic practices often left this class economically disadvantaged, though some were able to hold onto portions of their, or their kin's, allotment.[11]

To be clear, any description of the differences between "breeds" and "bloods" lends itself to potentially gross overgeneralizations. Particularly on twentieth-century Indian reservations, the labels themselves often have less to do with an individual's genetic makeup and relate more to the families or clans that individuals identify with. Still, these distinctions matter to tribal members generally, and they certainly mattered to the Northern Cheyenne. Cheyenne used these terms to identify fellow tribal members, explain their own values and actions, and draw lines between competing positions of political importance. Often, internal tribal politics pitted the two factions against one another, but within this landowners group, the two sides found common cause. Both feared the impacts of coal development on their land and community, and both sought to do something about it.

The news of Consolidation's July 1972 proposal sparked this group to action, but like Bill Bryan, the landowners initially lacked direction.

At the time, Marie Sanchez was living in Bozeman, attending and teaching classes at Montana State University, where she was part of a generation of tribal members taking advantage of belated federal support for Indian higher education. Like many in her situation, Sanchez also was becoming politicized by the American Indian Movement (AIM), a group that originated to assist urban Indians but now was developing a stinging critique of the federal government's long history of tribal treaty violations. AIM's new message was directed toward rural reservation Indians like Sanchez, and when the group's charismatic young leader, Russell Means, visited Bozeman in early 1972, she was determined to hear more. Seeking out Means to "get a statement that would stick clearly in my head for the rest of my life . . . that would *determine* my life," Sanchez found the AIM leader in the halls of Montana State's Student Union Building. Their encounter was brief but influential. As Sanchez later recalled, "At that point when I met Russell Means . . . I felt: Now look—for once here's an Indian who isn't on his knees." Hearing Means speak about the federal government's failure to uphold its treaty obligations throughout Indian Country sharpened Sanchez's already growing concern for the development planned for her reservation. It also strengthened her resolve to do something about it. When news of Consolidation's massive proposal reached Sanchez later that summer in Bozeman, she contacted Jim Goetz, who in turn referred her to Bryan.[12]

Coming together in that small studio apartment in Bozeman, Marie Sanchez and Bill Bryan seemed to give one another direction. Bryan explained to Sanchez and her colleagues his purpose for coming to Montana and offered his services to mobilize a community movement against reservation coal mining. Hearing details of the *North Central Power Study,* the gathered Northern Cheyenne began to understand Consolidation's project within broader energy development plans. They feared the impact of such large-scale development on their tiny reservation and gave Bryan a foothold to fight against regional mining.

Within days of the Bozeman meeting, Bryan appeared on the Northern Cheyenne Reservation. Marie Sanchez and her husband Chuck ushered him around to meet other Cheyenne landowners who would be adversely affected by coal mining. Bryan described these encounters in his monthly log: "It was some experience, as the Indians are about to lose their land for a few dollars to some upstanding corporations like Peabody Coal, Consolidation Coal, etc. Few realize what is about to happen and those that do feel almost powerless to act. There is no question that these people are in desperate need of help." Bryan was determined to provide this assistance, but he would not work alone.[13]

*

Pockets of anti-coal activists were popping up elsewhere too. Rumblings of discontent among non-Indian ranchers first appeared in the summer of 1971, before news of the *North Central Power Study* broke, when the Montana Power Company (MPC) announced plans to build a coal-fired power plant at the aptly named town of Colstrip, Montana. Located only a dozen miles north of the reservation, Colstrip had been a bustling refueling station for the Northern Pacific Railroad before the railroad closed its coal mine there in 1958. When both MPC and the Peabody Coal Company reestablished coal mining near the town during the late 1960s, residents reacted with optimism, hoping this industrial activity would create jobs and attract commerce.

But the decision to build a large, mine-mouth generating station at Colstrip turned local optimism into general concern over the potentially negative impacts to the region's air and water. Before area residents even had the opportunity to evaluate the power plant's potential impacts, local newspapers reported that MPC planned to expand the original facility design by adding two more boilers with the unprecedented capacity to produce 700,000 kilowatts of electricity. When the company began construction on the facility in the spring of 1972—before obtaining a permit from the state Board of Health, which would have entailed a public participation process—area residents were shocked at the speed of MPC's actions and scurried to halt construction.[14]

As these non-Indian residents near the Northern Cheyenne Reservation mobilized to prevent the Colstrip power plant, they discovered other ranching communities facing similar problems throughout the region. Just west of Colstrip on Sarpy Creek near the Crow Reservation, residents were fighting the Westmoreland Coal Company's efforts to purchase or condemn lands for a new coal mine. South of the Northern Cheyenne Reservation, a similar battle raged against coal companies seeking to open a series of mines from Decker, Montana, down through central Wyoming. And north of Billings, in the Bull Mountains, a landowners group had formed to fight Consolidation's plans for yet another coal mine there. These independent landowner groups organized to oppose what they thought were simply local energy projects threatening their land. But as details of the *North Central Power Study* became publicly available during spring 1972, the interconnected nature of the projects became apparent. The entire region and its way of life appeared under attack. As Steve Charter, a member of the Bull Mountain Landowners Association, explained to a *New York Times* reporter sent to investigate the commotion erupting on the Northern Plains:

> We feel, all of us, that this is our last stand, that there's no place else, now, that we could go to live the kind of life we've built. If we tear this land up and dam the rivers and dry them up and muck up the air with smokestacks and fill it full of people and ticky-tacky houses, there just won't be any place left, not in this whole country; there won't be anything left.

Concerned residents understood a more coordinated response was needed.[15]

That response came just months before Consolidation's historic proposal to the Northern Cheyenne, when on April 25, 1972, citizen activists formed the Northern Plains Resource Council (NPRC). Their goal, according to the *Billings Gazette,* was to provide a "unified, more powerful counterforce in public 'discussions' with the users of non-renewable resources (minerals), particularly including the coal strip-miners." Two of the existing landowners groups, the Bull Mountain Landowners Association and Rosebud Protective Association, spearheaded the NPRC's founding, but environmentalists from the Sierra Club and the Montana Wildlife Federation also were instrumental. This curious combination of socially conservative ranchers and young environmental activists made for an odd coupling, but their interests were well aligned. Wally McRae, an outspoken leader of the NPRC, explained his initial reluctance toward the alliance and his ultimate realization that both sides needed one another:

> Boy, I didn't want to join that outfit [NPRC], that bunch of wild-eyed, fuzzy-headed environmentalists. I said, "Man, I don't know. I think that I can do more good as an independent rancher, talking to other independent ranchers about the threats of coal development and what we've got to do. . . ." [But] about that time they were building this dang thing

[the Colstrip power plant]. . . . It is not the environmental things that concern me the most. It's the social things. It's the massive industrialization. It's just that the environmental numbers are all we have to fight them with.[16]

Both ranchers and environmentalists feared the impacts of energy development on the Northern Plains, if for slightly different reasons. Third- and fourth-generation Montanans like McRae may have prioritized social concerns, but they understood the need to protect certain environmental qualities, such as clean water and adequate vegetation, that made their ranching lifestyles possible. Southeast Montana ranchers thus flocked to the NPRC, making up the core of its membership and leadership, while the "wild-eyed, fuzzy-headed" environmentalists formed much of its energetic staff. Meeting in a small building across the street from MPC's Billings office, NPRC staffers dedicated themselves to publicizing energy development in eastern Montana, educating the public on its impacts, and challenging projects that threatened the region's ecology. In doing so, staffers remained mindful of their core ranching constituents, always connecting environmental concerns to the maintenance of existing economic and social patterns. As Pat Sweeney, NPRC's staff director, explained: "We would like to think of ourselves as not just an environmental group. We really have four purposes—communication, research, organization and advocacy."[17] In service to the ranching community, NPRC's mission was to provide a clearinghouse of information on coal development's social and environmental impacts and to lobby on this community's behalf.

As if a coalition of ranchers and environmentalists on the Northern Plains was not odd enough, NPRC's efforts to expose energy development's potential impacts also galvanized Indian opposition. The organization published its first newsletter the same month Consolidation offered its proposal to the Northern Cheyenne, dedicating the issue to the *North Central Power Study*. In it, NPRC not only detailed the enormous dimensions of the regional development scheme, but the group also provided Indian and non-Indian landowners with a list of "battle tactics" to prevent coal companies from securing more land. The following month, in August 1972, the organization orchestrated a contentious public hearing on MPC's Colstrip power plant, before suing to halt the facility's construction on the doorstep of the Northern Cheyenne Reservation. In September, NPRC hosted Harry Caudill, the famous anti–strip mine crusader from Appalachia whose 1963 book *Night Comes to the Cumberlands* publicized the depth of Appalachian poverty. This exposé had spurred President John F. Kennedy to establish the Appalachian Regional Commission to investigate the region's problems and contributed to Lyndon Johnson's focus on Appalachia in his War on Poverty. Caudill's current work now tied this endemic poverty to the adverse environmental impacts of coal mining. In fall 1972, he toured both the Northern Cheyenne Reservation and the region, sharing battle stories from the East.[18]

Each of these endeavors raised regional awareness of the impending energy projects and fulfilled the NPRC's primary mission to aid the ranching community, but Bill Bryan made sure the message also was heard on the Northern Cheyenne Reservation. Bryan met regularly with NPRC organizers and Northern Cheyenne activists during the fall of 1972, coordinating the two groups' efforts. In the week after his fateful encounter with Sanchez, for instance, Bryan spent days with NPRC leaders reorganizing and incorporating that organization before traveling on to the Northern Cheyenne Reservation to mobilize landowners there. Further, it was Bryan who picked Caudill up at the Billings airport, taking him to meet with local ranchers before ferrying him on to the Northern Cheyenne Reservation. And Bryan even flew to California with NPRC's lead environmental lobbyist, Kit Mueller, to drum up support from that state's powerful environmental organizations and seek additional funds for both the Northern Cheyenne and NPRC. Straddling both sides of the reservation, the "Northern Rocky Mountain Environmental Advocate" was instrumental in keeping communication lines open between these nascent advocacy groups that, for now, shared similar interests.[19]

The final push to mobilize concerned Northern Cheyenne tribal members into a formal, anti-coal organization came from the most unlikely of sources: the coal companies themselves. In early fall 1972, prospecting crews from the firms that had secured Cheyenne coal rights in the tribe's third lease sale began arriving on the reservation. The presence of these outsiders no doubt raised further awareness of the reservation's planned development. But it was not merely their presence; it was the damage they did. Throughout the fall, the federal government documented numerous incidents of roads being destroyed and rangeland disturbed. When warnings to clean up their operations went unheeded, BIA Superintendent Alonzo Spang even suspended several of the coal companies' drilling activities "due to surface damage and taking of water without prior permission." These careless deeds played directly into the hands of anti-coal organizers, providing tangible evidence of the destruction tribal members could expect when full-scale mining commenced. When this was combined with the community outreach efforts of Bill Bryan, Marie Sanchez, the NPRC, and others, the time for action seemed ripe. On October 20, 1972, concerned tribal members officially formed the Northern Cheyenne Landowners Association (NCLA), transforming the small group of landowners that had been meeting informally at Dave Robinson's ranch into a structured watchdog organization.[20]

"COAL: BLACK DEATH"

Poetically, the first attempt to organize the NCLA was disrupted on October 13, 1972, by a caravan of AIM activists headed to Washington, D.C. Leaving the West Coast in the early fall of 1972, this "Trail of Broken Treaties" planned to stop at reservations across the country to enlist recruits and draw attention to the federal government's long history of tribal treaty violations. This dramatic demonstration was just the latest in a string of high-profile protests AIM had coordinated. Inspired by similarly sensational tactics in the civil rights and antiwar movements, AIM had seized *Mayflower II*, the replica of the Pilgrims' ship, and painted Plymouth Rock red on Thanksgiving Day 1970. Activists then staged a July 4, 1971, occupation of Mount Rushmore. The organization also cultivated a public perception that it was involved in the 1969 Indian takeover of Alcatraz Island, although it had neither organized nor executed that protest. These events brought AIM great notoriety and, in the public's eyes, catapulted the organization to leadership of the burgeoning "Red Power" movement. Charismatic spokesmen like Dennis Banks, Clyde Bellecourt, and Russell Means articulated forceful critiques of federal Indian policy and offered a pan-Indian message of resistance that sought to elevate ethnic consciousness. All American Indians, AIM argued, had been harmed materially and culturally by Euro-American colonial practices. All must now unite to take dramatic, supratribal action to undo the damage.[21]

Considering the timing of the Northern Cheyenne's resistance to reservation mining, and, as we will see, the subsequent pan-tribal movement it launched to retake control of reservation resources, it is tempting to place the Cheyenne's struggle within this AIM-led Red Power movement. The association is fair, but only to a point. AIM's anticolonial rhetoric and direct action protests certainly inspired some tribal members, such as Marie Sanchez, to employ the same language and tactics in their fight against coal mining. However, as was the case on many rural reservations in the 1970s, AIM's 1972 caravan and its broader message received a generally chilly reception in Lame Deer. As tribal elder and council member Ted Rising Sun recalled, the dissimilar backgrounds of the mostly urban AIM members and the rural Northern Cheyenne made for awkward interactions when the caravan arrived in October 1972:

> AIM came to the school board and wanted sleeping bags to take on the trip; they wanted financial help. But we couldn't help them. They had a big rally . . . , [but] they didn't mix well because they didn't know any Indian songs, they didn't know the dances, they didn't know any Cheyenne. . . . They didn't do anything for guys like us. They were more of a disturbance than anything. People told them to leave.

Rising Sun's comments likely contain a hint of generational bias, as younger tribal members, such as schoolteacher Norma Bixby, remember that AIM's caravan "made a big impression," causing kids to jump "out of the windows" to view the spectacle. Still, most Northern Cheyenne struggled to identify with AIM's supratribal goals and militant tactics, which not only contravened established principles for addressing grievances with the federal government but also threatened the tribe's existing leadership. Again, Rising Sun explained the different approaches:

> We [the Northern Cheyenne] took over a BIA school without breaking a window. The tribe contracted from the BIA to run Busby school . . . [and] we set the model for Indian control of schools. This was in contrast to AIM. We knew they came from Minnesota. We read about Alcatraz Island. They could have really made a statement if they'd talked to people on the reservation and seen the problems with the BIA. Their approach was wrong. They could have taken their time, involved some of us here. We would have been glad to join them. But they didn't ask us.

Instead, AIM's brash tactics were such an affront to the Northern Cheyenne that not only did the community refuse support but the tribal government later joined a host of other Indian groups in condemning the caravan's November 1972 takeover of BIA headquarters. In the early 1970s, AIM may have modified its message to appeal to reservation Indians, but its members remained too urban and its tactics too militant to gain a foothold with the Northern Cheyenne.[22]

Where Northern Cheyenne members and AIM activists did share common ground was in their belief that immediate action was needed to protect Indian assets. Like AIM, concerned Cheyenne felt the federal government had failed to uphold its treaty obligations by allowing non-Indians access to reservation resources. But for tribal members, the cause was more desperate. It was *their* homeland under imminent attack, not a more general grievance against the treatment of all Native Americans. To the Northern Cheyenne who owned land and formed the core of early anti-coal resistance, the threat was palpable and obvious. Energy development would destroy their land and water and disrupt crucial ranching revenues. Rallying this group to the cause was an easy sell.

For the great majority of Cheyenne, however, who did not own reservation land, other motivations underlay their opposition to coal mining. One of the more prominent concerns troubling tribal members was the impact coal mining would have on the reservation's physical environment. A poll conducted by the Northern Cheyenne Research Project, which was organized to investigate coal mining's impacts, revealed that more than 40 percent of tribal respondents listed "environmental damage and loss of resources" as an expected "bad" consequence of reservation coal mining. This broad concern for the environment contained within it a series of more specific complaints, ranging from the loss of aesthetically pleasing landscapes to fears over pollution-based health problems. As one respondent to the poll noted: "The reservation is one of the most beautiful places in Montana. Let's keep it that way for our children." In the next breath, though, this person continued: "Pollution also creates health problems that we cannot afford. We've always had clear air, good water. Our land is very good. Why ruin it now?"[23]

Many held these dual concerns, while still others connected fears over land disturbances to beliefs about the sanctity of the earth and the Northern Cheyenne's sacred relationship to it. As another respondent noted: "Our people are of the earth, and we consider it to be sacred. My body will soon go back to the earth, and would you tear up your mother's body?" Former tribal president Woodenlegs shared this sentiment, explaining: "In our past we have a great concern for the earth. . . . We believe the earth is sacred because the Creator made it. We respect all living things because they are all made by the Creator. . . . Nothing is to be destroyed unnecessarily." Regardless of the specific nature of the environmental concern, fears over the physical destruction of the land were clearly prevalent, no doubt enhanced by the incessant work of NPRC and the army of environmental groups active in the area. These groups now included the Friends of the Earth, the Environmental Defense Fund, the National Resources Defense Council, and the Sierra Club. Thanks to their efforts, more Northern Cheyenne understood the massive land disturbances coal mining would bring and the vast quantities of water that power plants would consume. A substantial percentage of tribal members opposed development because of this.[24]

But more than anxieties over environmental disturbances, the greatest fear underlying Cheyenne resistance was that uncontrolled coal development would disrupt established social patterns and cultural norms crucial to maintaining the Northern Cheyenne as a distinct indigenous community. In the same poll that found 40 percent of Northern Cheyenne respondents feared environmental impacts, almost 80 percent noted that coal mining's "worst" effect would be the associated "social and community problems." To Cheyenne respondents, these problems included such things as the "breakdown of friendships, family and cultural values," "increase in crime," "non-Cheyenne population increase," and the "increase in Cheyenne/non-Indian intermarriages." Most often, these fears manifested as concerns over the massive influx of non-Indian laborers coal mining would bring and the inability of the tribe to control their actions. As one young Northern Cheyenne put it: "With more whites coming in, the Cheyenne way of life will soon be forgotten. There will be nothing but half-breeds and Indians thinking white, walking around." Another agreed, stating, "There will be total destruction of Cheyenne ways and culture, more social problems (crime, juvenile delinquency, etc.) and subserviency [sic] to dominant whites on the reservation." Others emphasized how the quick infusion of royalty cash could alter the existing relationships, values, and responsibilities that held their community together. Ted Rising Sun explained: "Preservation of our culture depends on us. [Coal mining] is going to disrupt our entire way of life. Who is going to pay attention to the real basic essentials of life if we all of a sudden get some money?" Countless more echoed these fears, arguing the influx of outsiders and money, over which their tribal government would have little control, would change existing lifeways and lead to the loss of Northern Cheyenne culture. Tribal member Ruby Sooktis put it most bluntly, "[Coal mining] would be the final destruction of our tribe."[25]

*

In a community with strong memories of past struggles to secure a homeland, worrying about the final destruction of the tribe was not farfetched. Like many other Indian groups, the Northern Cheyenne had experienced tragic episodes of violence and removal, and the collective retelling of these incidents served as an important source of tribal identity. In particular, the Northern Cheyenne's nineteenth-century removal to Indian Country and their improbable escape and return to Montana offered an especially compelling narrative uniting the tribe. Details of this episode are highly contested, but the basic story holds that after the Northern Cheyenne and Sioux defeated Custer at the Battle of the Little Bighorn, the military removed most Northern Cheyenne to Indian Territory. After a short stay under inhospitable conditions, a small group determined to return to their native homeland on the Northern Plains and left Indian Territory in fall 1878. Evading federal authorities and local militia through the winter of 1878–79, a portion of this group, led by Little Wolf, arrived safely in Montana the following spring. Another group, led by Dull Knife, was not so fortunate. This group suffered a bloody massacre at the hands of federal troops stationed at Fort Robinson, Nebraska, where the band had surrendered. Ultimately, the survivors of the Fort Robinson attack were permitted to join their brethren in Montana, and due to the outpouring of sympathy for their losses and Cheyenne efforts to pursue settled agricultural practices, President Chester A. Arthur awarded the tribe its reservation in 1884.[26]

More important than the details of this account is the way the Northern Cheyenne remembered it and employed the story to characterize coal development as the next attack on their sacred homeland. Anti-coal activists easily drew parallels between the nineteenth-century land grab that led to the Northern Cheyenne's removal and their current predicament, finding inspiration in their ancestors' actions. As tribal member Bill Parker explained:

> The parallels in history haunt us. In 1873 the country was in a financial panic brought on by the Civil War. Western mineral resources were seen as a key to putting the country back on a sound footing. Gold was discovered in the Black Hills. Only one problem remained. The land belonged to the Sioux and the Northern Cheyenne.
>
> Today the country is again in deep financial trouble. Reeling from the debts brought about by another country's war between North and South [Vietnam], the United States is looking to the "black gold" beneath our reservation. This time the "cavalry" comes in the form of the coal companies, Bureau of Indian Affairs and their lawyers. . . . The damn fools want the same thing again. Again we'll fight like the devil.

In fact, almost every articulation of Northern Cheyenne opposition to coal development began by explaining the connection between past sacrifices and the tribe's current efforts to protect its land base. When the tribe opposed the Colstrip power plant being constructed on its border, for instance, its official comments to the state of Montana emphasized:

> The position of the Northern Cheyenne Tribe must be understood in the context of the Tribe's history and its relationship to the lands which compromise its Reservation. These lands, quite simply, constitute the Tribe's Home Land. . . . After the Custer Battle in 1876, and the resulting relocation of the Northern Cheyenne Tribe, the Tribe literally walked backed from Oklahoma to re-establish its present Reservation as its Home Land. The Tribe paid dearly for this last, and finally successful, effort to secure its ancestral lands. The Northern Cheyenne Tribe presently occupies and cherishes these lands.

A few years later, when the Northern Cheyenne petitioned the federal government to declare their reservation a Class I protected air shed so as to halt expansion of the Colstrip power plant, the tribe articulated the importance of their reservation even more clearly:

> In order to understand what this petition for Class I air quality status means to the Northern Cheyenne people, it must be understood in relation to the Tribe's history, its current actions, and in terms of the reservation's meaning as a home, as a last retreat, and as the only foundation on which the Northern Cheyenne can retain their life and identity as a

people. It must be understood in the same context as the Tribe's walk against impossible odds and almost certain death a hundred years ago to reach its homeland, its consistent determination to maintain the integrity of the reservation, and its current refusal of instant riches for the sale of rights to violate this integrity. Redesignation to Class I is in the same spirit as everything else the Tribe has done during the last hundred years to secure its freedom and relative autonomy, and to retain the value and viability of its cultural identity.

Even the tribe's official stationery contained pictures of Dull Knife and Little Wolf, with the caption, "Out of defeat and exile they led us back to Montana and won our Cheyenne homeland which we will keep forever." For the Northern Cheyenne, the fate of this land base and their existence as a distinct people were inextricably entwined. Anti-coal activists argued their community had sacrificed too much to allow coal companies to finish what Custer had begun. As one young tribal member put it: "Our ancestors went through hell to return here. Why should we destroy our land and ourselves?"[27]

To foment action, the NCLA exploited the connections between past sacrifices, uncontrolled coal development, and the survival of the tribe. Days after officially organizing, NCLA leaders plastered the reservation with pamphlets detailing the enormous dimensions of the Consolidation proposal and calling for a public meeting to discuss the offer. Written by Bill Bryan, the pamphlets warned, "The ultimate end of the Northern Cheyenne Reservation and the removal of its people and the destruction of their culture seems [sic] inevitable unless measures are taken now to control the planned mining of coal on the reservation." Soon these pamphlets were followed by the appearance of stirring posters with the caption "Coal: Black Death" and depicting the Northern Cheyenne people walking mournfully into the jowls of a human skull labeled "Coal Co." (figure 2).[28]

The message was not subtle, but it was effective. On November 15, 1972, the NCLA's first public meeting attracted more than seventy tribal members, including Tribal President Rowland and BIA Superintendent Spang. No doubt, the presence of the tribe's elected leader was partly a reaction to the groundswell of sentiment generated by the NCLA. Rowland came to observe the power of this movement. It is also possible, however, that he came for another reason. K. Ross Toole reports that earlier that fall at an "Indian gathering," Edwin Dahle,

Figure 2. Coal: Black Death. Poster distributed on the Northern Cheyenne Reservation, 1972. Reproduced by permission of William L. Bryan, Jr.

a council member and close political ally to Rowland, crossed paths with George Crossland, an Osage attorney with experience defending Indian resource rights. In the course of their conversation, Dahle described the Northern Cheyenne's various coal leases to the Osage attorney, who immediately identified several federal violations. According to Toole, Crossland then began counseling Cheyenne leaders to cancel these deals and fight for better terms. Whether Rowland attended the NCLA meeting to gauge support for this new strategy, was genuinely concerned that coal development threatened tribal survival, or simply was assessing the reservation's shifting political winds, his presence represented a significant coup for the nascent NCLA. By the end of the meeting, both Rowland and Spang announced their tacit support for the organization. Two weeks later, when Consolidation representatives then returned to the reservation to discuss their proposal with the tribal council, a crowd of more than a hundred Cheyenne protesters greeted company executives. A week after that, on December 7, the NCLA staged yet another public forum. This time, the organization aimed to shut down all reservation mining.[29]

*

December 7, 1972, marked a turning point in the Northern Cheyenne's struggle to reassert control over reservation energy development. Attending the gathering were the usual local activists, but this time Bill Bryan brought national representatives from the Environmental Defense Fund and the National Resource Defense Council, and they brought their lawyers. Alvin Josephy, the prominent Indian scholar who had advised Interior Secretary Udall before becoming such a vocal critic of federal actions in the Southwest, was also there. But the most important attendee of the evening turned out to be Joseph Brecher, staff attorney for the Native American Rights Fund (NARF). Originally organized in June 1970 as a national offshoot of the California Indian Legal Services, NARF had cut its teeth defending southwestern Indian resources from that region's massive buildup of coal-fired power plants. Among its many lawsuits, NARF represented Hopi villagers seeking to overturn coal leases brokered by the BIA and their illegitimate tribal government, Navajo tribal members displaced by coal mining, and a consortium of southwestern Indians suing to halt regional coal development until a comprehensive environmental impact study was conducted in accordance with the National Environmental Policy Act. Brecher had joined NARF in December of 1970 and was involved in at least ten separate lawsuits challenging southwestern energy development. The newly supportive Northern Cheyenne Tribal Council, under Allen Rowland's leadership, had requested NARF's expert assistance in reviewing the coal deals previous council members, including Rowland, had negotiated. NARF, in turn, sent Brecher.[30]

Seasoned by the southwestern experience, Brecher understood that the key to making reservation mining work for tribal residents was asserting tribal control over the process. In doing so, the community could still reap revenues from their minerals, but their tribal government would be positioned to ensure that the pace and scale of mining did not upset social customs and cultural norms or substantially impair the reservation's ecology. Determined to carry this message to the Northern Cheyenne, the brash, young New Yorker arrived on the reservation declaring, "The landowners association woke the tribe up as to the environmental disaster that was about to occur, and also the loss of money, and now we are here to do something about it." Brecher proposed a three-prong attack: (1) enact a tribal tax code that would address inequitable financial terms and assure tribal revenue was fairly tied to coal production, (2) put in place tribal environmental ordinances that required reclamation of disturbed land and would control the pace and scale of mining, and (3) file legal actions to void all past coal deals, forcing coal companies to renegotiate with a more informed tribal council. The overall goal was to change the Indian approach to doing business with non-Indian corporations. Rather than non-Indians setting the terms of the deal and delivering them to ignorant tribal leaders, Brecher explained, "White men will wait in line to see what the Indians will give them."[31]

The approach of exercising tribal sovereignty to assert more control over resource development appealed to a Cheyenne leadership facing an impassioned movement from below. Within weeks, the tribal government suspended all prospecting activities and its leaders began to echo the same fears as their constituents. When asked why, given the desperate state of his reservation's economy, Rowland now resisted energy development, the tribal leader noted simply, "Because we would end up as a minority on our own reservation." James Dahle, chairman of the tribe's mineral committee agreed. "It scares me," Dahle admitted. "The biggest problem would be the influx of people working at the gasification plants. We aren't ready for that. We're like a foreign nation. We have no jurisdiction over non-Indians." Tom Gardner, the reservation's antipoverty and community action director, explained the threat facing his community in more apocalyptic terms:

[It is] a question of the white man's extinction of our way of life. We see prosperity from the coal, but we also see many thousands of white people—perhaps 30,000 miners and technicians and the people to serve them, when we are only a few thousand. We see a population explosion, with bars, beer taverns and discrimination against our people. My people are not competitive in the white man's sense and will be left out, swept aside. So it is not only some coal we would lose, and the damage to our lands, for a few million dollars. It is our life.

The grassroots message had clearly reached the top.[32]

Unified in their perception of the threat, the community also came together on the end goal of tribal control over reservation development, rather than an absolute ban on mining. NARF and Joe Brecher had presented the specific methods for obtaining such control, but tribal leaders and members bristled under Brecher's aggressive style. Ultimately, the Northern Cheyenne rejected NARF's representation in favor of a Seattle law firm specializing in Indian law, but they still implemented Brecher's plan. The tribal council began work on tax and natural resources ordinances to control mining should it occur. Then, on March 5, 1973, the council took the dramatic step of passing a resolution voiding all existing coal contracts, opening the way for renegotiations.[33]

The specific grounds for terminating the coal deals the tribe had worked so hard to obtain rested on a legal technicality: the BIA's failure to perform a "technical examination of the prospective effects of . . . surface mining operations upon the environment" pursuant to BIA regulation 25 C.F.R. § 177.4. Tribal correspondence with BIA Area Director James Canan, however, made clear the real goal was regaining control over the process. Lamenting that the BIA's failure to comply with its own regulations had placed the tribe "in the position in which the Navajo and Hopi Tribes now find themselves," the Northern Cheyenne demanded their existing leases and permits "be voided in order that new negotiations may proceed in the manner which is required." For the Northern Cheyenne, any new deals would have to affirm the tribe's right to control mining so as to protect the integrity of their land base, prevent the mass influx of non-Indians, and ensure the survival of the tribe. Council member Edwin Dahle put it concisely: "The name of the game is control. We don't have it right now, but we're trying to make damn sure that they [the coal companies] don't get it either. Without controls, we'll be eliminated."[34]

The Northern Cheyenne petition to halt reservation mining reverberated throughout Indian Country. Certainly this was not the first act to challenge energy development on Indian lands, but it was the first time a tribal community and its government acted in unison, armed with the legal and policy arguments to undue past actions. Responding to concerns over the nation's deteriorating environmental conditions, the Department of the Interior had only promulgated the regulation requiring a "technical examination" of reservation mining's environmental impacts in January 1969. More than simply an analysis of physical impacts to the land, the new rule required the BIA to "take into consideration the need for the preservation and protection of other resources, including cultural, recreational, scenic, historic, and ecological values." This provision foreshadowed the even more extensive demands of the National Environmental Policy Act (NEPA), enacted the following year, which required federal agencies to conduct an extensive audit of potential environmental impacts before taking "major Federal actions significantly affecting the quality of the human environment." Although both laws were on the books by the time the BIA authorized most of the Northern Cheyenne coal deals, agency officials were slow to fulfill their duties. At one point, the agency even denied that the National Environmental Policy Act applied to actions it took as a trustee over Indian resources. The Northern Cheyenne disagreed—as would eventually the Interior secretary and federal courts—and, together, these new environmental requirements provided the tribe with legal arguments not available to previous Indian groups. As Marjane Ambler, a journalist who covered Indian energy issues at the time, describes it, "Although the Black Mesa contracts [in the Southwest] made the problems clear, the Northern Plains tribes were the first that could act to avoid them."[35]

Beyond the opportunities afforded by the shifting legal landscape, the Northern Cheyenne also made their play for tribal control within a new policy environment. On July 8, 1970, President Richard Nixon announced to the nation the new federal Indian policy of "Indian Self-Determination," which explicitly rejected existing policy goals to terminate the tribes and assimilate their members. Instead, Nixon pledged to empower tribal governments so that they could effectively govern reservation programs and resources according to their community's desires. In truth, this bold announcement merely continued existing trends toward greater Indian autonomy begun under the Kennedy and Johnson administrations. But the message provided a formal endorsement of this approach and government-sanctioned rhetoric tribes could now use to their advantage. Arguing the current approach to Indian mineral development contravened the desires of their community, and thus failed the test of self-determination, the Northern Cheyenne demanded the previous deals be torn up and the current tribal council be allowed to determine the pace and scale of reservation development. This tribe intended to hold Nixon to his word.[36]

Faced with clear evidence that the BIA had failed to follow its own regulations and implement NEPA's requirements, the secretary of the Interior had little choice but to grant the Northern Cheyenne's petition in part and suspend all mining activities. Rogers Morton's June 4, 1974, ruling made clear that no reservation mining would commence without the support of the tribal government, and that the BIA was required to provide a careful analysis of the social and environmental implications of such development. Telling the parties he took seriously his trustee duty and "will not subvert [the Northern Cheyenne's] interests to anyone's desires to develop the natural resources on that Reservation," the secretary concluded, "the Tribe and the coal companies may be assured that the terms and conditions upon which mineral development may proceed on the Northern Cheyenne Reservation will require their joint agreement and support prior to any further approval by me." For the Northern Cheyenne, any such agreement would have to include tribal involvement in all phases of the mining project. There simply was too much at stake. The tribe could not afford to be disinterested landlords, receiving royalty checks yet having no control over operations threatening its community. As Allen Rowland explained in his typically colorful language, "We want to be involved in the goddam planning!"[37]

Unfortunately for the Northern Cheyenne, as Marjane Ambler notes, tribal actions to suspend this type of reservation mining left them with the unwanted and inaccurate reputation as the "antidevelopment tribe of the Northern Plains." This simply was not the case. In fact, only months after resolving to cancel their existing leases, Cheyenne leaders met with Montana's congressional delegation to discuss plans to mine their own coal deposits, rather than leasing the minerals to outside developers. In August 1973, the Northern Cheyenne apportioned $250,000 of tribal funds for a comprehensive study of reservation minerals, which by February 1974 was being used to put together a preliminary business plan to mine their own coal. Furthermore, the tribe continued to entertain offers from other energy companies, even visiting Peabody's St. Louis headquarters and touring its midwestern mines to evaluate reclamation efforts.[38]

Clearly, then, the Northern Cheyenne were not antidevelopment. They simply opposed mining they could not control for the very important reason that such development threatened the survival of their tribe. Refusing to accept the status quo where non-Indians dictated the development of Indian resources, the Northern Cheyenne set out to blaze a new path that entailed tribal enterprises developing tribal resources. And in this pursuit, the Northern Cheyenne harbored no illusions regarding the far-reaching impacts of their approach. As their February 1974 business proposal noted:

> The Northern Cheyenne intends to change Indians' historic roll of passive subservience to agencies who are charged with the administration of trust responsibility for the benefit of the Indian tribes and who in the past have evidenced little more than apathy toward this responsibility. . . . If the Northern Cheyenne are successful in the proposed undertaking the tribe intends to share their experience and to work with other Indian tribes to assist them in implementing the Federal Government's presently announced policy of "self determination" for Indians and Alaska natives.

In other words, the Northern Cheyenne intended to "give teeth" to Nixon's rhetoric, equipping Indians with the knowledge necessary to effectively exercise their sovereign powers so that tribal governments could determine the fate of tribal resources. This goal represented the fullest realization of Indian self-determination to date, and the movement to implement it began in this remote corner of southeastern Montana.[39]

5 Determining the Self

The Crow country is a good country. The Great Spirit has put it exactly in the right place; while you are in it you fare well; whenever you go out of it, whichever way you travel, you will fare worse. . . . The Crow country is exactly in the right place.

—Arapooish ("Sore Belly" or "Rotten Belly"), Crow leader, to Robert Campbell, Rocky Mountain Fur Company, c. 1830

SOME FIFTY YEARS after Arapooish described the bounty of his land to an intrepid fur trader, the dimensions of Crow country were changing dramatically. In 1884, Captain Henry Armstrong, the Crow's federal Indian agent charged with overseeing their progression from nomadic "savages" to "civilized" farmers, decided that the tribe's current location in the Stillwater Valley no longer fit its needs. This area in south-central Montana had served as a refuge for the Crow, protecting the tribe first from encroaching Native groups like the Teton Sioux, Northern Cheyenne, and Blackfoot, and then from an incessant stream of white prospectors, ranchers, and farmers moving into Montana after the defeat of the Sioux and Cheyenne in 1877. By the mid-1880s, however, the sanctuary no longer contained the elements required for subsistence. The game was gone and the area's upland topography made for difficult farming. Seeking better farmland on Montana's eastern plains and determined to claim this area before the recently extended Northern Pacific Railroad dumped more settlers in the region, Armstrong moved more than 900 Crow east to the Little Bighorn Valley. Justifying the relocation to his superiors, he declared confidently, "If any man can take a tribe of wild Indians and make anything out of them, I can."[1]

But, of course, the decision of what to make of this Indian group was not Armstrong's alone. As Frederick Hoxie shows, the move to the eastern plains set off a contentious debate within the tribe over the type of community the Crow would become. External factors certainly shaped the possibilities—the federal military prevented a full return to nomadic hunting. But the fundamental questions of group identity were still the Crow's to make. As Hoxie explains:

> The group's passage out of the mountains and into the valley of the Little Bighorn . . . brought a number of difficult issues forward for consideration. Who were the Crows? Were they hunters, warriors, farmers, ranchers, or all four? Was their community distinct? Could there be a Crow community in the new, reservation environment? If so, who would be this new community's leaders? And how could both leaders and followers identify themselves in a setting where they would soon be outnumbered by powerful outsiders? In short, what was their future as a people in this new land?

The picture Hoxie paints of those first years on the Little Bighorn is one of confusion and conflict. Some Crow supported the move, determined to adopt agriculture and accept rations as the best approach to securing peace, prosperity, and their own prestige within the community. Others were more reluctant, accepting the relocation but determined to pursue a mixed economy of ranching and hunting that more closely aligned with existing modes of subsistence. And a few, like the young warrior Sword Bearer, whose 1887 violent revolt against agency officials and subsequent death made him a martyr among the tribe, resisted at all costs. One thing is sure: as the parameters of Crow country shifted, the community calling this land home had to redefine itself, painfully and painstakingly selecting, as Hoxie explains, "a stable community leadership and a coherent cultural identity that both honored the past and served the future." Ultimately, the Crow would settle on a pragmatic compromise, adopting a defiant rhetoric that paid homage to Sword Bearer's independent values but working peacefully with federal officials to secure material necessities and retain as much control over their land as possible.[2]

Almost a century later, the dimensions of Crow country shifted again. Instability in global oil supplies; environmental legislation that increased the desirability of their vast, low-sulfur coal deposits; and an antiquated mineral leasing regime that made these resources readily available brought dozens of energy companies to the reservation's doorstep. Like other tribal groups, the Crow initially welcomed this interest in their minerals and consummated deals that promised unfettered reservation access to such multinational firms as Peabody Coal Company, Gulf Mineral Resources, and Shell Oil. Recognizing this fortuitous opportunity to secure revenue from their land, Tribal Chairman Patrick Stands Over Bull recalled Arapooish's famous words in a 1975 letter to his people:

> "The Crow country is good country. The Great Spirit has put it exactly in the right place." . . . Such were the words of one of our great chiefs, Arapooish (Sore Belly) in describing our land in the 1830s. Today is 1975 and, I believe, the Crow country is not only the right place but it looks like the Great Spirit was careful about what was under the Crow country! Billions of tons of tribally-owned coal underlie the southeast portion of our reservation and the ceded strip.

But like the Crow in 1884, changing land-use patterns in Crow country triggered fundamental questions about the future of the Crow community. Would the Crow become industrial laborers, wealthy landowners, or exploited victims of mining pollution? Would their tribal government be able to control the impacts of mining and non-Indian miners and protect their land base for future Crow generations? And what would it mean to be Crow if their reservation was overrun by white outsiders? Could the tribe continue to exist if mining rendered its members minorities in their own land, with tribal customs and values under constant pressure to change?[3]

As we have seen, energy tribes across the nation were asking similar questions as they debated how to capitalize on their suddenly valuable resources without compromising their existing community. Next door, on the adjacent Northern Cheyenne Reservation, a grassroots movement had emerged to warn of the threats posed by Northern Plains mining and unify that tribe against non-tribal controlled development. Forty miles west, the Crow heard this message and began debating what reservation mining would mean to their community. Continuing his 1975 message to the Crow people, Stands Over Bull captured the magnitude of the moment, articulating what many tribal leaders felt about the prospect of lucrative energy development: "If the Crow Tribe can control this development and maximize the beneficial aspects of mining on the reservation, we could realize economic self-sufficiency." "But," the tribal chairman warned, "if the proposed development is not controlled, the Crow people in fifty years could fade into the sunset as a landless, cultureless and powerless people." The fate of this people, and that of many other reservation Indians, was tied to how they managed their land in these changing conditions.[4]

A FRAGILE COALITION: MINING THE CEDED STRIP

In most things related to coal development, the Crow generally followed a few steps behind their Northern Cheyenne neighbors. Thus, in spring 1966, as the Northern Cheyenne and the Bureau of Indian Affairs were considering how to respond to Max Krueger's offer to commercially mine Cheyenne coal, the Crow received their own proposal from a start-up firm named Crow Coal, Inc. Organized in January 1966, the young company's founders included Crow executive council members Donald Deernose and Daniel Old Elk, a Crow geologist named Joseph Rawlins, and L. C. Scott, who formerly operated a small mine on the Northern Cheyenne Reservation. As tribal leaders and local coal operators, these men were in as good a position as any to judge the extent and location of Crow coal deposits. They proposed a twenty-five-year lease to develop coal on a 2,500-acre plot of tribal land, promising to pay royalties of 30 cents per ton, which was three times as much as Krueger offered the Northern Cheyenne. The new firm, however, also needed seed money, and thus it requested a $180,000 tribal loan, to be repaid at 5 percent interest. The offer was risky. Beyond the upfront loan, the tribal government would also have only limited control over the activities of Crow Coal, Inc., as it was a private firm operating under a lease. The proposal, however, did offer the benefit of a Crow-owned enterprise developing tribal minerals. Rather than hundreds of outside coal miners arriving to work the reservation, tribal members could expect that they would fill the bulk of new mining jobs.[5]

The historical record is silent on the Crow government's response, but considering that tribal and federal officials had long known the reservation contained valuable minerals, there must have been excitement over the possibility of finally securing revenue from these assets. Specific knowledge of the reservation's coal deposits dated back at least to the early twentieth century, when pressures to open Crow land to white homesteading caused the federal government to survey the reservation. Reporting the results of this survey to Congress in 1910, Interior Secretary Richard Ballinger noted the extensive coal mines being developed further south in Wyoming and concluded: "There is no doubt but that the valuable coal deposits there extend into the Crow Reservation. The value of these coal lands, as estimated by the Geological Survey, is upward of $100 per acres." A few years later, future Crow leader Robert Yellowtail placed the value much higher, telling a Senate committee that "the value of the land can only be estimated into the billions of dollars from the billions of tons of the largest coal deposits in the world." Yellowtail's assessment was tinged with more than a bit of optimism, but all parties understood that the reservation contained valuable minerals. The Crow's 1920 Allotment Act specifically retained tribal rights to all subsurface minerals for a period of fifty years, hoping the resources could be developed quickly to generate desperately needed revenue.[6]

That plan was not to be, though its failure stemmed not from a lack of effort. Tribal and federal officials worked diligently to establish mineral production on the reservation, particularly in the 1950s and early 1960s as rapid postwar growth demanded new fuel sources. Hoping to capitalize on this demand, the tribe issued numerous oil and gas permits to mining firms, but prospecting wells produced little return. Further, unlike the situation in the booming American Southwest, no viable coal market materialized on the sparsely populated Northern Plains. By 1967, then, the reservation's expansive mineral deposits had produced less than $4 million, forcing the tribe to lobby for more time to develop its minerals. Congress responded to tribal requests the following year with legislation permanently transferring reservation minerals to the Crow, but still little development occurred.[7]

The proposal by Crow Coal, Inc. offered a new opportunity to address this lack of production. However, despite the long, pent-up desire to realize mineral revenues, in 1966 the Crow were being advised by the same federal trustees who cautioned the Northern Cheyenne against accepting unsolicited offers without first testing the emerging western coal market. The Crow, no doubt, received similar advice. The tribal government thus made the seemingly prudent decision to forego a partnership with Crow Coal, Inc. in favor of cultivating interest from multinational companies with the capacity to develop larger and more lucrative projects.

*

To facilitate large-scale development of their mineral reserves, the Crow made fundamental changes to their methods for governing reservation resources. In 1948, the tribe had ratified a constitution that largely formalized political practices developed in the late nineteenth century, when the federal government sought to circumvent powerful Crow leaders by requiring the full tribe to consider and vote on land cessions. Over time, many Crow came to see this extensive public participation as a quintessential element of Crow governance. Thus, the 1948 constitution established a legislative "tribal council" that consisted of all adult members of the tribe. The Crow elected officers to execute this body's resolutions and an executive committee to set the council's agenda, but the constitution required the full tribe to consider all decisions regarding communally owned land and resources. This "direct democracy," however, had its limits. The Crow adapted even older political practices to this newer democratic model by creating strong factions that supported individual leaders who frequently spoke for their followers. Not for the last time, the Crow blended two separate political traditions into a workable governing structure.[8]

Despite the value the 1948 constitution placed on public participation, tribal members quickly realized that this deliberative form of government did not respond well to time-sensitive matters, such as offers to develop reservation resources that were tied to fluctuating markets. Therefore, almost as soon as the Crow passed their constitution, the tribe adjusted its governing structure by establishing, in 1952, the Oil and Gas Committee to "work with the Chairman of the Crow tribal council and the superintendent of the Crow Indian Agency to act for the Crow Tribe on the acceptance or rejection of bids on Oil and Gas lease sales." The tribe later clarified that this new committee's power included the authority "to transact any and all business which may become necessary in the leasing, or handling the mineral interests of the Crow Tribe," subject only to securing the tribal chairman's signature to execute mineral deals. Essentially, the tribe removed the constitution's public participation requirement from matters related to oil and gas.

Under this streamlined process, the tribe aggressively pursued development in the 1950s and 1960s, though as we've seen, other factors limited production.[9]

When interest in Crow coal suddenly materialized on the heels of this disappointing foray into oil and gas development, the tribe was determined not to miss another opportunity. After rejecting Crow Coal, Inc.'s 1966 proposal, multinational energy firms, such as Peabody Coal, Consolidation Coal, Humble Oil, and Shell Oil, began lining up to bid on Crow coal. Preparing for the opportunity, the tribe further centralized mineral development authority by granting Tribal Chairman Edison Real Bird unilateral power to issue prospecting permits and mining leases. The 1967 tribal council resolution conferring this authority left little question as to how the tribe expected Real Bird to wield his new power. Expressing frustration at past efforts to land lucrative development projects and explicitly noting that the "opportunity has arisen for direct negotiations with the biggest coal company of the world [Peabody]," the resolution instructed the chairman to "consider favorably a reasonable offer or offers . . . to produce coal." In relatively quick fashion, then, the Crow dispensed with "traditional," democratic governing procedures in favor of a highly centralized approach to mineral development. The tribe seemed poised to capitalize on their vast energy reserves.[10]

What followed next should sound very familiar. When Real Bird's administration authorized the Crow's first coal auction on April 2, 1968, the hoped-for lucrative deal did not materialize. Bidding on separate tracts without competition, Peabody and Shell each secured more than 80,000 reservation acres for relatively small bonus payments and fixed royalties at 17.5 cents per ton of coal mined, the same as the Northern Cheyenne's early deals. One year later, the Crow again tried their luck but again secured no competition. In this second auction, Gulf Mineral Resources obtained rights to an additional 75,000 acres under similarly meager terms. The frustrating process the Northern Cheyenne endured seemed to be playing out next door.[11]

Important differences, however, distinguished the Crow and Northern Cheyenne experience with coal development. None was more significant than the fact that the Crow owned minerals off the reservation. In 1899, under pressure from federal officials to open "unused" lands to white settlers, the Crow ceded to the United States all land north of the confluence of the Bighorn and Little Bighorn rivers, near the present-day town of Hardin, Montana. Consistent with federal policy at the time, the federal government then conveyed the surface rights for this "Ceded Strip" to incoming homesteaders but retained for itself all subsurface mineral rights. When Congress, in 1958, re-turned to the Crow "all lands now or hereafter classified as vacant and undisposed-of ceded lands," the mineral estate for the Ceded Strip once again belonged to the tribe. Thus at the beginning of the decade that brought increasing demand for western coal, the Crow not only owned mineral rights on the reservation proper but also held legal title to coal underlying more than a million acres just to the north.[12]

The third and final Crow coal sale focused exclusively on this Ceded Strip, and it was here that the Crow's long-awaited payday would come. Situated between the reservation and the already proven coal fields near Colstrip, Montana, there was little doubt these lands con-tained coal. In fact, the same geologist who put together the initial Crow Coal, Inc. proposal had been gathering state and private coal leases in this area for another local firm, Norsworthy & Reger. Hoping to add 35,000 acres of Crow lands to their existing holdings, Nors-worthy & Reger approached the tribe with an offer to bypass com-petitive bidding and negotiate directly for a coal lease. Tempting as this concrete proposal must have been, BIA officials resisted, choosing to follow protocol and require the Ceded Strip be offered at auction. Norsworthy & Reger would not, however, give up on their substantial investment in the coal lands north of the reservation. They convinced federal officials to at least open the auction to oral bidding so that the prospecting company could match other offers. When multiple en-ergy firms expressed interest in the Ceded Strip, Norsworthy & Reger's tactic to protect its investment ended up providing the mechanism to drive up Crow coal prices. After oral bidding on the Crow's third coal sale concluded on September 16, 1970, three mining firms, including the Westmoreland Coal Company—America's oldest independent coal company—paid more than $700,000 in bonuses for the rights to mine almost 70,000 acres in the Ceded Strip.[13]

Thrilled that the third coal sale had finally produced cash for their impoverished community, Crow leaders were determined to transform these prospecting contracts into viable mining enterprises with steady revenue streams. The ultimate form these projects would take, however, was still unclear and depended largely on distant markets that had not yet matured. Thus after quickly disbursing much of the signing bonuses in per capita payments to tribal members, these leaders worked with energy executives to fine tune their deals and make feasible a wide range of potential projects. The projects included possible mine-mouth power plants, gasification facilities on the reservation, or simply traditional mines that would ship coal to urban power generators.[14]

More than any other firm, the Westmoreland Coal Company aggressively pursued these options and was willing to invest in mining infrastructure before an established market existed. Crow efforts to move along energy development thus initially focused on that company's operations in the Ceded Strip. Westmoreland demonstrated its commitment by purchasing Norsworthy & Reger's coal rights, after which the tribe granted Westmoreland industrial water rights for a potential mine-mouth power plant. Tribal leaders then supported the construction of a railroad spur to the Ceded Strip, making possible the traditional option of shipping coal to urban power plants. The tribe also agreed to unify Westmoreland's numerous permits into one large lease so as to attract financing for a massive gasification project. Real Bird's administration even consented to modifying Westmoreland's financial terms to make Crow coal more competitive on the open market, though the full tribal council rejected these amendments. Nevertheless, Crow leadership clearly sought to tie the tribe's economic hopes to the fortunes of this coal company, and Westmoreland was committed to developing a viable project. When the mining firm elected to transform its prospecting permit into an outright lease in June 1972, the stage was set for mining to commence in the Ceded Strip.[15]

*

The timing of Westmoreland's lease was important; recall that the summer of 1972 was a dynamic season in southeastern Montana. News of the *North Central Power Study* filtered through the region and Bill Bryan, Marie Sanchez, the Northern Plains Resource Council, and their allies were beginning to ask important questions about the scale and costs of regional energy development. Many Crow were developing similar fears over potential environmental and social impacts, but of more immediate concern to tribal leaders was Consolidation's astonishing July proposal to their Northern Cheyenne neighbors. This offer of $35 per acre bonuses and 25 cents per ton royalties shattered anything the Crow had been able to secure from their energy "partners." This despite the fact that the tribal government had just spent two years renegotiating terms that Westmoreland insisted were necessary to make its project feasible. While elements within the tribe had already expressed dissatisfaction with the Westmoreland deal, Consolidation's offer to the Northern Cheyenne now united the Crow community and its leaders in a desire to go after better financial terms. By October, the newly elected tribal chairman, David Stewart, was leading yet another round of negotiations with Westmoreland.[16]

In these latest talks, the Crow used pressure applied by concerned regional ranchers and national environmental groups to push for better financial terms. In November 1972, for instance, environmental groups convinced a federal court that the National Environmental Policy Act required an environmental analysis for every Indian mineral lease. To meet this requirement and stay on schedule, the BIA and Westmoreland proposed an accelerated environmental impact statement for Westmoreland's lease, which the Crow endorsed on the condition it receive better royalty terms. Similarly, when the Sierra Club and six other groups filed a massive lawsuit in summer 1973 to halt all mining in eastern Montana pending a regional environmental analysis, the tribe seized another opportunity to trade its support for revenue. Intervening on behalf of the federal government and energy companies, the Crow claimed the suit violated its sovereign rights to develop tribal minerals by imposing a lengthy and bureaucratic environmental analysis process. Westmoreland aided the tribe by paying its attorney's fees, but the Crow were looking for more than free legal services. Tribal leaders demanded upward of a million dollars in advance royalties. Westmoreland President Pemberton Hutchinson argued to his fellow executives that the company should pay the demand so that "Cheyenne attitudes do not develop on the Crow Reservation." The two sides ultimately settled on other terms, but the Crow took every opportunity to remind Westmoreland that the tribal support it needed to get over the requisite environmental hurdles hinged on higher royalties.[17]

Crow leaders may have initially used the growing social and environmental movement against regional energy development to press for better terms, but as these critiques continued throughout 1973, many

The soil you see is not ordinary soil; it is the dust of
the blood, the flesh and the bones of our ancestors.
You have to dig down through the surface before you can
find Nature's earth. The upper.portion is Crow.

— Curly
Crow chief, 1908

Figure 3. Coal (Crow) Agency. Pamphlet distributed on the Crow Reservation,
1973. Reproduced by permission of Archivist, Little Bighorn College.

tribal members were becoming concerned about more than just financial returns. The Northern Cheyenne's March 5, 1973, revocation of
its coal leases crystallized the impact energy development could have
on tribal communities and heightened Westmoreland's concerns about
creating another "Northern Cheyenne situation" on the Crow Reservation. The coal company, however, appeared powerless to stop it. As
was the case with the Northern Cheyenne, anti-coal pamphlets soon
dotted the Crow Reservation, warning that "the very existence of the
Crow Reservation—as we know it now—could be lost forever to non-
Crows." These pamphlets extolled the sacrifices made by Crow ancestors to obtain their land and included images depicting coal mining as
the beast that would swallow the tribe whole (figure 3).[18]

By October, a reservation survey revealed just how prevalent these
fears about coal development had become. Ninety-four percent of
Crow respondents now favored a moratorium on all energy development until the tribe gathered more information on "how it will affect
our land, our culture, etc." Overwhelmingly, tribal members claimed

their leaders failed to disseminate details of proposed mining projects, arguing as one respondent did, "How can we ever know about any of our Crow affairs when only the ones who attend to the business keep it to themselves and their cronies?" Crow efforts to streamline its political process to move quickly on energy projects had created a citizenry unfamiliar with the plans laid for their land and fearful of potential impacts. Left in the dark by their leaders, oppositional groups stepped into the void, successfully pitching proposed mining projects as attacks on reservation land and lifeways. One respondent to the October survey summarized the tribe's general sentiment: "With all the outsiders coming here to work, we will no doubt lose our culture as well as our way of life. We will be exposed to the whiteman's dog-eat-dog way of life which again I am definitely against." The quote could have come directly from a Northern Cheyenne.[19]

Concerned their tribal leaders kept them uninformed and fearing the energy deals being brokered would compromise Crow land and culture, the community took action to return power to the people. In October 1973—the same month the reservation survey was released and, not incidentally, when OPEC's oil embargo began—the Crow Tribal Council created the new Mineral Committee composed of representatives from each reservation district, plus one member to represent off-reservation Crow. The enacting resolution charged this body with negotiating and enforcing all energy deals but, importantly, denied it the authority to execute mining permits or leases. Instead, reverting to the principles of the 1948 constitution, the resolution required that "all such matters must be submitted by the committee to a duly convened meeting of the Crow Tribal Council," which again included all adult tribal members. Rejecting the existing approach whereby the tribal chairman controlled mineral negotiations, assisted by the Oil and Gas Committee made up of political appointees, the Crow again amended their governing structure. This time, the tribe democratized authority over tribal resources.[20]

*

The new Mineral Committee hit the ground running. Faced with the increasing complexity of controlling reservation resources and understanding the potentially devastating consequences of bad coal deals, the committee turned to the one indigenous advocacy group with extensive experience in this area: the Native American Rights Fund (NARF). Daniel Israel, a NARF attorney, arrived on the Crow Reservation within weeks of the Mineral Committee's creation and told its members that the management of their coal was the most important issue currently facing American Indians. Coordinating with the Crow's community action program, Israel tapped federal funds to hire expert consultants to review existing deals and suggest terms for renegotiation. These consultants told the Crow what many members already knew, that their royalty terms were "unconscionably low and reflect[ed] inadequate preparation by the government and incompetent negotiation on behalf of the Crow Tribe." Suggesting the tribe collect or develop complete geological information on their coal deposits, put together their own estimates of mining costs, gather market data on their coal's value, and determine transportation and transmission rates to bring these resources to market, the consultants then offered a two-prong attack for negotiating with Westmoreland. First, with these data in hand, the tribe would be able to justify immediate demands for higher royalties. Second, once Westmoreland had recouped the capital invested in mining infrastructure, the tribe should then demand an equity partnership going forward. Much as it had done with the Northern Cheyenne, NARF and its consultants provided a blueprint to allow the Crow to realize monetary benefits from their minerals while maintaining control over mining.[21]

Implementing these plans, however, would prove more difficult than imagined. Throughout the winter of 1973–74, Israel and the Mineral Committee employed the two principles in negotiations with Westmoreland, hoping any deal would set a precedent for subsequent discussions with other coal companies. By late spring, the parties reached an agreement to significantly increase Crow royalties. Israel hailed the amended terms as "far and away the highest royalty existing in the United States for coal of this quality," but the Mineral Committee struggled to sell the deal to a tribal membership growing increasingly wary of coal mining. Tribal leaders held several public meetings to explain and justify the deal's terms, only to have a final decision postponed to allow for more consideration. The situation was further complicated by the impending Crow tribal elections, as hopeful candidates jockeyed for position by bringing in their own consultants to promote alternative negotiating strategies. With the waters significantly muddied, the tribal council shelved the Westmoreland contract until after the May 1974 elections, bringing the viability of Crow coal mining into serious question. When Westmoreland officer Howard Frey received news of the postponement, he could not help but doodle a bloody tomahawk in the margins of his company memo.[22]

With the issue of coal mining squarely on the ballot, the May 1974 elections brought the largest voter turnout in Crow history to elect a new tribal chairman, Patrick Stands Over Bull. Despite the interest generated, however, the change in leadership did not bring about a shift in energy policy, only an intensification of negotiating efforts. Announcing that he was "for coal development, but I'm for control," Stands Over Bull rallied his supporters to reject the Westmoreland deal and then attempted to reopen negotiations. But Westmoreland had grown tired of responding to the shifting sands of internal tribal politics. The firm simply ignored the latest offer to negotiate and began mining under the terms of the original lease. Buoyed by Interior Secretary Morton's June 1974 decision to void the Northern Cheyenne leases, the new tribal chairman responded with a resolution cancelling his tribe's coal contracts and establishing a "Green Belt Zoning Moratorium" for all reservation mining. This drastic measure certainly caught Westmoreland's attention and helped consolidate Stands Over Bull's support among his people, but it turned out to be little more than a negotiating tactic. In fact, despite the supposed mining moratorium, the tribal chairman continued to meet privately with Westmoreland officials, explaining that he did not want to cancel the coal company's lease but needed a better deal to sell to his members. At one point, Stands Over Bull even suggested the coal company send representatives to each reservation district to generate the grassroots support that would allow him to publicly champion an agreement. Like many tribal leaders before him, the pragmatic new Crow chairman sought to balance the need for revenue against his people's desire to control mining to limit its impacts.[23]

Ultimately, under the threat of Crow lawsuits and Westmoreland's continued extraction at the low royalty rate of 17.5 cents per ton, tribal leaders and coal company executives constructed a new deal acceptable to both sides. The amended terms included higher advanced royalties but also a tribal right to veto any mine-mouth generating facility or gas conversion complex within fifty miles of the reservation. Increased royalties certainly appeased many tribal members, but the veto authority meant the Crow could also prevent large-scale generating facilities that would attract unwanted outsiders and foul regional air and water. And not to be forgotten, Westmoreland's lease was located on the Ceded Strip, meaning any mining would occur off the reservation. Tribal members seemed willing to accept this arrangement as a compromise to generate revenue but protect reservation land and lifeways. When presented to the full tribal council on November 23, 1974, the tribe overwhelmingly approved the renegotiated Westmoreland deal, signaling the coalescence of a tribal coalition to support coal mining, but only on tribal terms.[24]

Of course, to arrive at this compromise, the Crow community and its government underwent important changes. First, the tribe streamlined its governing procedures to land potentially lucrative mining deals, but then returned to the 1948 constitution's democratic principles when this approach seemed to threaten the community's existence. The Crow also endured a crash-course education in energy development. Learning of potentially disastrous environmental and social impacts, the tribe retained outside experts to help structure a deal that returned more revenue while also maintaining a level of tribal control. By the end of 1974, then, the great majority of Crow members could agree that controlled coal mining off the reservation met the community's needs without threatening its survival.

A TRIBE DIVIDED: ON-RESERVATION MINING

The Crow had good reason for optimism in the winter of 1974–75. Tribal leaders had just successfully concluded difficult negotiations with an experienced and ambitious coal company that resulted in an immediate cash payment of over a million dollars, plus the promise of millions more in future royalties. The new tribal chairman touted a controlled approach to coal development, was advised by the Native American Rights Fund and their expert energy consultants, and appeared capable of building a tribal coalition to support his policies. Further, the recent Arab oil embargo, new federal air quality laws, and the 1973 federal moratorium on public coal leasing rendered the Crow's low-sulfur coal highly attractive to multinational mining firms. Once again, the tribe was poised to capitalize on its providential blessings.

But no sooner had the Crow put the finishing touches on their Westmoreland deal than energy companies sowed the seeds of tribal discord. Eleven days after the tribe overwhelmingly approved mining in the Ceded Strip, its consultants provided their recommendations on yet another proposal; this one to mine the reservation itself. Submitted by Shell Oil, the proposed lease would cover approximately 30,000 acres containing an estimated 300 million tons of recoverable coal. Extracting this stash could return royalties of $24 million per year over a fifty-year mining period, with more possible if Shell could construct a reservation power plant or gas conversion facility. The potential economic benefits were staggering, but so were the possible costs. Reviewing the proposal, NARF attorney Daniel Israel noted candidly that for the tribe "to prohibit *altogether* mining on the Reservation" meant "turning its back on millions of dollars of income." But, Israel warned, "the basic decision of whether to mine or not to mine requires a balancing of the Tribe's interest in preserving intact its cultural and natural environment versus its interest in obtaining a large and long-term revenue source."[25]

Having just reached a tenuous agreement to mine the Ceded Strip, the Crow were unsure how to proceed with on-reservation development. In a spring 1975 poll, 47.7 percent favored reservation mining, with 33 percent opposed and 18 percent withholding judgment. The same poll revealed, however, that a similar number, 46.4 percent, opposed reservation power plants, with 36.3 percent in favor and 16.7 percent unsure. Without a clear mandate, Stands Over Bull considered Shell's proposal but failed to pursue it with the same aggressive posture he took with Westmoreland.[26]

Shell officials could not afford to sit idly while the community weighed its options. One of the world's largest oil producers, Shell needed to act now to keep pace with other firms diversifying their holdings, and its Crow lease represented the company's primary investment in western coal. Thus when negotiations with tribal leaders failed to progress sufficiently, company officials appealed directly to the community, sending each tribal member a letter explaining that Shell's latest proposal included an immediate $200 per capita payment, a significant royalty hike over previous offers, and tribal control over any potential processing or power plant. For maximum effect, Shell timed the letters to arrive the week of a tribal council meeting that was to consider reservation coal development and one month prior to the tribe's annual Crow Fair, when the need for spending money was high. Understanding that the current Crow political system gave tribal members ultimate authority to determine land policy, Shell went straight to the people.[27]

Had Shell officials understood equally well the developing concerns among many Crow about the potential impacts of reservation development, they may have chosen another path. Certainly, opposition to coal mining was nothing new. After all, recall that the October 1973 tribal survey revealed that 94 percent supported a mining moratorium. However, thanks to the newly established Crow Office of Coal Research, by 1975 this resistance was taking on a much more structured and informed character. Funded by federal grants to the Crow's community action program, the "Coal Office" had two mandates: (1) "to compile objective data concerning the physical, economic, socio-political, and legal aspects" of Crow coal mining, and (2) to disseminate this information so tribal members could "make an informed decision concerning the utilization of their coal deposits." To carry out its mission, the office began issuing reservation-wide "Information Sheets" that summarized the treaties and laws governing reservation resources and explained the tribe's various mineral contracts.[28]

The Coal Office also organized a delegation of tribal members to visit the Navajo and Hopi Reservations in the American Southwest. According to trip organizer Angela Russell, the overall goal was simple enough: to see with their own eyes "what might be involved should the Crow Tribe decide to proceed with mining coal within our own reservation." In fall 1975, eighteen Crow, representing each reservation district, toured the Black Mesa strip mines and power plants and met with Hopi and Navajo members living nearby. Not surprisingly, the trip left a lasting impression. Before the visit, members of the delegation were split evenly on whether they favored reservation mining. Afterwards, 60 percent opposed mining and only 33 percent still supported it. Even more astounding, when asked before the trip whether participants believed reservation coal mining would be good for the Crow people, 53 percent answered "yes," and 29 percent said "no." After the trip, only 20 percent still believed reservation mining would benefit the community; 67 percent now thought reservation mining would bring harm. Faithful to its mission, the Coal Office made sure to publish details of the trip and disseminate the results of the participants' survey.[29]

In publicizing the growing sentiment among tribal members to oppose reservation mining, the Office of Coal Research claimed it simply was reporting the objective data it collected. Many within the tribe, however, were not so sure and came to view the institution as an agent of anti-coal forces. To those suffering under immense reservation poverty, reports of potentially adverse mining impacts and negative descriptions of other, existing reservation projects threatened the financial relief promised by coal mining, specifically from the most recent Shell proposal. The fact that young, educated Crow, like recent graduate student Angela Russell, and non-Indian experts, such as Dr. Lloyd Pickett of the Montana Cooperative Extension Service, ran the Coal Office furthered suspicions that it failed to serve ordinary tribal members. As one Crow critic of the Coal Office explained in a December 1975 open letter published in the local paper:

> Instead of getting expert people to help us, the Coal Office has been using its money to just fight coal development rather than learn about coal. It looks like the ranchers and environmental people have taken over the Coal Office and are just telling us bad things about coal.... The fact that our people need jobs, and per capita payments is easy to forget when you have a nice warm job that will last as long as Crow Coal is *not* developed. What about the rest of the people who do not have a nice warm place to work like that?

Tribal Chairman Stands Over Bull was sensitive to such complaints, for his political viability rested on improving his constituents' lives. Supported by a coalition desiring controlled coal development, the tribal chairman did not misread his mandate. He understood that many Crow still coveted mining revenue, even if they wanted to mitigate the worst of its impacts. If these members viewed the Coal Office as a threat to that possibility, he needed to respond.[30]

Sensing that the growing anti-coal sentiment limited his ability to deliver new mining projects, Stands Over Bull moved to reestablish his leadership over Crow coal development while at the same time strengthening his negotiating position with coal companies looking to mine the reservation. Denouncing Shell's direct appeal to tribal members as "at best presumptuous and misleading, and at worst fraudulent," the tribal chairman filed a lawsuit to void all existing coal contracts, except the renegotiated Westmoreland deal. In doing so, however, Stands Over Bull made sure his actions were not misinterpreted as an absolute, anti-development policy. Instead, his goal was to force Shell and other coal companies into even better agreements affording greater tribal control. In a public statement released concurrently with the lawsuit's filing, the chairman assured mining companies and tribal members alike that the legal action "does *not* mean that the Crow people are opposed to the development of our resources. We simply believe that if we are to permit the mining of our coal, we must adequately plan and prepare for the impacts of such development so that we can preserve our culture, our heritage, and our reservation." A major part of this preparation included enacting tribal ordinances to mitigate future mining impacts, such as a law and order code, a tribal tax on coal extraction, and reclamation requirements for any future mines. The tribe thus set to work on drafting these measures, and then, as a precondition for resuming negotiations, the tribal chairman demanded all coal companies agree to abide by them. Further, reflecting the increasing sophistication of tribal leaders looking to control reservation mining, Stands Over Bull required that all future mining projects include the tribe as an equity owner.[31]

Having strengthened his hand with energy firms, Stands Over Bull next moved to consolidate power within the tribe. In October 1975, over objections of several tribal members, the tribal chairman orchestrated new Mineral Committee elections that put in place officials supporting his plan to develop reservation coal in compliance with tribal regulations. The move not only signaled that on-reservation mining was firmly on Stands Over Bull's agenda but also effectively removed the Mineral Committee as a counterweight to the chairman's power. Essentially, the tribe returned to the centralized governing structure that produced the massive, reservation-wide energy deals Stands Over Bull had been elected to control. This time, however, the chairman claimed tribal ordinances and his own good judgment would mitigate the worst effects of mining while still offering new revenue streams. With institutional controls in place and his authority unchecked, Stands Over Bull reopened negotiations with coal companies to develop reservation coal.[32]

As might be expected, not all Crow were confident in the ability of their leader and his ordinances to prevent the worst effects of reservation mining. Following the enactment of the tribal regulations in January 1976 and the reopening of talks with energy companies, tribal members turned out in force at the spring tribal council meeting to demand their government focus solely on Ceded Strip mining. When Stands Over Bull ignored these calls and continued to negotiate, anti-coal advocates went after the chairman's job, peppering complaints about his coal policy with claims of public drunkenness. Despite these attacks, Stands Over Bull narrowly survived reelection in May 1976, though voting results show the victory was more the product of his numerous opponents splitting the anti-coal vote and less an affirmation of his policies. In fact, no less than four candidates, including Stands Over Bull's own vice chairman, ran opposed to their chairman's coal strategy. Had these competitors unified their supporters, their collective votes would have tallied 1,070 for an anti-coal candidate to Stands Over Bull's 608 votes. Acting as a referendum on plans to mine the reservation itself, the heated election signaled the end of the tribe's fragile pro-coal mining coalition.[33]

*

To be clear, energy development did not create entirely new divisions among the Crow. Rather, coal mining provided the latest, potentially dramatic shift in reservation land use that brought tribal factions to the fore. In fact, prior to energy development dominating tribal politics, the Crow had ruptured in the 1950s over federal plans to dam the Bighorn River. One faction, known as the "River Crow" or "Southsiders," argued for selling reservation land to the federal government, while another, the "Mountain Crow" or "Northsiders," fought federal ownership of the dam site, proposing instead that the tribe only lease to the federal government usufruct rights. These labels, "Mountain Crow" and "River Crow," had nothing to do with the early, nomadic bands of the same names that constituted two of the three major pre-reservation Crow groups. Instead, the labels reflected deep divisions within the tribe over how to deal with external desires for Crow land and resources. Twentieth-century River Crow generally supported a more cooperative approach with outsiders, working with the federal government and others to develop Crow land to produce revenue. Mountain Crow, in contrast, tended to favor greater tribal control over land and were reluctant to turn over property rights to developers, even if that meant foregoing economic opportunities. Enforced by kinship and clan ties and maintained through a pervasive political patronage system, these basic divisions loosely structured Crow politics—including energy debates—during the second half of the twentieth century.[34]

Understanding Crow debates over coal development, however, requires more than simply identifying these two factions and placing specific Crow families within their respective camps. While these divisions remained present and inescapable throughout the postwar period, they never completely determined an individual's position on a particular land issue, and certainly not for all times. Northsider/Mountain Crow Sonny Yellowtail, for instance, could break with his famous father, Robert Yellowtail, and vote to sell land for the Bighorn River dam, whereas Southsider/River Crow Patrick Stands Over Bull could lead efforts to halt mining only to pursue development later. Moreover, these dividing lines often receded when the benefits of a proposed land-use project seemed unquestionable or the impacts so drastic that all either favored or opposed the project. Such was the case with the original 1960s coal contracts. Without sufficient knowledge of potential impacts and desperate for revenue, tribal members from all sides overwhelmingly supported these deals. Yet, as the potentially adverse consequences of uncontrolled development became apparent in the early 1970s, the tribe almost uniformly supported a reservation moratorium, consenting only to energy development in the Ceded Strip. Only when plans to mine the reservation placed pressure on this tribal consensus and disagreements formed over the costs and benefits of reservation mining did the old factions reemerge to help structure coal debates. In this latest battle over the management of Crow land, Southsiders tended to support their tribal chairman in his efforts to develop coal on the reservation while Northsiders resisted.[35]

But as was the case in previous controversies over the dispensation of Crow land, important generational differences also informed this most recent battle between the Crow factions. Young, educated Crow who had spent time away from the reservation, and who perhaps still lived in the nearby cities of Billings or Hardin, tended to oppose reservation mining and support the Northsiders. Many like Angela Russell, Ellis Knows Gun, and Dale Kindness worked at or with the Office of Coal Research, where they gained firsthand knowledge of coal development's potential impacts. Privy to such information—or perhaps predisposed to seek it out—these Crow echoed the Northern Cheyenne's concerns that mining would bring outsiders to disrupt social customs and alter cultural values, plus leave the Crow with untold environmental harms. Rendered minorities on their scarred reservation, Northsiders feared coal mining could eliminate the community altogether and jeopardize their status as American Indians. As the young leader Dale

Kindness explained, "We Indians have very little [land] left. If we lose it, America's historians will write the final chapter on American Indians, beginning soon, and the chapter will be entitled 'Coal.'" Curiously, these younger Crow who often resided elsewhere looked to the reservation as a refuge that would preserve the essential characteristics of their tribe. Consequently, they placed a strong emphasis on protecting the social, cultural, and physical integrity of this place.[36]

With the homeland seemingly under attack, Crow coal opponents constantly sought to strengthen the powers of their tribal government to prevent the worst of coal mining's impacts. Here their interests lined up perfectly with Stands Over Bull's. Through their work with the Coal Office and its connection to outside experts, they understood that tribal control was the key. As Kindness once again explained: "If we are to continue as Indian people with our own values, society and culture, we have to stand up straight and get our stuff together. We have to come up with some zoning ordinances, reclamation and environmental laws, we have to make the most out of this development if we are to have it . . . , while at the same time providing safeguards for our land and environment." Considering this emphasis on strengthening tribal powers, many young Crow supported, and even proposed, the tribal ordinances Stands Over Bull pushed through the tribal council. *But the dividing line for these tribal members supporting their chairman's coal policies was located at the reservation border.* Mining in the Ceded Strip under carefully controlled tribal regulations that would ensure impacts did not spill over to the reservation represented the perfect compromise. It allowed the tribe to reap financial benefits without disrupting reservation land and customs. Once Stands Over Bull attempted to extend mining on to the reservation, he lost this important faction.[37]

Several among this youthful group drew additional inspiration from the growing chorus of militant Indian protests erupting across the nation in the 1970s. As was the case with the Northern Cheyenne, the Crow Reservation was never a hotbed of Red Power activism, but neither was it immune from these activities. In fact, during the June 1976 centennial celebrations of the Battle of the Little Bighorn, the reservation became the focal point for protests when former American Indian Movement leader Russell Means interrupted the planned festivities by leading a procession of Native protesters up Custer Hill. Coming on the heels of Stands Over Bull's narrow and contentious May 1976 reelection, Means announced to a shocked audience: "Nothing has changed in 100 years. Custer came and invaded us over gold. Today we have a much more sophisticated invasion by the corporate giants of America over mineral wealth, but this time it is for coal." As news of the protests spread quickly through the reservation, Stands Over Bull curtly dismissed the actions, telling reporters, "What happens up there [on Custer Hill] has nothing to do with us." The tribal chairman, however, may have done better to pay closer attention, for standing with Means were several young Crow, including his own vice secretary, Ellis Knows Gun. Knows Gun announced to the audience that his tribe was "fighting for our very existence" and called for a unified Indian struggle against mineral developers. If only temporarily, these young, energized Indians tapped into the Red Power Movement's anticolonial rhetoric to reclaim the meaning attached to this historic battlefield and cast Crow coal development as the "last stand" for American Indians.[38]

But although the Red Power Movement at times inspired young Crow activists, these tribal members ultimately rejected direct action protests in favor of working within the tribe's political system to stop reservation mining. Arguing that Stands Over Bull's unilateral pursuit of such mining violated the 1948 constitution, this group took over the tribe's October 1976 council meeting and narrowly established (by vote of 393–321) yet another committee to handle all mineral development activities. Dubbed the "Crow Coal Authority" this new entity was intended to be more than just a negotiating body. Instead, the tribe's latest consultant, Charles Lipton, an international attorney renowned for advising postcolonial countries developing their oil reserves, advised the Crow to establish the Coal Authority to serve as a tribally owned operating company. As such, it was vested with the power to enter into partnerships with energy firms or to contract with them to perform mining, but under either approach, the tribe would remain owners of the project and retain authority over the pace and scale of operations. Importantly, the enacting resolution directed the Coal Authority to negotiate only with coal companies operating in the Ceded Strip, and it required that all finalized deals be sent back to the full tribal council for approval.[39]

The creation of the Crow Coal Authority not only usurped the chairman's negotiating power and returned the tribe to the 1948 constitution's democratic principles, but it also sought to remove coal development from day-to-day, contentious Crow politics. Rather than debate energy policy at each tribal council meeting or allow the elected leader to handle all negotiations himself, the resolution vested authority to negotiate in a semi-autonomous, continuously sitting body with representatives from across the reservation and beyond. For young Crow activists, this new governing structure represented all the benefits of a modern and efficient corporate enterprise while retaining what they viewed as the crucial component of Crow governance: majority rule after full vetting before the tribe. It also guaranteed no coal companies would operate on the reservation, removing the largest perceived threat to tribal survival.

These young Northsiders, however, did not hold a monopoly on the discourse of tribal survival. They may have constantly painted reservation coal mining as the primary threat to the Crow's existence, even tweaking the tribal government to prevent this from happening, but older, on-reservation Indians viewed the young, brash leaders as the real risk to the tribe. Characterizing the young Turks as off-reservation meddlers with little respect for established customs, Stands Over Bull's supporters urged the BIA not to recognize the Coal Authority. Longtime Tribal Secretary Eloise Pease submitted a formal protest, arguing that the October 1976 meeting violated a host of tribal procedures and that the new governing body failed to "recogn[ize] the traditional status of the Crow Tribal Chairman." As the BIA considered the matter, Stands Over Bull continued to defiantly meet with Shell officials, creating the confusing situation of two competing Crow factions negotiating with different coal companies. The tribe called a December 22, 1976, special tribal council meeting to clarify which Crow entity held the authority to negotiate, but fistfights broke out after Dale Kindness introduced a resolution to convey all negotiating authority to the Coal Authority. When Stands Over Bull abruptly adjourned the meeting and left under a police escort, almost a third of the 900 attending Crow remained to pass a resolution suspending the chairman for a ninety-day period.[40]

Although the BIA's Board of Indian Appeals later declared Stands Over Bull's suspension invalid, this attempted removal set the agenda for tribal politics over the coming year. The suspension action quickly grew into calls for Stands Over Bull's impeachment, and the heated rhetoric intensified during the January and April 1977 tribal council meetings. With the specter of violence in the air, many of the chairman's most fervent supporters denounced the opposition group as "half-breed" radicals unfamiliar with suffering on the reservation whose actions threatened the tribe's existence. Not all went this far, but even moderate Stands Over Bull supporters like Eloise Pease pleaded with the chairman's critics not to alter the tribal government. "We should not try to break down the Chairman's office," Pease urged. "We have precious things that is [sic] ours—our land, mountains and we have our water back. The Constitution and Bylaws is the only protection that you Crows have!"[41]

But Stands Over Bull's opponents refused to relent. Turning to the BIA's Board of Indian Appeals, the opposition group secured a ruling that the tribal council must take up their petition for impeachment. The showdown was set. The tribe's July 9, 1977, meeting would determine the fate of the Crow leader and the future of tribal energy policy. Wrapped up in both issues was a determination of what type of community the Crow would become.[42]

*

On a warm and stormy July evening, in a tightly packed gymnasium, which included armed police to protect tribal officers from the violence erupting outside, more than 1,200 Crow engaged in a lengthy debate over the future of their tribe. To position themselves as authorities on this question, both factions attempted to establish their side as the protector of authentic Crow values and governance. Pat Stands Over Bull's mother arrived in nineteenth-century Crow garb, long braids, and high moccasins to defend her son, while tribal elder Silas Big Medicine refused to speak in English, instead berating Stands Over Bull in Crow for working against the wishes of the majority. On this point, impeachment advocates seized upon the rhetoric of sovereignty and self-determination to defend what they saw as the "traditional" Crow value of public deliberation and majority rule. Opposition leader Duane McCurdy asserted that sovereignty rested with the Crow people, not tribal officers like Stands Over Bull who sought to unilaterally strike energy deals. McCurdy argued:

Pat Stands and his administration have attempted to dissolve the sovereignty of the Crow Nation. . . . He has failed to protect the best interests of the Crow Nation. He has allowed special interest groups to put their foot in the door without putting up a fight. The Crow Nation never allows anybody to take our lands. Therefore, we cannot allow this man to stay in office to sell out or phase out the statue of the Crow Nation.

But Stands Over Bull's supporters turned this sovereignty rhetoric on its head, countering that the opposition was being run by half-breeds and whites, not Crow Indians. As Joe Alden pleaded to his tribe, certainly this was not self-determination:

You are letting some half breeds do your talking and you are just sitting back, why don't you talk for yourself? I don't agree with your actions. . . . You are Crows, why are you taking actions against your own? One of our past leaders once said if ever these half breeds run our affairs, you Crows would be lost. I think that day is here.

This bitter divisiveness extended even to the rules governing the meeting, as Stands Over Bull's opponents narrowly passed a motion (675–618) to replace the common voting method of walking "through the line" with secret balloting so that tribal employees could vote their conscience rather than be beholden to the political patronage system. Further, when the opposition succeeded in appointing the tribe's white attorney as the meeting's parliamentarian, the chairman's supporters nearly walked out. Ted Hogan exclaimed that all the talk of self-determination "seems to be a double standard here in that we just elected a white guy to be a parliamentarian to tell us how to run our council." At one point in the meeting, past tribal chairman Edison Real Bird turned directly to the television cameras broadcasting the event and tried to explain that impeaching their leader was "not the [typical] behavior of the Crow Tribe of Indians." Of course, what was "typical," "authentic," or "traditional" Crow governance was exactly what was being debated that night.[43]

What is striking about the arguments deployed by both factions—besides their intensity—is the similarity of rhetoric. Beyond the one-sided use of ethnic slurs to disparage the chairman's opponents, both groups described their position as embedded in "traditional" Crow values. Young Crow believed the use of experts and the Coal Authority were necessary to protect the land base—a vital ingredient of their Crow identity. They argued that their method of resource management maintained traditional governing practices by vesting ultimate authority in the full tribal council. Seen through this perspective, the true threat to the tribe lay in exploitative contracts negotiated by naïve or corrupt leaders that portended disastrous consequences for the community. Meanwhile, Stands Over Bull's supporters decried the delegation of power to the Coal Authority as a nontraditional, non-Indian way of doing business. Seen in this light, their use of ethnic rhetoric to deride their opponents was less a description of biological qualities and more a characterization of the Northsiders' proposed mineral policies and practices. To this group, on-reservation energy development could actually save the tribe, and they believed Crow political tradition gave the tribal chairmen the authority to make these deals. Altering the existing structure in favor of a semi-autonomous body populated by "half-breeds" and advised by outside experts threatened to turn the tribe into non-Indians. As Phillip Beaumont described it, "We have followed Crow traditions and come this far, but if we impeach the Chairman today, we have changed to the whiteman's way of doing things."[44]

These agonizing debates over the fate of their chairman, their energy policy, and the survival of their tribe continued throughout the warm July night. At 10:40 a.m. the following day, the weary tribe finally adjourned the meeting having impeached their chairman, broken with traditional modes of voting along clan lines, and established a coal development policy that prohibited mining on the reservation itself. Beyond these rather obvious results, the tribe also emerged with an altered conception of what it meant to be Crow. The new, dominant meaning foregrounded the importance of an Indian-only land base and the use of efficient, expert-driven mechanisms for protecting this reservation refuge. The new coal policy also paid homage to the past, reestablishing the governing values of public deliberation and majority rule that young, educated Crow held to be vital components of their "Crowness." Through the process of debating energy policy, the Crow fixed specific governing values and remade their tribal identities in ways that, as Frederick Hoxie observed, "honored the past and served the future." It was a struggle their 1884 ancestors would have recognized as similar to their own.

3

THE NATIONAL CAMPAIGN

6 Taking the Fight National

BY THE SUMMER of 1974, the view from southeastern Montana was improving. Responding to perceived attacks on the homeland, both the Northern Cheyenne and Crow had taken control of reservation mining and were exploring options to develop their resources in ways that ensured their communities' survival. The Northern Cheyenne's successful petition to the Department of the Interior had halted reservation mining and put the tribe in a position to extract the coal itself. The community was unified and prepared to reverse American Indians' historical role as passive observers to the development of their own resources. Next door, the Crow would soon fracture over the issue of reservation mining, but in summer 1974, the tribe's newly elected chairman, Patrick Stands Over Bull, had established a reservation mining moratorium and was focused on developing only the Ceded Strip. All Crow agreed that tribal control over energy projects was necessary to mitigate harmful social, cultural, and environmental impacts. Benefiting from difficult lessons learned elsewhere, both tribes stood ready to reap economic benefits from development pursued only on tribal terms.

Yet as important as these actions were for the Crow and Northern Cheyenne communities, those involved in these battles recognized that the war over Indian energy could not be won solely in southeastern Montana. Events beyond regional and national boundaries ensured

127

continual pressures to develop reservation resources across the West, pressures that could be met only with a similarly broad campaign to equip tribal leaders with the tools and knowledge needed to control development. Thus, in the months following President Nixon's November 1973 announcement of Project Independence—an ambitious response to OPEC's October oil embargo that called for expanding domestic production to make the country "energy independent" by the end of the decade—tribal leaders made several attempts to mobilize a consortium of similarly situated tribes to share experiences, consultants, and funding to prepare for the coming onslaught in energy demand. If the country wanted Indian resources, energy tribes could facilitate the process, but they had their own set of demands. These groups organized to ensure their communities received the bulk of benefits from reservation development.

STANDING GROUND: "A DECLARATION OF INDIAN RIGHTS"

Ironically, the federal government planted the seeds for the first pan-tribal association to defend Indian energy rights. On October 3, 1972, Interior Secretary Rogers Morton announced a joint, interagency, federal-state task force "to assess the potential social, economic and environmental impacts which would result from future development of the vast coal deposits and other resources in the five Northern Great Plains States." Involving a dozen federal agencies and a handful of states, the Northern Great Plains Resource Program (NGPRP) followed two previous attempts in the decade to coordinate energy development in the region. Like its predecessors, which included the ill-fated *North Central Power Study*, the NGPRP explored the possibility of a massive, interjurisdictional, region-wide development scheme to transform the thinly populated Northern Plains into an "energy belt" to meet the nation's growing needs. But unlike the previous studies, which focused solely on maximizing the rate of production for valuable resources, the Department of the Interior intended the NGPRP to take a more holistic approach. Multiple scenarios for regional development would be studied, and potential impacts assessed across a wide range of economic, social, and environmental values. In fact, in explaining the NGPRP as "an outgrowth of public concern in the region [over] prior studies of the region's resources by Federal and State governments as well as private organizations," Secretary Morton left little doubt that his agency had heard the complaints of Northern Plains' ranchers and environmentalists who feared energy development would disrupt their livelihoods and landscapes. Responding to these concerns, the secretary promised a more thoughtful approach to regional development.[1]

The same attention, however, was not paid to the region's first occupants, as once again, no one had bothered to solicit Native American input for the proposed plans. Anxious tribes could only watch as the Interior secretary promised other constituencies a more calculated approach to Northern Plains' development while declaring confidently that "these major coal deposits will be developed, that is inevitable, but how they are developed is of national interest." Excluded from the process, Indians felt their apprehension over the potential use of tribal resources increase as President Nixon delivered a series of unprecedented addresses in 1973 that stressed the need to expand domestic energy production, particularly from the nation's vast coal reserves. Never before had a president featured energy policy in a message to Congress or the American people. Now, even before the October 1973 Arab oil embargo, Nixon was highlighting the disparity between the amount of coal the country possessed—according to him, over half the world's reserves—and the amount being used to meet domestic energy needs—again by the president's estimate, less than 20 percent. To remedy this disparity, in his April 1973 address the president urged "that highest national priority be given to expanded development and utilization of our coal resources," including those along the Northern Plains. When Nixon again emphasized these vast untapped coal reserves in his November 7 announcement of Project Independence, the message from the top was clear. Energy development was coming to the Northern Plains and the federal government was paving the way.[2]

The nation's newfound commitment to Northern Plains coal development was on a collision course with indigenous peoples' commitment to community survival. Sensing tribal resources would again be sacrificed for the good of the country, Indian leaders reacted to Nixon's call for energy independence by organizing a historic gathering of Northern Plains tribes for December 18, 1973, on North Dakota's Fort Berthold Reservation. The one hundred plus delegates who arrived at the reservation shared by the Mandan, Hidatsa, and Arikara tribes planned initially to discuss the NGPRP's impact to tribal water rights. The conversation broadened quickly, however, to include a general denunciation of the regional development program and a plan for a coordinated defense. Unable to ignore a gathering of this many disgruntled stakeholders, especially those with precious water and mineral rights, NGPRP Director John Vanderwalker scrambled to attend the meeting and placate Indian concerns. He did not receive the reception he had hoped for. Instead, the gathered tribal leaders made clear their strong resolve to oppose regional development without Native input, leaving the director with little choice but to bring the tribes into the NGPRP process. Yet Vanderwalker's view of the tribes' appropriate role was telling of the government's notion of tribal sovereignty, even under the new self-determination policy. Labeling these groups as special "consultants," the NGPRP director invited the tribes merely to submit formal comments on the final report. Apparently, the insensitivity of belatedly asking American Indians to "consult" on a plan that would deeply impact their resources and communities was lost on Vanderwalker.[3]

The insult was not missed by tribal delegates. Those in attendance seized the opportunity to submit comments on the NGPRP as a chance to organize collectively and articulate broader concerns regarding the expropriation of Indian resources. Before disbanding at Fort Berthold, delegates established a temporary committee to draft their comments and enlisted the assistance of Native American Rights Fund (NARF) attorney Thomas Fredericks, himself a Mandan tribal member. At the time, NARF attorneys were already busy on the nearby Northern Cheyenne and Crow Reservations restructuring or canceling existing mining projects. This experience, combined with NARF's earlier work on behalf of Hopi and Navajo tribal members, positioned Fredericks's relatively small public-interest law firm as the nation's foremost expert on protecting Indian mineral rights. It also allowed NARF attorneys to develop a common legal strategy that entailed first asserting tribal control over natural resources—and defending this claim in legal or administrative actions, if necessary—before entertaining proposals to develop them. Fredericks shared this message with his new clients, several of whom, like committee member and Northern Cheyenne President Allen Rowland, were already fighting their own tribal battles to control reservation mining. Under Fredericks's guidance and with Rowland's support, the temporary committee's task to provide specific comments on the NGPRP morphed into a general defense of indigenous rights over all Northern Plains resources guaranteed by past treaties.[4]

As the broader scope of this undertaking became clear, those involved understood that a simple declaration of rights was not sufficient to defend legal claims to highly valuable resources. A formal organization was required to carry the fight. Thus when the Northern Plains tribes gathered again in Billings, Montana, on January 17, 1974, to review their draft statement on Indian resources, delegates formed another ad hoc committee to not only finalize the statement but also draft a constitution and bylaws for a new federation to protect tribal rights. None other than Northern Cheyenne Tribal President Allen Rowland chaired this new committee. Working throughout the winter, Rowland and his fellow delegates returned to Billings in March to approve what was now titled the "Declaration of Indian Rights to the Natural Resources in the Northern Great Plains" and finalize founding documents for the Native American Natural Resources Development Federation (NANRDF). By May, the new organization had elected former and future Rosebud Sioux Tribal President Robert Burnette as its chairman. In addition to his tribal duties, Burnette also was the former executive director of the National Congress of American Indians and the visionary behind the Trail of Broken Treaties. Clearly, he possessed the leadership qualities and experience necessary to make NANRDF a force to be reckoned with on the Northern Plains. Within a few short months, the indigenous outrage at being excluded from the NGPRP process had blossomed into a full, pan-tribal alliance to protect tribal resources and communities.[5]

Much like the Northern Cheyenne and Crow revolts, organizers of this pan-tribal alliance understood their mission as a desperate defense of tribal homelands, and the Native American Rights Fund made sure to make this point in terms all Americans could understand. Dedicating its spring 1975 newsletter to the formation of NANRDF, NARF staff drew explicit comparisons between the saga unfolding on the Northern Plains and the American Revolution. The Northern Cheyenne and Crow, NARF explained, were the Sons of Liberty that ignited the insurrection. The Billings meetings played as a modern-day Second Continental Congress, producing a Native Declaration of Independence and a confederation to manage the anticolonial war. And just as the complaints of the Boston patriots had found their fullest expression in the exalted prose of the Founding Fathers, the arguments first articulated by the Northern Cheyenne and Crow were now being expounded upon by the twenty-six founding members of NANRDF. Their Declaration of Indian Rights explained how the international energy crisis "makes the vast coal resources of [the Northern Plains] very appealing for immediate development," and that such pressure to develop "threatens the viability of our environment and the continued existence of the 26 tribes which occupy the Northern Great Plains." Defiant in its defense of these communities, NANRDF put the world on notice that its members intended to "maintain their ownership to the priceless natural resources which are geographically and legally related to their reservations" and warned federal agencies that any attempt to divert or use tribal resources "shall be at their own risk." The line in the sand had been drawn.[6]

To defend its position, NANRDF set out not only to represent its members' interests in federal and state planning efforts but also to construct an indigenous network of knowledge to help tribal leaders make sound resource development decisions. In fact, of NANRDF's four founding purposes—(1) to coordinate efforts to describe and quantify Northern Plains Indians' cultural and natural resources, (2) to develop scientific data and expertise to make informed management decisions for these resources, (3) to represent affected Indians in federal and state planning programs, and (4) to provide assistance to individual tribes in managing their resources—three were dedicated to generating and sharing information on appropriate resource management techniques. This focus on gathering knowledge about minerals and markets and educating tribal leaders on the nuances of energy development mirrored the approach taken by the Crow and Northern Cheyenne. The affinity was no accident. The very same leaders and advisors involved in those struggles were applying similar tactics in this concomitant effort to build a pan-tribal alliance.[7]

ON THE OFFENSIVE: CREATING THE COUNCIL OF ENERGY RESOURCE TRIBES

By the summer of 1974, the revolution launched in Lame Deer had gained solid footing in tribal communities across the Northern Plains. The government's latest coordinated efforts to tap regional energy reserves triggered indigenous resistance among numerous potentially affected communities. Conditioned by the Cheyenne, Crow, and southwestern experiences, the Northern Plains groups issued a declaration of rights drawing attention to the government's latest exploits and formed a pan-tribal organization to combat them. NANRDF was the first entity of its kind, uniting dozens of tribes behind the single purpose of protecting valuable tribal minerals.

But for all of its importance, the Northern Plains' coalition was still regional in scope and defensive in nature. It was an appropriate response, for it reflected the particular threat posed. The Department of the Interior's actions to exploit Northern Plains' resources represented an older, Progressive-era approach to western development, one where the government directed resource management and reflexively ignored tribal input. In the 1970s, however, new federal agencies were exploring innovative partnerships with groups outside the federal bureaucracy that could increase domestic energy production nationwide. If Interior's actions on the Northern Plains called for a defensive response, this novel approach provided common ground for energy tribes and federal officials to work together. It also provided a platform to expand the Northern Plains alliance into a national consortium to represent the interests of all energy tribes. Tribal leaders formed NANRDF to fight Department of the Interior actions in the North, but they would establish the Council of Energy Resource Tribes (CERT) in partnership with new federal efforts to cooperatively expand domestic energy production.

A familiar warrior triggered the search for common ground between energy tribes and the federal government. On February 13, 1974, George Crossland, the Osage attorney who had first counseled the Northern Cheyenne to tear up their coal leases, wrote to Stuart Jamieson of the National Congress of American Indians (NCAI) advocating for a "tribal energy coalition" to help tribes maximize the long-range benefits of their energy resources. Crossland was not involved in NANRDF's creation, but he understood what Project Independence meant for Native resources. He warned Jamieson that the country's excessive growth would continue to place extreme pressures on these resources and argued that tribes needed a common strategy to protect their minerals or else "we shall see the experiences of the Osages and Navajos-Hopis repeated: the depletion and consumption of the resources base." Following up a month later, Crossland submitted a more extensive memo to NCAI Executive Director Chuck Trimble that included data on the nation's increasing energy use and quotes from its top energy policy makers. According to the longtime tribal rights advocate, these indicators "lead inevitably to the conclusion that the Bureau [of Indian Affairs] and [the Department of the] Interior are quite willing to sacrifice Indian people, in the first instance, for the gain of the energy industry." "Therefore, if the 'past is prologue,'" Crossland continued, "the tribes must be more informed than ever before if they determine to utilize their natural resources. In the headlong rush to meet the nation's energy demands, it is entirely conceivable that the loss of tribal viability will be considered just one of the nation's 'social costs.'" One of the nation's foremost experts in defending tribal resource rights was raising the alarm to the country's largest Indian rights group and asking the NCAI to organize its members for a mutual defense.[8]

As it turns out, Crossland's plea fit perfectly with an important policy shift occurring within the NCAI to empower tribes to develop their own, Indian-led reservation economies rather than relying on outside capital to build non-Indian enterprises on the reservations. Founded in 1944 to fight federal efforts to terminate the special trustee relationship between tribes and the federal government, the NCAI had consistently worked "within the system" to protect tribal treaty rights and enhance indigenous communities. During the 1960s, this approach meant largely eschewing the combative tactics of more militant groups, such as the National Indian Youth Council or the American Indian Movement, to focus on extending President Lyndon Johnson's Great Society programs to impoverished American Indians. To stimulate reservation economies, the NCAI thus obtained status as a national Community Action Agency and administered an Indian Economic Development Program designed to bring industrial activity to rural reservations. As the NCAI explained in a proposal to the Economic Development Administration, this approach involved "a series of 'industrial show-type' seminars wherein Indian Tribes would set up booths extolling the benefits of locating industry on their respective reservations . . . and booths were [also] provided for industries to display their products for consideration by the Tribes." To develop reservation economies, the NCAI acted essentially as a national Chamber of Commerce seeking to site private industries on Indian reservations.[9]

By the early 1970s, however, the organization was reexamining this model. Member tribes were rejecting the "industrial show" approach due largely, as the NCAI noted, to the "growing nationalistic emphasis of the Tribes on the development of Tribal government and development of their natural resources." Proposing a shift in tactics to the Economic Development Administration in 1974, the NCAI explained that in this "year of national introspect[ion]" caused by the Arab oil embargo, tribes "are engaged in widespread governmental and economic development, and are beginning to look increasingly to the development of their [own] human and natural resources." To lead this transition to Indian-centered reservation economies, the NCAI proposed a series of intensive, multiday seminars that would educate tribal leaders on the specific industries most appropriate for their reservations. These included commercial fishing seminars for Pacific Northwest tribes and agribusiness primers for those in the Great Plains, but the NCAI argued that "potentially the most important seminar on the proposed schedule" was a panel on energy resources intended for the "Indian 'Energy Belt' extending from western North Dakota diagonally southwestward through Arizona." In this time of soaring energy demands and limited international oil supplies, the NCAI looked to Indian energy development as the potential flagship for its new approach to reservation economies.[10]

And, of course, who knew more about the intricacies of the Indian energy industry than the tribes and consultants currently fighting to control their minerals? NCAI staffers thus reached out to the Northern Cheyenne, Crow, and other Northern Plains tribes to help organize the first ever "Indian energy conference" for late summer 1974. Dan Israel and Thomas Fredericks—NARF attorneys who represented the Crow and NANRDF, respectively—responded with a series of memos to conference organizer Stuart Jamieson, sharing their extensive experience with Indian energy development and outlining everything from general topics to be addressed to specific panel structures and suggested participants. Unsurprisingly, the issues topping NARF's discussion points reflected their experience on the Northern Plains, including developing tribal capacity to control reservation resources, educating tribal leaders on how to negotiate contracts that retained tribal ownership over mining ventures, and discussing the role of the recently formed NANRDF. When the NCAI announced details of the August 1974 energy conference in its national newsletter, the proposed agenda mirrored the format and topics suggested by the NARF attorneys. And if the influence of the Northern Plains energy tribes was not clear enough, the conference was scheduled to take place in Billings and would be cohosted by Northern Cheyenne President Allen Rowland and Crow Chairman Patrick Stands Over Bull.[11]

*

The NCAI-sponsored Indian Energy Conference marked an important transition in the movement for tribal control over reservation resources. Coming together for several days of debate and discussion, tribal leaders began to reconceive their mission as not only defending reservation resources against perceived threats to tribal survival but also proactively using these assets to expand tribal sovereignty and reservation economies. Of course, both the defensive and proactive strategies were needed to replace non-Indian mining with tribal-led ventures, and both views were represented at this conference. Allen Rowland, for instance, opened the meeting by deriding the federal government's failure to uphold its trustee duty and explaining that NANRDF had been formed specifically to fight federally led development. "Where's our trustees?" Rowland asked the audience rhetorically, "Well by God, that's a damned good question. I've been looking around for them for a hell of a long time now, about 15 years. And every place I go, I find them working against us. . . . [S]o what's got to happen, the way I look at it, is the Indian people got to band together to save what we have left." Rowland was not alone in his continued calls for a mutual defense. Suggesting specific tactics to strengthen tribal resistance, Crow activist Dale Kindness warned that coal development would spell the end of many indigenous communities unless tribes established reservation zoning ordinances and environmental codes to shape planned mining. Kindness pleaded, "If we are to continue as Indian people with our own values, society and culture, we have to stand up straight and get our stuff together." Clearly, the experience of the Crow and Northern Cheyenne as the test subjects for Northern Plains' energy development had produced powerful sentiments against non-Indian mining.[12]

But the other message offered at this unprecedented gathering moved beyond defensive posturing and suggested an innovative approach to capitalize on the tribes' vast resources. Interestingly, this view was articulated most clearly by an outsider, Arjun Makhijani, who was a project specialist at the Ford Foundation's Energy Policy Project. Since 1971, the Ford Foundation had been committing its substantial resources to resolving what it saw as an unsustainable rate of American energy consumption. As part of this effort, Makhijani worked with a group of distinguished economists, scientists, engineers, and policy experts to explore the range of available energy choices and to suggest new policies for responsible energy use. Completing its final report, entitled *A Time to Choose*, earlier in 1974, this team recommended a "conservation oriented energy policy" to reduce America's energy demand, which would address the associated problems of energy shortages, environmental and social concerns arising out of increased domestic production, and the growing power of Middle Eastern oil exporters. At the end of their three-year study, the Ford Foundation group represented perhaps the country's foremost gathering of energy experts. They had the knowledge energy tribes lacked.[13]

Recognizing the need for expert assistance, the NCAI had approached the Ford Foundation for help on its Indian Energy Conference. Directed to Makhijani, NCAI Director Chuck Trimble met with the energy expert and explained the tribes' predicament. "We're ground zero on this," Trimble acknowledged. "We don't know what we have, and therefore we don't know where we're going, and that's what this conference is about." Makhijani responded by admitting he knew very little about American Indians, but he nevertheless accepted Trimble's invitation to apply his vast knowledge of the global energy industry to reservation development. The indigenous network of knowledge was expanding.[14]

Arriving in Billings as the featured speaker on the opening panel, Makhijani captivated the conference by offering the stunning suggestion that energy tribes model their approach after the Organization of Petroleum Exporting Countries (OPEC). The Ford Foundation's energy expert first explained the central role energy held in the global economy and then walked the attending tribal leaders through OPEC's history from exploited colonial states to "one of the most dominant economic forces in the world." This remarkable transition, Makhijani explained, was due to its collective management of oil, and energy tribes could do the same with coal.[15]

Of course, evoking the specter of an "a Native American OPEC" less than a year removed from the October 1973 Arab oil embargo and the infuriating fuel shortages it produced was a dangerous proposition.

Makhijani thus was careful not to emphasize OPEC's cartel power in withholding oil and setting prices. Instead, similar to the benefits NANRDF organizers touted, he argued OPEC's biggest attribute was its ability to collect and share information on global energy projects to ensure its members pursued similar strategies with their oil company partners. The same type of an organization, Makhijani argued, could serve the tribes well by "permit[ting] you to get a lot of knowledge about what your resources are [and] what the relation of those resources [are] to the U.S. and world energy picture." Once these data were obtained, Makhijani continued, "it should be relatively easy for Indians to go into business for themselves, rather than lease to coal companies from which they're usually not deriving adequate benefit." Clearly encapsulated, this was the message of Indian-led economic development the NCAI had gathered the tribes to hear.[16]

With Makhijani articulating the path forward, subsequent speakers focused on the specific steps to carry out this project. Northern Cheyenne and Crow attorneys reviewed the actions they had taken to halt existing mining, but then focused their comments on how to develop reservation codes to shape future mining. George Crossland bashed existing federal regulations that restrained Indian entrepreneurship before he and others proposed changes to federal law that could give tribes flexibility to enter into promising commercial ventures beyond the standard lease form. Each of these suggestions reflected a new, forward-looking perspective that envisioned Indians controlling their own resources, and each called for a collective effort to make this goal a reality. Barney Old Coyote, a Crow tribal member and president of the American Indian National Bank, created to finance tribal ventures, used a football analogy to support the strategy. "You can have the best defensive unit in football," Old Coyote told the audience, "but if you don't have the ball, and you're on the defensive all the time, you're never going to win the ball game." The energy tribes were ready to go on the offensive.[17]

*

At the end of the two-day Indian Energy Conference, Barney Old Coyote continued his football analogy by announcing that one of the offensive "plays" he and others had been exploring was a partnership with the Federal Energy Office. Created in the wake of the Arab oil embargo to allocate reduced oil supplies and control prices, this temporary crisis-management office had become the hub of energy policy and planning under the Nixon administration. When the president and Congress created the permanent Federal Energy Administration (FEA) in summer 1974, the new agency largely absorbed the responsibilities and expertise of the Energy Office, including the search for ways to make the country energy independent. To carry out this goal, the FEA started exploring partnerships with groups outside the federal government, offering grants to fund private, domestic energy projects.[18]

And here is where Old Coyote and his fellow tribal leaders saw an opening. Rather than have this new agency support mining projects designed by energy firms that rarely owned mineral resources yet profited greatly from their development, Old Coyote questioned the gathered tribes, "Why not have the Energy Office . . . start dealing [directly] with the Indian owners of resources and of energy in this country?" It was a question worth considering, even for a group conditioned to be wary of federal involvement in the development of their resources. Those in attendance began to recognize that they, as individual tribes or a consortium, could contract directly with the federal government to obtain funding to support mineral studies and development plans to produce energy for the nation and revenue for themselves.[19]

The idea of forming a national coalition of energy tribes that would interface with the federal government to gather and share energy information quickly gained momentum. Six weeks after the energy conference in Billings, many of the same participants gathered at the NCAI's national convention in Denver to share their insights with a broader audience. Arjun Makhijani, who, as NCAI Director Chuck Trimble explained, had "become famous overnight" within the Indian community, once again offered OPEC as a template for shifting "your tactics in a very fundamental way from defensive battles to assertion and recognition of your rights before anything happens [to your resources]." Makhijani cautioned, however, that in order to assert these rights, the energy tribes first needed to know exactly what resources they possessed. "You first of all have to know what you have got," he warned. "If you don't have this knowledge, then you will be at the mercy of the government and the companies, from the very start, as you have been in the past." George Crossland echoed these comments, arguing the tribes' first step was to coordinate a national inventory of Indian resources, particularly those water rights so precious to any western development scheme.[20]

Makhijani's and Crossland's warnings took on added importance in the winter of 1974–75 as it seemed that some federal agencies still planned to appropriate Northern Plains' resources for Project Independence. On February 24, 1975, the Department of the Interior and the Army Corps of Engineers entered into a memorandum of understanding to market Upper Missouri River Basin water—much of which was committed to Indian reservations—for industrial purposes. Sensing their fears were coming to pass and that Indian resources would be auctioned away without their input, the energy tribes launched into action. Northern Plains' tribal leaders traveled to Washington, D.C., to lodge their objections with federal officials and then submitted a formal letter of protest to President Gerald Ford, threatening a lawsuit that could tie up valuable water rights in litigation for years. It was the standard defensive tactic, but it was complemented by NANRDF's and NCAI's outreach to the new FEA Administrator Frank Zarb. Hoping to head off the federal appropriation of tribal water rights, these organizations requested that Zarb provide "heavy federal funding of engineering, economic, and socio-cultural studies to determine the presence and quantity of natural resources and the social and economic impact of development of those resources on Indian resources."[21]

Tasked with exploring all options to increase domestic production, FEA officials were eager to engage tribes possessing significant energy resources. On April 22, 1975, at an FEA "consumer workshop" in Denver, Deputy Administrator John Hill met with tribal groups from both the Northern Plains and the Southwest who had formed a unified "Indian caucus" to press their concerns. After meeting with Hill, this group issued a formal statement demanding that the president reaffirm the federal trustee duty to protect Indian assets and develop these resources "only with the informed consent, concurrence, and the active participation of each tribe." Days later, many of these same caucus members then flew to Washington, D.C., to attend a meeting arranged by the NCAI between FEA Administrator Zarb and NANRDF representatives. While the Northern Plains group had scheduled the meeting to discuss FEA assistance to tribes in their region, when NANRDF members made their play for federal funds, the southwestern tribes demanded their fair share as well. The hoped-for unity among energy tribes was being tested over the allocation of federal support, and the FEA began to understand how difficult it could be to formulate national policy for a diverse Native America.[22]

Despite the lack of unity displayed by the energy tribes—or because of it—this April 25 meeting set in motion the process that would produce the Council of Energy Resource Tribes. Once the diverse interests of the energy tribes became clear, Zarb commissioned an FEA task force to develop a comprehensive Indian energy position paper that evaluated the role of all Indian resources in meeting national energy goals and considered the environmental and socioeconomic impacts of reservation resource development. In typical bureaucratic fashion, the resulting position paper suggested an additional "interagency/Indian tribes task force" to obtain more tribal input for FEA's national Indian energy policy. After a meager attempt to organize this new task force in San Francisco in June 1975 attracted only a handful of tribes, the FEA pushed for a much larger gathering in Washington, D.C., the following fall. This time, with both FEA Administrator Zarb and Bureau of Indian Affairs Commissioner Morris Thompson scheduled to attend, and travel expenses provided, representatives of more than twenty energy tribes from across the country arrived to discuss how the FEA could facilitate tribal energy development.[23]

In the halls of the Federal Energy Administration, the Council of Energy Resource Tribes was born. On September 16, 1975, attendees at this latest round of meetings spent a long opening day hearing from federal officials about how the FEA intended to increase domestic energy production and where Indian resources could fit into this goal. Tribal representatives understood the need for collective action, but as individual groups with diverse interests and concerns, the tribes debated how to respond. After spending two more days trying to organize themselves and develop a unified position, LaDonna Harris of the Americans for Indian Opportunity decided to aim for something lower. Seeing the tribes struggle to agree on substance, she gathered a small group of volunteers to focus on process. This group, which included NARF attorney Charles Lohah and Jicarilla Apache attorney Robert Nordhaus, then drafted an organizational charter to provide energy tribes with an institutional mechanism for communicating tribal desires to federal officials. The organization would be a mouthpiece but little more. By the end of the day on September 18, fourteen of the twenty-three tribes present had signed the two-page charter drafted by Harris and company. They then proceeded to elect the charismatic chairman of the Navajo tribe, Peter MacDonald, as their leader. Common ground had been found over procedure, but not all were sure of the impact of their actions. Leaving the FEA's Washington headquarters at one o'clock the following morning, LaDonna Harris recalls Charles Lohah turning to her and asking point blank, "What have we done?"[24]

GROPING TOWARD AN IDENTITY: CERT'S FORMATIVE DAYS

CERT had been birthed by the federal desire to develop domestic energy sources but driven by energy tribes' determination to take charge of reservation development. Its founding documents reflected the confused nature of its origins. Along the lines of the OPEC-style organization Arjun Makhijani proposed, CERT's organizational charter envisioned a coalition of similarly situated tribes that would share energy information and cooperate to "promote the general welfare of the Energy Resource Tribes." But issued concurrently with this charter was a longer list of recommendations to the FEA that emphasized the need for partnership between CERT and the federal government to respond to "the present 'Energy Crisis' and potential 'Energy Disaster.'" This second document called for the creation of yet another task force under the newly created, cabinet-level Energy Resources Council—which Frank Zarb also directed—that would include the leaders of all energy tribes. This task force would work with the federal government to review the needs and practices of Indian resource development, make available federal assistance to support such projects, and monitor reservation mining. It seemed a worthy proposal, but together the two documents suggested conflicting organizations. On one hand, CERT's charter called for an independent coalition of mutual interest to share information and strengthen each member's negotiating position with energy companies and federal agencies; on the other, the position paper proposed an intimate, institutional connection between energy tribes and the federal government that blurred the lines between the two. Certainly, the tribes took momentous actions in Washington that September, but it was hard to ascertain exactly what these actions meant.[25]

The creation of CERT confused even those tribes and tribal leaders that spearheaded the movement for a national coalition of energy tribes. Writing to NCAI Executive Director Charles Trimble a week after the FEA meetings, Northern Cheyenne President Allen Rowland noted that his and a few other important energy tribes had not signed the organization's founding documents and suggested an Indian-only meeting, free of federal interference, to clarify CERT's purpose. Like NARF attorney Charles Lohah, Rowland was not sure what CERT was. Responding dutifully, the NCAI brought the energy tribes back to the same Billings facility where Rowland and Crow Chairman Patrick Stands Over Bull had hosted the inaugural Indian energy conference a year earlier to better define the new organization.[26]

At this latest gathering of the energy tribes, confusion reigned. Was CERT an independent organization of energy tribes or simply a task force of the FEA? If an independent organization, what was its relationship to the Northern Plains federation known as NANRDF? Did their purposes align or would the organizations compete for federal funding and tribal membership? Would CERT subsume NANRDF? After hours of debate, NARF attorney Thomas Fredericks, who was now NANRDF's executive director, attempted to clear the air. Believing CERT and NANRDF had similar goals but different functions, Fredericks recounted the series of meetings that led to CERT's creation and then argued that "both groups can co-exist" because CERT's only purpose was to act as "the organization or the vehicle to supply the administration with the consensus . . . of the Indian community as to what they feel about energy development on reservation lands and Indian country." According to Fredericks, CERT was not an independent cartel but rather served as an important advisory body to federal policy makers, especially those agencies with money to invest in domestic energy production. "I think the whole concept of CERT," Fredericks explained, "was that by having a voice in the administrative arm of government, that the monies that were available to really develop this energy could be . . . channeled to the Indian tribes because of the potential that exists on most reservations." Fredericks and others used organizational charts depicting the federal bureaucracy to point out where

CERT would give Indians "a voice in the upper echelons of the energy policy makers to [force them to] come up with programs that would be relevant to the Indians' needs." The explanation seemed to quiet the controversy. After making his case, Fredericks then focused the meeting back on CERT's demands to the FEA, walking the audience through a line-by-line analysis of its earlier list of recommendations. If CERT truly was a mouthpiece to provide Indian input into federal energy policy, crystallizing these demands was its most important task.[27]

This interpretation that CERT's primary role was to work within the federal government to advise policy makers and lobby for aid in Indian energy development set the organization's early agenda. Cultivating federal connections, CERT requested $1 million in federal seed money to conduct a resource inventory study and then opened offices in Denver and Washington, D.C., to give the organization one foot in Indian Country and another in the Beltway. The organization also used federal funds to hire its first executive director, Ed Gabriel, an FEA staff member who was instrumental in forging the federal-tribal partnership. Apparently, raiding the federal bureaucracy to lead a pan-tribal organization charged with developing indigenous resources barely raised an eye. As Marjane Ambler explains, Gabriel "was a logical choice" due to the closeness of the CERT-FEA relationship. Be that as it may, tribal leaders that had been inspired a year earlier by calls for a "Native American OPEC" to wrest back control over reservation development must have wondered how their cause became so intimately entwined with the federal government.[28]

*

Fortunately for those desiring a more independent federation, the honeymoon between federal policy makers and CERT was short-lived. In March 1977, with a new Democratic administration prioritizing energy policy and promising a comprehensive energy program within its first ninety days, CERT Chairman Peter MacDonald challenged Jimmy Carter to address Indian energy concerns or else risk losing access to these valuable minerals. During the previous year and a half, MacDonald and his fellow tribal leaders had worked their federal connections to advance CERT's mission, but they were becoming frustrated with the lack of results. The organization's $1 million initial request, for instance, had not been met, and the BIA was blocking the FEA's encroachment onto their traditional bureaucratic turf. MacDonald complained publicly, "We have gone to [multiple federal agencies] and pleaded for resources to inventory our minerals—pleaded for the kind of technical assistance necessary to achieve self-sufficiency," but to no avail. Now, with the change in administration, MacDonald determined the time was right to deploy alternative tactics to secure the support tribes needed. Delivering a public speech in Phoenix, the Navajo and CERT chairman issued a not-so-veiled threat to federal officials:

> Now, as some of you know, a dozen Indian nations have formed a do-mestic OPEC. We call it CERT. . . . We ask [for assistance] now quietly and constructively. We will not ask much longer. We will withhold future growth at any sacrifice if that is necessary to [tribal] survival.

In a few short lines, MacDonald made public an option energy tribes had been discussing for years. If the federal government would not will-ingly provide the tools energy tribes needed to intelligently and respon-sibly manage their resources, the Indians would convert CERT into an OPEC-style cartel to withhold desperately needed energy sources.[29]

Reflecting this bold, new approach, CERT members moved quickly to reframe their relationship with the federal government. Meet-ing days before President Carter's April 18, 1977, "unpleasant talk" with the nation wherein he described the present energy crisis as the "moral equivalent of war," CERT members issued a revised statement of demands that omitted any reference to the energy tribes acting as a task force within the executive bureaucracy. Instead, the statement repositioned CERT as an independent coalition of resource owners controlling "55 percent [of the nation's] uranium, 30 percent of coal and 3 percent of petroleum and natural gas." Considering this substan-tial tribal stockpile, CERT demanded "direct and constant" access to the secretary of energy. Never willing to give up on the federal-tribal partnership, though, CERT also dangled the possibility of cooperation if the federal government took four specific actions: (1) fund a com-prehensive energy resource inventory, (2) help energy tribes construct alternative development agreements to the standard lease contracts, (3) provide capital for energy tribes to develop their own resources, and (4) educate tribal leaders in proper energy resource planning. Although not new requests, energy tribes' crystallized their most crucial demands for tribal control. And if the demands were not new, the negotiating strategy certainly was. If the feds wanted access to Indian resources, they now would have to engage with an independent cartel threatening to withhold energy resources crucial to the country's growth.[30]

Apparently, federal officials were unmoved by the new tactic, and so in the summer of 1977 MacDonald dramatically upped the ante by transforming the OPEC analogy into a potential partnership with the oil-exporting countries. In July, the CERT chairman met with several OPEC members in Washington, D.C., of all places, to discuss how these former colonial nations had gained control over their valuable resources. Noting that "federal red tape and foot dragging" had left him no other options, MacDonald assured national reporters covering these meetings that he was "not looking for advice on how to impose an embargo" but instead "our purpose is more long range," seeking technical assistance on how to structure mineral development deals, plan for sustainable development, and market Indian minerals. Still, news of Arab and tribal leaders meeting in the nation's capital to discuss potentially withholding valuable energy resources garnered much attention, which was exactly what MacDonald intended. On his own reservation, the Navajo tribal chairman had made a political living framing energy projects as a colonial appropriation of Indian resources to feed American growth. For years, he had even compared the Navajo nation to the exploited OPEC states and advocated that his tribe follow a similar anticolonial approach to resource management. "From now on," MacDonald had announced in the *Navajo Times* in March 1974, "the Navajos intend to use the same kind of tactics that oil-rich Arabs have employed. Our goal is the same: a bigger take from our desert Kingdom." Now, in 1977, the CERT chairman hoped that by cementing a formal relation with these Middle Eastern states—or at least appearing to—he could goad the federal government into following through on promises of support for all energy tribes.[31]

Seeking a partnership with OPEC and, more important, cultivating CERT's public image as the "Native American OPEC" was a bold move with, at best, mixed results. The strategy got the federal government's attention and perhaps produced initially a few more federal dollars. But as Marjane Ambler reports, it also ignited a public backlash against "unpatriotic Indians" who appeared to be withholding American energy. This anti-CERT sentiment hit a fever pitch in January 1979, when an exiled zealot named Ruhollah Khomeini led an Islamic Revolution that toppled the Iranian monarchy. The loss of oil from the world's second largest exporter disrupted global markets, and although other Middle Eastern states worked to offset the deficit, panic quickly set in. Oil companies and consumers alike rushed to obtain the petroleum they feared would not be available the next day. In a repeat of the 1973 energy crisis that had heightened demand for Northern Plains' coal, the nation endured its second bout of frustrating fuel shortages. America's disdain for foreign oil producers had never been higher.[32]

The same was true of the country's feelings toward energy tribes. CERT continued to request more and more federal dollars throughout late 1970s, including $2 million in 1978 and an astonishing $60 to $70 million in 1979. But in the wake of the second energy crisis, these requests now appeared to most Americans as blackmail during the country's time of need. As the *Denver Post* editorialized in 1979: "Supposedly we are to pony up cheerfully so the noose of escalating energy prices can be tightened around our necks? The energy crisis is too important for confrontational politics, which, if pursued likely will boomerang and hurt the Indian cause rather than help it." This is exactly what happened. CERT kept requesting money, but federal officials could not justify supporting an organization touting its ties to the Middle East.[33]

Peter MacDonald was not deaf to the events capturing the nation's attention and understood the need for another shift in strategy. Writing to President Carter days after his famed July 15, 1979, "crisis of confidence" speech, wherein the president challenged the nation to fight "on the battlefield of energy [so] we can win for our nation a new confidence," MacDonald maintained his defiant tone but recommitted Indian energy to the fight. Telling the president he was disheartened Native Americans had not been included in Carter's new energy program, the CERT chairman nevertheless affirmed, "Today I offer my support, and that of the 24 other CERT energy-producing tribes, to the president and his Administration, and will await his direction." Of course, that support would come with a price, but MacDonald was reaching out to change the trajectory of federal-tribal relations.[34]

Carter soon took the CERT chairman up on his offer to provide Indian energy to the nation. Within the month, Charles Duncan, the newly confirmed secretary of energy, met with Peter MacDonald and then dispatched his assistant director, Richard Stone, to CERT's December 1979 annual meeting. At that gathering, CERT members unveiled proposals for several new reservation energy projects, including two large coal-fired generating plants, an oil refinery, and a coal gasification facility. Impressed by the Indians' efforts, Stone responded with the federal commitment CERT had been seeking. His $24 million pledge included $10 million for specific tribal projects, $7 million for an Indian resource inventory, and another $2 million to cover CERT's day-to-day operations. In the heat of a yet another "energy crisis," MacDonald and his fellow tribal leaders learned that playing the role of an independent broker for Indian energy resources worked far more effectively than the alternative of an antagonistic cartel threatening to withhold valuable minerals.[35]

*

With this lesson learned, the 1979 CERT annual meeting should have presented a scene of congratulatory celebration for the young organization. Instead, reaching its goal of obtaining federal support caused yet another round of deep introspection by CERT's members. Those Indians, like many within the chairman's own Navajo tribe, who had adopted a nationalistic stance toward controlling their minerals now questioned CERT's authority to speak for their tribal governments and commit reservation resources to the American market. According to Marjane Ambler, other tribal members who desired to halt all reservation mining protested what they saw as CERT's new position as "an elitist broker of Indian resources . . . prostituting its members' land and people in exchange for energy agency dollars." Winona LaDuke even describes one group of "traditional people" from the Navajo Reservation crashing the 1979 Phoenix meeting, demanding "that the indigenous members of CERT realize their traditional and spiritual ways of survival and their responsibility to the earth and their people." Ironically, at the height of its influence with federal officials, CERT appeared to be crumbling from the inside. As CERT's executive director, Ed Gabriel, later admitted, "We got what we asked for [at the 1979 Phoenix meeting], but it took us more than a year to recover."[36]

To restore legitimacy in the eyes of all its constituents, CERT shifted focus from selling the benefits of Indian energy development to federal officials and toward proving the organization's value to tribal leaders and members. The first step was to clarify that the bulk of federal dollars CERT secured would go directly to benefit tribal energy programs, not into the organization's coffer. Thus, just days after the Phoenix meeting, CERT explained in its newsletter that the government's $24 million pledge would fund specific reservation inventories and feasibility studies "and not be channeled through CERT." The organization then focused its activities on providing consulting services to individual tribes desiring development—which, of course, could be paid for with these new funds—rather than assume the role as spokesperson for all energy tribes. To do so, CERT grew its technical assistance center in Denver, where by 1981 two-thirds of its sixty employees were located, leaving only a small lobbying team in Washington. The geologists, energy consultants, and former federal employees in the Denver office understood the type of information tribes needed to pursue development, and most important, they knew how to obtain funds to gather that information. Through assisting tribes in putting together federal grant applications and private lending documents, CERT officials claimed that, by 1981, they had secured $17 million for tribal energy projects that would not have been available otherwise. Federal bureaucrats also recognized CERT's value in this endeavor. Energy Department official Richard Stone explained that in this period of unprecedented federal investment in energy development, federal money "goes to those who produce good paper, [and] the paper CERT has produced on behalf of the tribes has been of consistently good quality."[37]

By producing "good paper" to secure funding for potential energy projects, CERT was positioning energy tribes to finally capitalize on their vast and valuable resources if they chose to do so. A voluntary coalition of independent sovereigns, CERT itself had no authority to commit Indian resources. Instead, the grants and loans it helped secure would fund reservation inventories and feasibility studies to allow tribal leaders to make their own informed decisions. Of course, CERT often benefited by conducting these studies itself, getting paid with the same federal dollars it secured for tribal governments. The individual projects CERT helped evaluate included a natural gas refinery on the Jicarilla Apache Reservation; a hydroelectric facility for the Nez Perce; oil, gas, and geothermal projects with the Cheyenne River Sioux; and the nation's first synthetic fuel facility on the Crow

Reservation. Clearly, CERT worked to develop tribal energy, but by the start of the new decade, the OPEC template was dead. In its place was something more closely resembling a professional consulting firm. CERT had become a pan-tribal organization with the business experience and technical expertise to empower tribal governments to manage their own resources.[38]

Not all American Indians, however, were happy with this outcome. CERT's close ties with—and some would say, dependence on—the federal government continued to draw criticism that the organization was a pro-development entity ignoring the concerns of ordinary Indians. Winona LaDuke, the Ojibwe environmental activist and future Green Party vice presidential candidate, complained that of the approximately one hundred studies CERT was conducting or had completed by 1980, only five focused on mineral development's harmful impacts. The rest, she concluded, supported "non-renewable, extractive, and technologically-advanced development scenarios." When CERT officials defended its focus on development by reminding LaDuke that "CERT does only what the tribal chairmen request," the activist responded by reminding them that "the choices and options presented to each tribe originate in reports from the CERT staff." Those studies, of course, overwhelmingly supported large-scale energy projects oriented toward exporting Indian resources off-reservation.[39]

The criticism was fair, but it failed to resonate widely. For a majority of American Indians who knew only suffocating poverty, the chance to develop reservation minerals under the control of their tribal governments was too great an opportunity to forego. In the end, disgruntled Indians like LaDuke were not CERT's clients; the tribal governments were. The organization thus focused on expanding tribal capacity by securing funds to study energy projects and educate elected officials on the institutional controls necessary to shape mining operations. Ed Gabriel admitted freely that his goal was to transfer his organization's expertise over to the tribes so that CERT could close its technical assistance center by the mid-1980s and focus purely on lobbying. Its members shared this goal, as Hugh Baker, director of energy for the Three Affiliated Tribes of the Fort Berthold Reservation, explained:

> People who have problems with CERT should think of the concept behind forming it. I continually remind the CERT staff, "You're here to put yourselves out of business by teaching me. When we, [the tribes] get

rich on [energy resources], maybe you can come work for us. Until then, help us get rich." [40]

CERT worked in many ways to transfer knowledge to its tribal clients, but perhaps the greatest lesson it offered was that tribal governments must control the pace and scale of mining to ensure profits without sacrificing community. Gathering mineral and market data was an important first step, but mainly because this information better positioned tribes to negotiate the mineral agreements that controlled mining operations and profits. As for these agreements, CERT consultants constantly hammered home the need for tribal leaders to reject mineral "leases," which afforded tribes little control, and instead pursue "alternative contracts" that retained tribal ownership over mining ventures. Ownership, they lectured, guaranteed control.

And at least initially, the federal government seemed to agree. BIA officials tentatively supported the use of alternative contracts as a way to open reservations to development under tribal terms. As we will see, however, these officials eventually questioned whether federal law provided tribal governments with the authority to develop their own resources under these alternative contracts. The old concerns about Indian capacity to responsibly manage their assets, which were embedded in the 1938 Indian Mineral Leasing Act, came back to the fore. Energy tribes, facing the possibility that they would be denied the right to exercise their newly developed capacity, once again would have to mobilize to protect this most basic principle of sovereignty. This time their fight would take them all the way to the halls of Congress.

7 Recognizing Tribal Sovereignty

AS THE ENERGY tribes gathered for the September 1980 annual meeting of the Council of Energy Resource Tribes, they had good reason to be optimistic. Earlier that year, the federal government had made good on its $24 million pledge to support Indian energy development. The tribes had put these funds to work developing an extensive Indian resource inventory, conducting feasibility studies for new energy technologies, breaking ground on tribal mining projects, and continuing to educate tribal leaders on resource management techniques. In addition to the flow of federal dollars, the Department of the Interior had also just proposed new regulations for mining on Indian lands that promised to minimize "any adverse environmental or cultural impact on Indians, resulting from such development" as well as guaranteeing the tribes "at least, fair market value for their ownership rights." The key to delivering these results was a new provision authorizing Indian mineral owners to enter into flexible mineral agreements that "reserve to them the responsibility for overseeing the development of their reserves." These "alternative contracts" to the standard lease form would finally provide tribes with the control necessary to ensure mining did not threaten their indigenous communities.[1]

Reflecting the improved relationship with the federal government, CERT held its 1980 annual gathering in Washington, D.C. There, Chairman Peter MacDonald explained that the meeting's purpose was to further explore "how to go about building a truly meaningful energy partnership between the tribes and the federal government." Federal officials played their part enthusiastically: Energy Secretary Charles Duncan delivered the keynote address, and numerous governors, senators, and members of Congress attended the event to endorse the strengthening tribal-federal relationship. The three presidential candidates— Jimmy Carter, Ronald Reagan, and the independent congressman John Anderson—either personally attended or sent congressional delegates to voice their support for tribal autonomy and lobby for CERT's endorsement. Speaking at the concluding press conference, Senator John Melcher of Montana captured the shared sentiment: "No longer can the federal government dictate the terms of energy development on Indian lands [and] no longer can the government decide what is good for the Indian people." All the years of work seemed to be paying off. Again, optimism abounded.[2]

But to those paying close attention, there were rumblings of trouble in the recesses of the conference's meeting hall. In fact, despite the recent contribution of funds, promising new regulations, and supportive messages, Wilfred Scott, CERT's vice chairman, noted "mixed signals" coming from federal officials over whether tribes had the legal authority to manage their own minerals. The specific source of these concerns was a recent oil and gas deal struck between the Northern Cheyenne and the Atlantic Richfield Company (ARCO) that deviated from standard lease form and procedure. This agreement, like a lease, conveyed exploration and production rights to the oil company, but it retained for the Northern Cheyenne certain ownership interests in the project. Moreover, the Northern Cheyenne procured this alternative oil and gas contract through private negotiations rather than via the standard public notice and bidding process. Government officials wondered aloud whether federal law allowed a deal that failed to comply with the 1938 Indian Mineral Leasing Act, even if it represented a clear exercise of tribal sovereignty. After delaying approval until a tribal referendum established that a majority of Northern Cheyenne supported the project, the Department of the Interior grudgingly authorized the arrangement only after ARCO agreed to assume the risk should a court later invalidate the contract.[3]

More troubling than the reluctant approval, however, was Interior's announcement made shortly after CERT's annual meeting. The Northern Cheyenne contract had forced the agency to review the law governing reservation mineral rights, and the department's new lead attorney, Clyde O. Martz, did not like what he saw. A former University of Colorado law professor and oft-described "father of natural resource law," Martz reasoned that "the Indian Nonintercourse Act prohibits contracts that convey interest in land unless they meet the requirements of the 1938 Mineral Leasing Act." Finding no other statutory authorization for alternative contracts like the one just entered into by the Northern Cheyenne, the solicitor told CERT staff that any contract conveying Indian minerals "other than the traditional lease, may currently be illegal." Once again, the federal government threatened to constrain tribal sovereignty.[4]

Martz's statement regarding the legality of alternative contracts sent shockwaves through the energy tribes' community. Peter MacDonald called it the "final betrayal," rendering "everything CERT tribes have been doing or want to do . . . illegal." This strong reaction stemmed from the fact that tribes had come to view alternative agreements as the linchpin for exerting control over reservation development. They were the mechanism that allowed tribal leaders to apply their increasing expertise to secure desirable terms and oversee mining operations. Without non-lease contracts, the progress of the previous decade could be lost, turning back the clock to the days of federally run bidding procedures, standard lease terms, and minimal tribal control. Martz's opinion even threw the legality of his own agency's recently proposed rulemaking into question. How could an executive agency promise to allow tribes "to enter into contracts which reserve to them the responsibility for overseeing the development of their [mineral] reserves" if federal statutes limited energy contracts to the standard lease form? Federal officials had promised Indian self-determination but now seemed poised to invalidate clear exercises of tribal sovereignty. Certainly, energy tribes had come a long way in developing the *capacity* to manage their own resources. Now, it appeared, there was work left to be done to ensure that federal law recognized their *authority* to do so.[5]

"THE MOST IMPORTANT TRIBE IN AMERICA," REPRISE

The Northern Cheyenne's measured pursuit of energy development forced federal officials to address the disconnect between federal laws governing Indian resources and tribes' increasing capacity to manage these assets. Since the Northern Cheyenne's successful 1974 challenge to its inequitable coal leases, the tribe had been working to develop its vast energy reserves in a manner that balanced the need for revenue with the desire to preserve its indigenous community and environment. The first step in this process was ensuring that the tribe, not individual allottees, actually owned the minerals underlying the reservation. Like the Crow's allotment law, the Northern Cheyenne Allotment Act had reserved subsurface mineral rights to the tribe, but only for a period of fifty years. The intent was to provide the initial means for an economic base but ultimately to have these rights flow to individual landowners. Prior to the 1960s, however, there was no viable market for Cheyenne oil, gas, or coal. Sensing the tribe had missed its opportunity to capitalize on communal resources, both federal and tribal officials lobbied to have the mineral rights transferred to the tribe in perpetuity. In 1968, Congress obliged, passing a law effectuating this permanent transfer.

But federal support for tribal ownership of mineral rights came with conditions. Not wanting to create liability from an unconstitutional taking of private property rights, the 1968 law conditioned the permanent transfer on a determination by a federal court that the 1926 Northern Cheyenne Allotment Act had not created vested mineral rights in allottees. In other words, Congress practically demanded litigation, placing the Northern Cheyenne in the unenviable position of having to sue its own members to settle property rights. Seeing little alternative, the tribe commenced legal action in summer 1970 against several allottees who stood to gain mineral rights at the end of the fifty-year period. By 1976, the case had made its way to the United States Supreme Court, where, in *Northern Cheyenne Tribe v. Hollowbreast,* the court upheld the permanent transfer of minerals to the tribe. Specifically, the unanimous opinion found that the conveyance conformed to the 1926 act's original intent that the tribe benefit from their minerals, which clearly had not yet happened.[6]

In the same year the Northern Cheyenne confirmed tribal rights over reservation minerals, the tribe also forged new legal ground to shape regional energy projects threatening its reservation. Recall that in 1972, the planned construction of the Colstrip Power Plant at the reservation's border had helped unite the tribe with area ranchers and environmentalists against regional coal development. This partnership spread concerns about impending energy projects and produced the Northern

Cheyenne's historic petition to cancel all reservation leases. It did not, however, stop construction at Colstrip. By 1976, two coal-fired boilers were in operation with plans announced for two additional units that were twice the size of the originals. All told, this facility had the potential to produce 2,100 megawatts of electricity, making it larger than the country's dirtiest power plant, the Four Corners facility, located on the edge of the Navajo Reservation.[7]

With a massive power plant planned at the reservation's border, and just beyond the reach of the tribal government, the Northern Cheyenne got creative. The tribe turned to new relief offered by the 1970 Clean Air Act and announced in July of 1976 that it would reclassify the air above its reservation as a Class I air shed. Under the pioneering 1970 environmental law, the Environmental Protection Agency had established a nationwide area classification system to prevent the deterioration of air quality in regions with relatively clean air. Initially the EPA designated all air sheds as Class II areas, which would allow for some air quality degradation due to light industry. The implementing regulations, however, gave state and tribal governments the option to protect specific areas from virtually any change in air quality by requesting an upgrade. In June 1976, the state of Montana approved the Colstrip plant's expansion based on modeling that showed its air emissions would not violate the region's Class II standards. Two weeks later, Northern Cheyenne President Allen Rowland announced plans to reclassify his downwind reservation to the higher, cleaner standard.[8]

As the first land manager in the nation, whether state or tribal government, to request an upgrade in air quality protection, the Northern Cheyenne garnered many accolades from the environmental community. One publication even named the tribe "Environmentalist of the Year" for 1976. But more than a defense of the natural environment was at play. The tribe took action primarily to ensure the integrity of its social and cultural community. This was the same concern that rallied tribal members to halt on-reservation mining. Massive energy development on *or* near the reservation would despoil the Cheyenne's land, air, and water, but even more so, it would bring outsiders to disrupt social customs and cultural norms that defined the tribe. Numerous tribal members and groups, including the Northern Cheyenne Landowners Association, made this exact point to the state of Montana during Colstrip's permitting process. The tribal government's official comments warned that development on the reservation's border "portend[s] nothing but adverse environmental, social and cultural consequences for the People of the Northern Cheyenne Tribe, their way of life, and the natural resources of their Reservation Lands." These comments further explained the tribe's opposition within the context of its long and difficult history to secure the reservation:

> Not only is the Reservation the Northern Cheyenne Tribe's Home Land; as a Tribe, as a People, it is their *only* place in this world. The Tribe's life as a People, as the Tribe knows and desires to maintain it, is unqualifiedly dependent upon maintaining its Reservation free from outside environmental insult and destructive social and cultural impact.

But these pleas went unheeded and the state of Montana issued Colstrip's permit. The tribe was now forced to take its argument to the federal level. Writing to the EPA to request the redesignation of the reservation's air shed, Allen Rowland was clear about Cheyenne intentions:

> We are not requesting this redesignation because we are against progress, either here or anywhere else. Our Tribe has been struggling for progress and self-determination for years. . . . For us, progress means developing *our* environmental resources in renewable and compatible manners. . . . Not only are such activities our livelihood, they are the cores of our value systems as a people.

The Northern Cheyenne did not oppose energy development per se, just projects beyond tribal control because they threatened the community. The tribe thus exercised its sovereign rights under the Clean Air Act to prevent a project that would change the fabric of its region and reservation.[9]

As powerful as this argument was, the Northern Cheyenne could only shape, not preclude, regional energy development. The EPA granted the tribe's request to upgrade their air designation and stepped in to halt Colstrip's expansion based on expected impacts to the new Class I air shed. Colstrip's owners responded, however, by adding new pollution control technologies that they claimed would drastically reduce emissions. The move satisfied EPA officials, whose focus remained on protecting environmental quality. In fall 1979, the agency approved the issuance of Colstrip's long-awaited expansion permit.[10]

But again, the Northern Cheyenne had broader concerns than just the environment. The tribe filed a legal challenge to the EPA's approval, and the longtime head of the Natural Resources Committee, Edwin Dahle, began exploring a negotiated settlement that would allow for Colstrip's construction *and* alleviate tribal fears over the unhealthy influx of non-Indians and pollutants. Ultimately, Colstrip's owners and the Northern Cheyenne settled on what CERT Executive Director Ed Gabriel described as "a precedent-setting, multi-faceted agreement" whereby the facility would install more stringent pollution controls, fund reservation air quality monitoring, provide $350,000 to the tribe for continued socioeconomic impact analyses, and guarantee employment and job training at Colstrip for tribal members. Certainly the outcome did not please all Cheyenne, but these concessions addressed the tribe's major fears. As Dahle explained, the agreement reduced the threat of unwanted people and pollutants and meant "wealth will be coming into the reservation, not just flowing out, as it has in the past." Dahle also believed the agreement would help the tribe "develop a trained workforce for the day when the Cheyenne might develop our own coal."[11]

*

The Northern Cheyenne's willingness to negotiate and tailor the Colstrip facility to address specific tribal concerns signaled a shift in the tribe's approach to energy development. Throughout much of the 1970s, the tribal government had found itself on the defensive, fighting to prevent projects it did not control rather than pursuing energy ventures that could bring wealth. This approach began to change, however, with the fall 1978 election of new council members eager to explore development options. This rush of new blood coincided with mounting debt accrued through the tribe's various legal battles and the real possibility of reduced federal support for tribal programs. Now that the tribe had secured its authority over reservation resources—not to mention demonstrated its ability to shape off-reservation development—the time had come to exercise this power to produce revenue. As Allen Rowland explained, "We've made millionaires out of several lawyers"; now it was the tribe's turn.[12]

This shift toward a more assertive pursuit of tribal-controlled development was evident on the very first day the new council members took office. Sworn in on September 13, 1978, by none another than Marie Sanchez, who by now was a tribal judge, the newly elected leaders endured a crash course in reservation energy development. CERT consultants were brought in to lead a three-day orientation program featuring CERT Executive Director Ed Gabriel, National Congress of American Indians President Chuck Trimble, Native American Rights Fund attorneys John Echo Hawk and Scott McLaroy, and the tribe's own attorney, Steven Chestnutt, who had spearheaded the petition to halt uncontrolled reservation mining. The new officers also heard from Dick Monteau, director of the Northern Cheyenne Research Project (NCRP) that had been established after the first round of harmful coal leases in 1973 to investigate coal mining's impacts. Supported by federal funds, the NCRP was a quasi-independent arm of the tribal government that gathered economists, geologists, anthropologists, and energy consultants to inventory Cheyenne resources and evaluate mining proposals. It provided the internal, institutional expertise the Northern Cheyenne had lacked when the tribe eagerly auctioned away reservation coal rights in the early 1970s. In evaluating potential energy projects, the NCRP also was guided by the founding principles of "maintaining survival [of the Northern Cheyenne] as an ethnic group" and "aiding in the maintenance of Tribal identity and sovereignty."[13]

With the Northern Cheyenne's renewed interest in energy development, it did not take long for the NCRP to prove its worth. In summer 1979, several energy companies approached the tribe with new coal mining ventures, and the tribe referred these proposals to the NCRP for analysis. The staff there quickly concluded that although cloaked in the language of joint partnerships, these latest deals shared similar deficiencies with the previous leases. Namely, they provided no tribal control over the pace and scale of development. Without such control, the NCRP warned the tribe would be unable to protect its community and environment. Hearing these critiques, the Northern Cheyenne rejected the offers out of hand.[14]

But more than tribal control was now required for on-reservation energy projects. Among the general membership, concerns about coal development's impacts had grown so strong that even when a proposal provided control, tribal members were wary to authorize strip-mining. In response to the deficient 1979 deals, for instance, tribal consultant George Crossland—the Osage attorney who initially found fault with the Northern Cheyenne's earlier coal leases—introduced a coal mining proposal from the Fluor Corporation that would have allowed the tribe to retain complete ownership over the venture. Fluor, the world's largest construction firm, offered to operate the proposed mine under a service contract. But even this was too much. The wounds of the recent coal mining wars were fresh, and tribal members rejected this promising deal structure. Council member Joe Little Coyote explained the reaction: "Because of the impact on our socio-economic and cultural development, coal mining is not an option at all at this point." Tribal members simply could not overcome the idea that massive strip mines would disrupt community relations and despoil their landscapes.[15]

With reservation coal mining a dead issue, pro-development tribal leaders quickly turned to the seemingly less invasive option of oil and gas drilling as the vehicle for economic growth. Ironically, the initial push for this form of development came from the NCRP, which, according to employee James Boggs, typically operated under "a policy of caution and skepticism towards large-scale leasing." Considering this viewpoint, the organization's director, Richard Monteau, had for some time been exploring the possibility of a small, tribally owned and operated oil and gas project as an alternative to massive strip-mining. When tribal members rejected all coal mining offers in the fall of 1979, pro-development council members appropriated the idea for oil and gas production and expanded the scope of Monteau's small proposal to fit their larger objectives. In December 1979, these leaders then consolidated authority over energy development decisions by passing a resolution bringing the NCRP under the direct supervision of the tribe's Planning Committee, which was controlled by the pro-development wing. In protest, much of the NCRP's staff, including Director Monteau, resigned. With the cautious NCRP eviscerated, the path was cleared to pursue large-scale oil and gas projects.[16]

To land such a deal, the Northern Cheyenne turned the typical, federally controlled process for soliciting and evaluating energy proposals on its head. Rejecting the standard public notice and bidding process, the tribe advertised directly for mining partners in national oil and gas trade journals. By February 1980, Tribal President Allen Rowland could report that the response was "very good ... proposals are coming in daily." But to evaluate these offers, the Northern Cheyenne turned not to federal officials; instead, it relied largely on its own expertise, augmenting this knowledge where necessary with some Bureau of Indian Affairs technical assistance. Several tribal members argued that the loss of the NCRP had left the tribe unprepared to effectively evaluate drilling proposals, but Harvard-educated tribal member Joe Little Coyote skillfully led negotiations with potential energy partners. In May, the tribal government settled on an agreement with the independent oil firm Atlantic Richfield Company that gave the tribe a $6 million upfront bonus and a 25 percent production share. Beyond these unprecedented financial benefits, the contract also stipulated that the Northern Cheyenne would retain joint ownership over all geological data and would hold approval authority over all operating plans, and that ARCO would fund a Tribal Oil and Gas Office to monitor drilling activities. This was not your typical lease. Instead, it resembled more a service agreement in which the drilling company would prospect and produce reservation oil and gas in exchange for a share of the profits. Importantly, the Northern Cheyenne retained control.[17]

Most, though certainly not all, tribal members viewed the ARCO deal as a sensible compromise between all-out development and none at all. Opponents pointed to the relatively hasty manner in which the deal was constructed and the absence of the NCRP to evaluate its impacts. But when these concerns were put to the entire tribe in the form of two referenda on the ARCO agreement, an overwhelming majority sided with their tribal government (82 percent in the first, 88 in the second). Yes, the tribe would open its reservation to an outside developer, but most were comfortable with the tribal government retaining oversight over drilling operations and ownership of geological data. Furthermore, many defended the deal on environmental grounds. Allen Rowland noted simply that drilling pads leave smaller holes in the ground than do coal mines, and Joe Little Coyote concurred that oil wells "are a lot more environmentally acceptable than coal mining." The Department of the Interior also agreed, describing the ARCO project in its environmental assessment as "the first major energy development on the reservation, but it is small-scale when compared to other energy development alternatives such as strip-mining." In a world of trade-offs, the impoverished Northern Cheyenne determined that some energy development, operating under the supervision of its Tribal Oil and Gas Office, was better than none at all.[18]

*

The Northern Cheyenne's increasing sophistication in managing its valuable energy resources was emblematic of advances occurring throughout Indian Country. Since 1975, numerous tribes had positioned themselves to negotiate alternative contracts that included better financial terms than the BIA's standard leases. Although not all deals resulted in tribal-led mining ventures, each evidenced the tribes' increasing capacity to tailor contracts to reflect specific reservation conditions. For example, on the Navajo Reservation, where the tribal government had the most experience with mineral development and possessed ample geological and market data, the tribe brokered a 1977 uranium deal with the Exxon Corporation that netted a $6 million bonus and included the option for a joint venture operation. On the Blackfeet Reservation, however, where less geological information existed, tribal leaders willingly gave up bonus payments in favor of an oil and gas agreement with the Damson Oil Corporation that included percentage royalties plus half of all production revenue once the company recouped its start-up costs (potentially 58 percent of all profits). In this case, Blackfeet leaders may not have secured ownership over the energy project, but they understood that a back-loaded service contract was necessary to encourage the small, independent oil company to prospect in a relatively unproven area. And like other tribes, the Blackfeet knew federally orchestrated leases did not meet tribal demands. As one BIA area director explained, "The difference [now] is that the tribes are fully informed about the market value of their holdings and the [problems with the] leasing strategy." Kenneth Black, the director of the National Tribal Chairman's Association, summed up the demands of these newly enlightened leaders: "No more leases—we want a percentage of the deals."[19]

Tribal efforts to secure more beneficial agreements certainly indicated a rising level of sophistication, but their alternative contracts also put the Department of the Interior in the difficult position of trying to support Indian self-determination while also enforcing the letter of the law. Federal agents did their best to juggle these competing duties, employing a host of innovative legal theories to approve negotiated contracts that deviated from the 1938 Indian Mineral Leasing Act. One such theory applied a broad reading of the term "lease" contained in the statute, rationalizing that the 1938 Congress surely intended to authorize whatever form of mineral contract was favored by industry standards, and thus joint ventures must be allowed. Another approach justified non-lease mining agreements based on an obscure federal statute authorizing tribes to enter into "service contracts," though this law had been previously applied only to approve contracts for tribal attorneys. By 1980, then, the Interior Department had approved a handful of alternative contracts based on these legal theories, but the piecemeal approach left the law unsettled. Serious concerns remained as to the authority of tribes to negotiate their own contracts and participate directly in the development of reservation resources.[20]

With the Northern Cheyenne–ARCO agreement, Interior Solicitor Clyde Martz had seen enough. After first delaying his review of the contract until the September 1980 tribal referendum confirmed that a strong majority supported the deal—again, more than 80 percent were in favor—Martz then suspended federal approval until two issues could be resolved. One, the solicitor questioned whether the contract conveyed a property interest in Northern Cheyenne minerals, making it a "lease" that then failed to comply with the 1938 Indian Mineral Leasing Act. Two, Martz wondered whether any other laws beyond the 1938 act authorized such a mineral agreement. Hoping to slap a pragmatic solution onto a sticky legal question, the Northern Cheyenne and ARCO quickly executed a "Statement of Intent" noting the parties themselves did not consider the agreement a lease but instead a service contract authorized by existing law. For good measure, ARCO also agreed not to sue the federal government if a court later invalidated the agreement.[21]

This stop-gap solution eased some of Martz's immediate concerns, but the former law school professor was most interested in a long-term fix that could clarify tribal authority once and for all. Martz was sympathetic to tribal aims, but his hands were tied without further congressional action. Pulling in Montana Senator John Melcher, all parties thus agreed to support legislation that would, according to Northern Cheyenne Vice President George Hiwalker, Jr., "remove any uncertainty that may exist regarding the Secretary's . . . authority to approve such agreements, and to provide Indian tribes with a clear alternative to the 1938 Minerals [*sic*] Leasing Act." With a legislative solution proposed, and ARCO's promise not to sue, Interior Secretary Cecil Andrus had enough assurances to approve the Northern Cheyenne–ARCO agreement on September 23, 1980. A few days later, Martz made the startling announcement that, without clarifying legislation, other alternative agreements may be illegal. As he did so, however, both Senator Melcher and the Solicitor's Office had already begun work on legislation to recognize tribal authority to enter into these vital contracts.[22]

"DOING BUSINESS WITH INDIAN TRIBES": THE 1982 INDIAN MINERAL DEVELOPMENT ACT

Just as it had done in stopping inequitable leasing practices earlier in the decade, the Northern Cheyenne provided the specific impetus for changing federal law to recognize tribes' sovereign control over reservation development. But the tribe, of course, did not operate in a vacuum. Broader changes in federal Indian affairs created a sense of urgency that helped push the new legislation through Congress. These changes were set in motion barely a month after the Department of the Interior approved the Northern Cheyenne–ARCO agreement when the country elected Ronald Reagan as its fortieth president. A California conservative who sought to extend many of the policies of his fellow Californian Richard Nixon, Reagan proclaimed his support for Nixon's Indian self-determination policy and its goal of strengthening tribal governments so as to lessen federal dependency. But like Nixon, Reagan inherited a sputtering national economy and a burgeoning federal bureaucracy, two problems he aimed to remedy with deep cuts in government spending. Perhaps unsurprisingly, Indian programs topped the list of expendable items. The president's first budget proposed more than $1 billion in cuts to the 1982 federal Indian budget, representing a 34 percent reduction. These cuts included a 77 percent reduction in economic development programs and a 46 percent reduction to programs assisting Indian energy resource management.[23]

But the real blow to Indian energy development was actually much worse. The only Indian energy programs Reagan proposed to leave intact were those run by the BIA to inventory Indian minerals and oversee mineral leasing; the Department of Energy's entire tribal energy program, which provided the backbone of support for CERT and specific Indian energy projects, was on the chopping block. Adding insult to injury, the president also appointed western attorney James Watt as the new Interior secretary. As president of the Mountain States Legal Foundation, Watt had just filed an amicus brief to the Supreme Court challenging tribal rights to tax energy companies operating on their reservation. The multifront attack on tribal-controlled energy development so alarmed energy tribes that CERT Chairman Peter MacDonald immediately wrote to Congress complaining that the new administration seemed determined to "return to an era of . . . giveaways of tribal oil, gas and coal resources."[24]

Energy tribes fought hard against Reagan's budget cuts in Congress, but the unmistakable trend of diminishing federal support forced tribal leaders to reassess their strategies for pursuing energy development. With 74 percent of CERT's 1981 budget pegged to federal funds, energy tribes could not simply wait and hope that Congress would reverse the trend. These groups needed immediate cash to continue consulting services and capital for mining projects already in development. To fill the financial gap left by a retreating federal government, CERT reached out to private industry. Styling its 1981 annual meeting as "Doing Business with Indian Tribes," CERT's Executive Director Ed Gabriel pressed hard for industry attendance, touting the tribes' vast natural resources and assuring potential investors that "the Indian people are amenable to bold, innovative business proposals of all types." The only stipulation, Gabriel noted in his letter to industry invitees, was that the deals must "recognize and respect [the tribes'] own cultural, environmental, and economic values and priorities."[25]

The 1981 meeting featured speakers who continued the message that tribal leaders stood ready to consider serious business proposals. In his opening remarks, Peter MacDonald implored the assembled tribal leaders and corporate officers to demonstrate the power of private investment by turning economically depressed reservations "into new growth zones that would transform the economy, the nation, and the future for us all." "I encourage you to gamble," the CERT chairman continued, as "the odds are much better here than at Las Vegas. There is risk—but the risk is far less than the danger we face if we fail to seize the opportunity of the moment." MacDonald's call for investment was followed by energy consultants explaining the procedures for doing business in

Indian Country and by testimony from corporate executives already working with tribes extolling the potential for profits. And as if on cue, the keynote speaker at the conference, Houston oilman Michael Halbouty, a close energy advisor to President Reagan and a member of Secretary Watt's Commission on Fiscal Accountability of the Nation's Energy Resources, concluded the meeting by telling the audience, "It is about time that the entire business community of the United States realize that it can do business with the Indian tribes."[26]

This shift by energy tribes toward actively courting private investment was certainly not the first time these groups looked outside the federal government to support their quest for economic self-sufficiency. The tribes had made similarly eager overtures in the 1960s, when energy companies first descended on western reservations looking for low-sulfur coal. This time, however, tribal leaders understood what was needed to make the tribal-private partnership work for both parties. Years of work by CERT and others to educate tribal leaders and provide market and geological data created negotiators well equipped to demand fair royalties. But as Peter MacDonald explained at the 1981 CERT meeting, "Simply bargaining for higher royalty rates is not enough and [the energy tribes] must explore issues involving ownership, management, up-front payments, and differentiation of agreements to authorize development." The tribes were hungry to strike deals, but this time they understood that the agreements must give Indians an active role in the ensuing ventures.[27]

To ensure the outcome they desired, CERT members concluded their annual meeting with a series of resolutions supporting measures that would give energy tribes the authority to control reservation resource development. In emphatic terms, MacDonald declared these initiatives would inaugurate "the dawning of a new era for [the federal-tribal] relationship: an era of recognition of our right to freedom from the shackles of federal restrictions on our ability to do business, to look after the needs of our people and to shape our own future." After first demanding that tribes receive the same regulatory status as states in every "federal program that delegates authority," tribal delegates turned their attention to the ongoing efforts to amend the 1938 Indian Mineral Leasing Act. Clearly, energy tribes supported any action enlarging—or more accurately, recognizing—their sovereign authority over reservation resources. But CERT had not been consulted on this important piece of new legislation and the energy tribes wanted a voice in the process. The organization's lawyers at the Native American Rights Fund opined that tribes "probably" already possessed the legal authority to negotiate alternative agreements, but like Senator Melcher and the Department of the Interior, CERT began drafting its own piece of clarifying legislation. Until its version was considered and its officers consulted, the organization resolved to oppose the other bills. The energy tribes would go it alone, if necessary, working their congressional connections to promote their own legislative proposal.[28]

*

By fall 1981, then, no less than three different versions of legislation to amend the 1938 Indian Mineral Leasing Act were in circulation. While they differed in the details, all shared the goal of clarifying tribal authority to negotiate alternative mineral contracts. The proposals drafted by Senator Melcher and by CERT were similar in that they offered a clear, straightforward authorization for tribes to enter into whatever type of agreement they desired, subject only to the federal government's subsequent approval. This shared approach provided ground for dialogue between the energy tribes and the senator, dissolving CERT's opposition to his bill. When the Department of Justice endorsed Melcher's proposal, finding "no reason to differentiate between lease and non-lease arrangements" in the law, the senator introduced his bill to Congress on November 30, 1981. Rather than supplant the old 1938 Indian Mineral Leasing Act, however, the proposal left that statute intact to give tribes the option of using competitive bidding procedures and standard lease forms if they so desired. The bill also included a provision retroactively ratifying all previous alternative agreements.[29]

Energy tribes and their corporate partners quickly rallied to support the proposed legislation. At special on-site hearings held in Billings in February 1982, nine western tribes—including the Northern Cheyenne, Crow, and Navajo—voiced their support for the legislation's general concepts. They argued again that increased tribal sophistication meant their governments deserved the flexibility to craft deals meeting their specific needs. As Navajo spokesman Gilbert Harrison explained,

In the last decade, the Navajo Nation has upgraded its internal capacity to plan, evaluate and develop various energy projects. No longer is the Navajo Tribe satisfied with the old standard federal leases, which only emphasized and relied on royalty return. New concepts which could be formalized will address alternative forms of agreements keyed to assumption of control and efficient development of its energy resources and these agreements will pay a higher return to the tribe.

Knowledgeable mining companies agreed, noting, as ARCO representative Curtis Burton did, that the days of Indian ignorance in energy negotiations were gone:

Our recent experience in conducting business with representatives of Indian tribes is that the tribes, represented by their elected authorities and by retained experts, bring to the negotiating table a level of sophistication and trading skill that rebuts any alleged need for a status resembling guardianship for the protection of tribal assets.

Witnesses expressed similar sentiments a month later when these hearings continued in Washington, D.C. There, Peabody Coal Company, Amoco, and oil and gas prospector Mission Resources added their names to the list of corporate supporters.[30] Existing law may have treated American Indians as incapable wards, but business people engaged with tribal enterprises understood how inaccurate that perception was.

Not all interested parties, however, supported a bill designed to ease the tribes' ability to develop reservation resources. Indian allottees formed the most forceful opposition to Melcher's proposal, arguing the new law would subject them to the same pressures and unbalanced negotiations that had produced inequitable coal leases with tribal governments a decade earlier. Norman Hollow, chairman of the Assiniboine and Sioux tribes on the Fort Peck Reservation, where 90 percent of minerals were owned by individual allottees, distilled their complaints:

The fundamental thing wrong with [the bill] is that it provides the tribes and individual Indians with no protection or advice during the most important time; that is, when the company or its agent is soliciting a lease or contract from the individual Indian. Perhaps most tribes will have the means and will to hire independent consultants. But [Melcher's bill] leaves the uneducated and uninformed Indian on his own.

Tribal governments may have come a long way in developing the expertise to manage reservation resources, but many believed the same could not be said for individual Indians who happened to own valuable mineral rights.[31]

This allottee opposition reflected the diversity of Indian experience with mineral development and the differing ownership structures on reservations. But energy tribes had come too far in developing their institutional capacities to allow individual Indians to now derail the expansion of tribal authority. The fix, they proposed, was not to discard the new law but to tie the fate of allottee mineral owners to their presumably better-equipped tribal governments. Melcher's Senate select committee thus amended the bill to remove allottees' authority to negotiate their own alternative agreements and give these individuals only the right to join a tribal agreement. As the committee report explained, everyone agreed allottees should receive the same flexibility to develop their minerals as the tribes themselves, but there was no way to ensure they would be adequately prepared and protected. Therefore, since "it is, of course, expected that tribes are in the best position to protect their own members from exploitation," the committee amended the bill to "retain the Secretary's authority to approve the inclusion of allottees in a tribe's negotiated agreement." For allottees on the Northern Cheyenne, Navajo, Fort Peck, and other reservations whose plans for mineral development differed from their tribal governments, the response to their fears of being exploited must have provided cold comfort.[32]

With allottee concerns addressed, though perhaps not alleviated, supporters refocused the debate on the proposed legislation's primary benefit: recognizing tribal *authority* over reservation resources to match the tribes' expanded *capacity* to craft smart energy deals. At the bill's final hearings, CERT Executive Director Ed Gabriel reiterated that his members were prepared to govern their own minerals and that energy tribes "were no longer content to sit on the sidelines while their resources were being taken from them under unfair terms." This law, Gabriel argued, was thus "a critical element" for Indian self-determination, not to mention for "all Americans, as our country strives to become more independent of foreign energy resources." The Department of the Interior concurred, sending letters of support to both the Senate and House committees explaining that the flexible mineral agreements authorized by the legislation would "provide the vehicle by which tribes can become directly involved in management decisions," thereby "enabling them to gain management experience and contributing significantly to the goal of self-determination." Tribal capacity and authority thus formed a mutually constitutive relationship. Increased tribal skills and knowledge justified tribes' having the authority to strike their own deals and participate in mineral development, and this participation would further increase tribal capacity to effectively manage reservation resources. Capacity without authority, however, thwarted the goals of Indian self-determination.[33]

With the support of federal agencies, mining companies, and energy tribes, Melcher's bill gathered bipartisan support as it worked its way through Congress. Reported unanimously out of the Senate Select Committee on Indian Affairs, the full Senate passed the measure on June 30, 1982. On the House floor, Arizona Democrat Morris Udall and Nebraska Republican Douglas Bereuter coordinated the easy passage of a slightly amended bill, which they explained updated antiquated federal laws passed early in the twentieth century when tribes did not have the capacity to effectively manage their minerals. Melcher and Udall avoided a time-consuming conference between the Senate and House by negotiating mutually agreeable amendments that both chambers passed unanimously on December 8 and 10, respectively. As Melcher explained on the Senate floor, the new law would provide the flexibility Indians needed to develop their resources, which "should help tribes to become economically self-sufficient and the rest of the Nation to become less dependent upon foreign energy sources." On the House side, Congressman Bereuter agreed, noting the law "is strongly supported by Indian tribes, the administration, and by companies interested in working with tribes to develop reservation mineral resources. It represents a large and positive step toward the future economic well-being of a large segment of the Nation's Indian population."[34]

With all parties in support, on December 22, 1982, President Reagan signed the bill into law as the Indian Mineral Development Act. The bill's sponsor, Senator Melcher, hailed the act as an opportunity for tribes "to play an active role as opposed to the passive role permitted under the 1938 Act." He further explained that "in the last decade, many Indian tribes, under self-determination, have begun to build solid governmental infrastructures, as well as trained management and planning personnel." The president followed up one month later with his administration's first, and only, formal statement on Indian policy. In it, Reagan reaffirmed Nixon's self-determination approach and pledged "to assist tribes in strengthening their governments by removing the federal impediments to tribal self-government and tribal resource development." The statement announced the transfer of the White House's Indian affairs personnel from the Office of Public Liaison to the Office of Intergovernmental Affairs, thereby recognizing the tribe's "rightful place among the governments of this nation." Then, in a clear nod to the recently passed Indian Mineral Development Act, the president noted:

> Tribal governments have the responsibility to determine the extent and the methods of developing the tribe's natural resources. The federal government's responsibility should not be used to hinder tribes from taking advantage of economic development opportunities. . . . The federal role is to encourage the production of energy in ways consistent with Indian values and priorities. To that end, we have strongly supported the use of creative agreements such as joint ventures and other non-lease agreements for the development of Indian mineral resources.

Almost a half century after the 1938 Leasing Act coded into law paternalistic assumptions of Indians' inability to manage their affairs, tribes finally secured explicit federal authority to develop reservation resources however they deemed fit.[35]

The ground for this remarkable expansion of tribal sovereignty was prepared over the previous decade by energy tribes' coordinated efforts to increase their capacity to responsibly and effectively manage reservation assets. Once adequately prepared, tribal leaders pursued innovative deal structures meant to realize their desire for tribal-controlled development. The Northern Cheyenne were both leaders in and emblematic of this movement. After first confirming ownership over reservation minerals and asserting legal rights to shape regional development, the tribe negotiated a sophisticated oil and gas agreement that promised both revenue from and control over drilling operations. But the deal also forced federal officials to reckon with an outdated and ineffective law that seemed to foreclose the Cheyenne's and other energy tribes' chosen path to self-determination. Undeterred, these groups redirected their energies toward changing that law. Working under the pressures of massive federal budget cuts and with a consortium of federal officials and energy executives, energy tribes orchestrated the passage of the 1982 Indian Mineral Development Act to provide the legal authority to match the tribes' recently expanded governing capacity.

Epilogue
New Era, Similar Results

IRONICALLY, AS FEDERAL policy makers, energy executives, and tribal leaders collectively hailed the 1982 Indian Mineral Development Act as a momentous victory for tribal sovereignty, several of those most responsible for its passage were not present to share in the celebration. One month before President Reagan signed the act into law, at the Council of Energy Resource Tribes' annual meeting in Denver, the organization announced plans to replace its longtime director, Ed Gabriel. A former Federal Energy Administration official, Gabriel had led CERT from the beginning, using his contacts to secure federal support and push through legislative changes that empowered tribal governments. Gabriel had tactfully guided the organization's evolution from an Indian advisory body for federal policy makers to the polemical "Native American OPEC" and ultimately into a professional association dedicated to improving tribal governance. He was an integral player in CERT's rapid rise to becoming a formidable national institution capable of empowering tribal leaders and enlarging tribal sovereignty.[1]

But Ed Gabriel's departure signaled a shift within an organization that had come of age. His replacement, David Lester, was the current commissioner of the Department of Health and Human Services' Administration for Native Americans and could match Gabriel's understanding of the federal bureaucracy. He also possessed attributes his predecessor did not. As an enrolled member of the Creek Tribe of Oklahoma, Lester would be CERT's first Native American director. The move held great symbolic meaning, representing the passage of responsibility and expertise for reservation energy development from federal to Indian hands. Yet David Lester's hiring was more than just a symbolic act. His unique skill set would shape CERT's new direction. As commissioner of the Administration for Native Americans, Lester had administered a multimillion-dollar federal grant program to aid social and economic development on reservations. He also was a former economic development specialist for the National Congress of American Indians and former director of the United Indian Development Association. His experience in growing reservation economies replaced Gabriel's aptitude for lobbying for federal support, and over the next several years, Lester would oversee the closing of CERT's Washington, D.C., office to focus on providing technical assistance to tribes seeking to develop their resources. With tribal governments now possessing clear legal authority over tribal minerals, energy tribes shifted their attention from the nation's capital back to the reservations. More than at any time in their history, the tribes were well positioned to capitalize on their vast resources.[2]

Sadly for these groups, forces beyond their control would thwart the successful execution of their recently clarified authority over reservation development. Not only did Ronald Reagan's budget cuts inflict financial woes on CERT and its members, but the same president who signed into law the Indian Mineral Development Act also pursued energy and economic policies that made the development of Indian energy, particularly low-sulfur coal, economically nonviable. Reagan accelerated President Carter's deregulation of oil prices, which produced a temporary surge in domestic oil supplies as producers moved reserves into the unregulated market to take advantage of higher prices. The expected increase in domestic output, however, was matched by an unexpected rise in global exploration and production by non-OPEC countries seeking to capitalize on higher international oil prices following the "energy crisis" of 1979. In the face of higher international prices, OPEC's discipline broke down, and its members raced to capture the economic windfall. By 1983, OPEC was frantically trying to regain control of global supplies and prices by lowering its production quotas, but the damage was done. The world was flooded with oil, and the demand required to consume this across-the-board increase failed to materialize. Reagan's austere fiscal and monetary policies exacerbated a global recession, and conservation measures instituted during the Ford and Carter administrations contributed to an overall decline in energy consumption. With demand waning and production soaring, the "energy crises" of the 1970s turned into the "oil glut" of the mid-1980s.[3]

Cheap oil collapsed the market for Indian energy just as tribes had secured the authority to develop their minerals. Low-sulfur Indian coal development was particularly hard hit—why buy coal when oil was so cheap? Tribes struggled to find development partners to invest in reservation coal mines, and those that had negotiated potentially lucrative deals now saw the projects shelved. In 1980, for instance, the Crow had secured the nation's first alternative coal agreement with the Shell Oil Company, but by 1985 Shell had determined that the project was economically infeasible. In a curt letter to the tribal government, the multinational energy firm explained that due "to the current status of the coal market," it must surrender all rights to Crow coal. The Westmoreland Coal Company had reached a similar conclusion a few years earlier, releasing rights to portions of its Crow coal lease.[4]

Tribes possessing oil and gas deposits faced similar struggles. Many rushed to exercise their newfound flexibility to negotiate energy deals only to find their bargaining position undercut by the oil glut. In these altered economic conditions, the new negotiated contracts began to resemble the old leases. Better-informed tribal leaders were able to secure important concessions like tribal hiring preferences, environmental protection clauses, and fluctuating royalties tied to market prices, but energy companies now refused to give up control over mining operations. With an abundance of oil, developers had little reason to begin new projects in which they could not dictate the pace and scale of development. Without control, tribes remained subject to corporate decisions over whether or not to develop and at what scale. The glutted market meant reduced oil and gas production, and the drilling that did occur produced diminished revenue because royalties were now tied to declining market prices. Tribal revenue from oil and gas development reached its peak of $198 million in 1982, then plummeted by 60 percent over the next four years. The same energy tribes that had successfully increased their governing capacity and altered federal law to authorize tribal control of reservation development found mastery over a shifting global energy market to be more elusive.[5]

Ongoing intratribal disputes over whether to pursue development, and on what terms, also continued to challenge energy tribes. The Crow example is again instructive, for after the contentious July 1977 impeachment of Tribal Chairman Patrick Stands Over Bull, the Crow community shuffled through a series of leaders as it debated energy development. In fact, of the five tribal chairmen elected in the twenty years following the first serious coal proposal in 1966, only Edison Real Bird (1966–1972) escaped calls for impeachment. Two leaders, Stands Over Bull (1972–1977) and Donald Stewart (1982–1986), were either forcibly removed from office or had all executive powers stripped by tribal resolution. And in every impeachment episode—each of which mirrored in intensity the debates surrounding Stands Over Bull—the driving argument for removal was the alleged mismanagement of tribal energy resources.[6]

These passionate internal debates both did violence to communal relations and drove away potential energy partners. Firms desiring Crow minerals found the tribe's constantly changing political landscape confusing and too risky for business. After Stands Over Bull's impeachment, energy companies pleaded with the Department of the Interior to provide clarity as to which Crow faction held the authority to strike coal deals. Mindful of the new policy of Indian self-determination, however, federal officials responded by refusing to "substitut[e] [their] judgment for that of the tribe's in an internal dispute of this sort." Without clarity, several energy firms abandoned development plans, and those that continued to pursue Crow minerals pushed the tribe to restructure its government to provide a more stable negotiating body.[7]

Ultimately, the Crow tribe responded to pressures to develop by, once again, altering its governing structure. In 1980, a new majority disbanded the cautious Coal Authority and authorized the tribal chairman to aggressively pursue development projects. But as indicated by Shell's and Westmoreland's surrender of Crow coal rights, market conditions hampered these efforts. Ongoing battles within the tribal council, which still included all adult members of the tribe, also continued to drive away potential investors. By 2001, a frustrated majority had seen enough and took dramatic action to overhaul the entire tribal government structure. The Crow ratified a new constitution that replaced its hyper-democratic tribal council with a system based on the United States' model of representative government, including separation of powers and a strong executive branch.[8]

Finally, with this new governing structure in place and oil prices again skyrocketing due to disruptions in global supply, the Crow negotiated a 2004 agreement with the Westmoreland Coal Company to allow the first commercial coal mining on the reservation. The deal, in fact, merely extended the company's ongoing operations in the Ceded Strip southward onto the reservation proper. Most years, revenue from this enlarged Absaloka Mine provides two-thirds of the tribal government's nonfederal budget—more than $20 million in 2010. The mine also employs a 70 percent tribal workforce. The relationship between the Crow and Westmoreland has become so strong that Tribal Chairman Darrin Old Coyote recently affirmed to a congressional subcommittee that "without question, [the Absaloka Mine] is a critical source of jobs, financial support, and domestically produced energy. [Westmoreland] has been the Crow Nation's most significant private partner over the past 39 years."[9]

But on a reservation with 47 percent unemployment and a per capita income less than half the U.S. average ($11,987 to $27,334), coal mining's benefits still do not reach all tribal members. The tribal government thus continues to explore more development opportunities, largely with the blessing of the tribal majority. Since Westmoreland's extension, the Crow have granted the mining firm more coal rights in the Ceded Strip and also announced three new energy ventures with other companies on the reservation itself. One of these projects could be the nation's first mine-mouth, coal-to-liquids gasification plant; the others look to export Crow coal to Asia. Billions of tons of coal and millions of dollars of tribal revenue are once again on the table. Of course, not all are thrilled about the prospect of impending development and some tribal members continue to fear the potential impacts. The tribe will continue to wrestle with these decisions. But while it is too early to judge the effects of these potential projects on the Crow community and landscape, it is clear that a restructured tribal government, informed by decades of energy development experience, possesses the clear legal authority to make the deals.[10]

With global oil prices remaining relatively high in recent years, the Crow tribe is not alone in using its sovereign authority to once again explore tribal-led energy projects. On the Navajo Reservation, where the postwar exploitation of tribal minerals began and rampant poverty remains, the tribe has taken a two-step approach to exerting control. First, the community has acted largely in unison to shut down dirty and unwanted projects. Second, some portions of tribe have pushed for tribal-controlled ventures to replace them. In 2005, for instance, the tribal government passed a moratorium on uranium development and, in partnership with the Hopi Tribal Council, withdrew tribal water rights necessary to operate Peabody Coal Company's Black Mesa Mine. That same year, Indian and non-Indian environmental groups forced the closure of the Mohave Generating Station after the facility failed to install costly pollution control technology. These actions delivered death blows to some of the reservation's more notorious energy projects, but Navajo energy development was far from dead. Starting in 2003, the Diné Power Authority, a tribal enterprise, pursued plans to build its own coal-fired power plant on the reservation, the Desert Rock Energy Project. This facility was proposed to provide electricity to another ambitious tribal endeavor, the Navajo Transmission Project, which would have provided the infrastructure needed to carry reservation-produced electricity to distant markets. Neither project, however, was realized. Local environmental opposition emerged from the outset and the requisite permits were never obtained.[11]

Undeterred, the Navajo tribal government now has gone back to the infamous mine that began the tribe's tumultuous experience with commercial coal development. On December 31, 2013, the Navajo Transitional Energy Company, another tribal enterprise, bought the Navajo Mine from the world's largest mining firm, BHP Billiton. This massive facility—once the planet's biggest strip mine—had fed coal for over fifty years to the Four Corners Generating Station—once the country's dirtiest power plant. Now the Navajo own it. But the community cannot agree on whether this is a good thing. Proponents point to the protection of Navajo jobs and the secure revenue stream gained by continuing to sell coal to the Four Corners plant, which would have likely shut down had Billiton not found an interested buyer to keep the mine open. These supporters also hail the deal as a victory for tribal sovereignty, positioning the tribe to control the future of these coal reserves, whether that be exploring cleaner coal gasification technology or exporting coal to Asian markets. Opponents, of course, question the sanity of now participating in an industrial process that has brought so much harm to the community. Detractors also fear the environmental liabilities the tribe has inherited and argue that buying a worn-out coal mine to supply an outdated power plant makes little business sense. The arguments on both sides are fair. But these are the dilemmas faced by a sovereign government representing diverse constituencies and attempting to wield its power to participate in a risky global energy industry.[12]

In the thirty-four years since the Northern Cheyenne negotiated the oil and gas deal with the Atlantic Richfield Company that triggered fundamental changes to federal Indian law, the tribe's reservation has seen little development. In the early 1980s, ARCO drilled dozens of prospecting wells, but most came up dry. By 1984, the company was forced to walk away, leaving behind unreclaimed drill sites and a community becoming more, not less, impoverished. Two years after ARCO shuttered its operations, reservation unemployment reached 60 percent—up from 34 percent in 1979. It has remained there ever since. According to the 2000 census, the per capita income was only $7,247, and more than 50 percent of the population was mired below the poverty line. No doubt, the Northern Cheyenne's 1970s actions allowed the tribe to maintain control of its resources and protect the reservation. That place is still the Cheyenne homeland, free of the non-Indian interlopers tribal members worried so much about. But it is also free of desperately needed economic development.[13]

Further, the Northern Cheyenne's success in keeping its land a distinctly tribal space has not protected the community from the pernicious influences of the outside world. Today, the reservation is completely encircled by coal development. A dozen miles to the north, the Colstrip Power Plant continues to burn coal extracted from a massive adjacent strip mine. On the eastern border, Arch Coal, Inc., the nation's second largest coal company, is developing the vast Otter Creek Tracts, which span more than 8,000 acres and are estimated to hold over 1,200 million tons of coal. Twenty-five miles to the south, several strip mines operate in the vicinity of Decker, Montana, and the reservation's the western boundary is flanked by the Crow Reservation and its impending development. Testifying to Congress in 2014, Tribal President Llevando Fisher complained that the surrounding activity puts constant pressure on the Northern Cheyenne's inadequate public services and facilities and "produces major influxes of newcomers to the area [that] leads to undesirable socio-economic effects on the Tribe, including on-reservation crime, traffic, and accidents." But the tribe reaps none of the financial rewards that would help combat coal mining's ill effects. As Fisher explained, "We suffer the impacts of development but receive no revenues that would allow us to minimize the ills inflicted by this development."[14]

For this reason, the Northern Cheyenne—the tribe that halted the exploitation of tribal energy resources and was labeled as the anti-development tribe—will soon vote on whether to pursue reservation coal mining once again. Already once, in 2006, a tribal referendum directed the tribal government to do just that. Intervening elections, however, have placed a succession of alternating pro- and antidevelopment leaders in the tribe's highest office. The community is clearly divided on the issue. On February 13, 2014, President Fisher, once a coal mining opponent, asked for clarity. Explaining that "the bleak financial future facing our nation" had persuaded him to now personally prefer development, Fisher announced that he would nevertheless "let the people decide." "We may not all agree," he warned, "but we'll let the majority decide . . . [and] if the Northern Cheyenne vote yes by a majority for coal development on our reservation, we will go strongly in that direction." Considering the mountains of coal underlying the Cheyenne Reservation and the tribe's historical importance to Indian energy development nationally, federal officials, energy executives, and other tribal leaders look on anxiously as the tribe deliberates its decision.[15]

In each of these cases of potential reservation development, the debates over tribal survival continue. The infighting is particularly intense when changes to tribal governing practices are proposed to facilitate energy development, as they often are. Some Indians hail the creation of tribal enterprises or new governing committees endowed with the authority to dispense tribal property as necessary improvements to tribal governance. Employing modern and efficient management techniques, they argue, will help the tribes conduct business and alleviate poverty. Others deride the new governing methods as an affront to traditional tribal practices and a threat to the continued existence of the tribe. Of course, the labels of "modern" and "traditional" forms of governance are deeply problematic. Both assume the authenticity of a particular governing structure and then argue that exterior forces either demand change or require its preservation. The labels are, in essence, ahistorical. But the point here is that the battles over resource development, tribal governance, and indigenous identities continued unabated after energy tribes secured authority to control development. Changing the law to recognize tribal sovereignty was an incredible victory; taking back control over reservation development saved the tribe. But this victory was not the end of the struggle to capitalize on reservation resources. Tribal communities remain subject to the same national and global pressures that first brought energy companies to their doorstep. For that matter, so do indigenous peoples worldwide. Here in the United States, these communities sometimes have been able align the desires of the tribal majority with market forces and reap mining revenues. More often, they have not. Their responses to these forces, however, continue to shape their communities, their landscapes, and the tribal governments that patrol both.[16]

*

In yet another example of the inner turmoil that often accompanies tribal energy development, CERT's 1982 annual conference not only witnessed the departure of Executive Director Ed Gabriel, but it also marked the last meeting for CERT and Navajo Tribal Chairman Peter MacDonald. Just two weeks before the Denver gathering, the Navajo Nation voted MacDonald out of office in favor of Peterson Zah, the head of the DNA People's Legal Services, which represented individual Navajos fighting energy projects often supported by MacDonald's administration. Zah's position with DNA had given him a political base to attack MacDonald's pro-development policies, and MacDonald's defeat meant the longstanding chairman could no longer serve as CERT's leader. At exactly the moment energy tribes secured authority to develop their own minerals, CERT was faced with replacing its entire leadership team.[17]

Like its new director, David Lester, CERT's new chairman, Wilfred Scott, brought a different perspective to Indian energy development. Scott's Nez Perce tribe did not possess substantial hydrocarbons and showed little appetite for pursuing large-scale energy projects. In fact, the Nez Perce had recently rejected a hydroelectric facility due to potential harm to its tribal fishery. In addition to this different perspective,

Scott also brought a different leadership style, replacing MacDonald's combative bluster with a conciliatory approach that cultivated cooperative relationships between member tribes, CERT officials, and federal agencies. The new leadership tandem of Scott and Lester continued to advocate for tribal control of mining projects and made available CERT's consulting services to tribes desiring development. But in contrast to their predecessors, they did not push mineral development as a panacea for tribal problems. More wary of the potential social and environmental impacts of development, CERT's leaders counseled tribal governments to take calculated approaches to reservation development that considered their preparedness to manage potential projects and their community's support for them.[18]

The difficult market conditions of the 1980s also meant there was little upside to pushing hard for development until tribes were ready to manage and support it. In the interim, energy tribes focused on improving their capacity to regulate mining and consolidated legal authority over tribal resources. CERT continued to provide technical assistance to help tribes determine their resource inventories, improve accounting systems to better track royalties, and, with the increasing support of the Environmental Protection Agency, monitor environmental impacts of existing development.[19]

To match this continued growth in capacity, the tribes pushed through a series of new federal laws designed to further extend tribal control over reservation development. The 1992 Indian Energy Resources Act directed the Department of the Interior to help tribes develop a "vertically integrated energy industry on Indian reservations," and the 2003 Energy Policy Act provided grants and technical assistance to achieve this end. Tribal control over energy development reached its legal apogee in 2005 with the passage of the Indian Tribal Energy Development and Self-Determination Act, which authorized tribes to completely forego federal approval of development projects once they had established a "tribal energy resource agreement" (TERA). Serving as "master agreements" between individual tribes and the federal government, TERAs must include adequate procedures for constructing tribal energy deals, provisions related to the tribe's economic return, lists of all tribal laws governing reservation mining, and assurances of the tribe's capacity to monitor and manage environmental and social impacts. Once a TERA is approved, a tribe has complete regulatory authority over reservation energy development, from contract negotiations to enforcement of the deal's terms. Critics argue that TERAs remove important federal protections for tribal lands—such as the requirements of the National Environmental Policy Act and the National Historic Preservation Act—but these agreements represent the fullest manifestation yet of Indian self-determination. Such autonomy has always come with risks, as well as benefits.[20]

The significant change in CERT's leadership that accompanied the passage of the 1982 Indian Mineral Development Act thus ushered in a new era in the tribes' approach to energy development. New leaders counseled a more measured, though still active, pursuit of development, and energy tribes continued to expand their knowledge of and sovereignty over reservation resources. Distant market forces and intratribal turmoil, however, stifled potential projects, leaving the end results, for now, largely unchanged. Energy tribes continue to wait for the day when they can capitalize on their valuable minerals, which they now possess the capacity and authority to do.

Beyond ushering in a new era in Indian energy development, the 1982 changeover in CERT's leadership also provided an opportunity to reflect on how far the tribes had come. Seizing the moment, outgoing chairman Peter MacDonald delivered a farewell address at CERT's annual meeting that recounted the entire history of the organization he helped create. The flamboyant leader did not disappoint. Applying a Star Trek metaphor to characterize CERT's voyage as a long-imperiled mission with little hope of success, MacDonald began by listing the many challenges facing "Starship CERT" at its outset. These included the energy tribes' immense diversity, their lack of geological and market data, and the resistance of federal agencies to relinquish control over Indian resources. He also noted the universal hostility created "just by dubbing ourselves the 'Native American OPEC'" and the criticism CERT received from some American Indians when it obtained "the thing that we feared most . . . a federal grant, and not just one federal grant, but numerous federal grants." The early days of CERT, the chairman recalled, were characterized by confusion over its mission, the ignorance of its members, and the reluctance of federal officials to faithfully carry out their trustee duty.[21]

But the message MacDonald hoped most to convey was that despite these long odds, CERT survived in the same way American Indians had survived since European contact, by adapting to constantly changing circumstances. In his words, the organization "evolved from a MEANS to increase bargaining leverage to an END in itself—a forum for giving tribes power in national politics." Now that CERT and its allies had exercised their power to change federal law and clarify the tribes' expansive sovereignty, MacDonald predicted:

> CERT will become a SYMBOL for the next voyage of the human species—a voyage to a post-industrial world. It is a voyage which Native Americans are uniquely equipped to make. . . . We retain our traditions, our sense of community, and the medicine bundles of sacred soil, brought from previous worlds and preserved to enable us to achieve harmony in a new world, yet unknown. . . . Spaceship CERT is ready for its next five-year voyage—ready to create the think tanks, the social experiments, the new institutions, and the new linkages for our peoples, the First Americans. We are equipped by long tradition and practice to adapt, adjust, and yet survive with our identity miraculously preserved.[22]

MacDonald's last point was the most important to American Indians. The onslaught of demand for tribal resources had brought the world's largest energy firms to reservation borders, where a flawed legal regime invited them in. Proposed mining not only imperiled reservation landscapes, but it threatened to erase established customs and norms that defined the communities living there. Yet, as alluded to by MacDonald, the energy tribes survived with their identities intact. Belying perceptions encoded in federal law that American Indians were incapable wards, these tribes mobilized a defense of their homeland and developed the institutional capacity to regulate industrial activities within that land. Based on this increased capacity, the 1982 Indian Mineral Development Act recognized tribal authority to direct reservation development, which subsequent laws strengthened. Now equipped with the legal authority to pursue development in line with their communities' desires, only the successful execution of that power is left unfinished. The fact that external, often global, structures continue to limit the exercise of this sovereignty—while internal debates rage over how to respond to these pressures—does not diminish the energy tribes' accomplishments. Rather, it makes them historical actors like any other, operating among forces they can shape but not fully control.

Notes

1. "Proceedings of the Native American, Environmentalist, and Agriculturalist Workshop" (Northern Rockies Action Group, December 10, 1975), 15, in author's possession.

2. 31 U.S. 515 (1832), 559. A staunch federalist, Marshall limited his defense of tribal sovereignty to internal tribal matters within tribal lands, maintaining that the federal government held superior authority over the tribes' external relations. In fact, he followed the quote about Indian nations being distinct and independent with the words "with the single exception of that imposed by irresistible power" of a conquering nation. This recognition of federal supremacy, however, does not affect Marshall's legal opinion that tribes retained the right to manage resources within their lands. As to Jackson's quotes, see Felix S. Cohen, *Cohen's Handbook of Federal Indian Law* (Newark: LexisNexis, 2005), 50, n. 304; Ronald N. Satz, *American Indian Policy in the Jacksonian Era* (Lincoln: University of Nebraska Press, 1974), 49, n. 31; Francis Paul Prucha, *The Great Father: The United States Government and the American Indians* (Lincoln: University of Nebraska Press, 1984), 212, n. 61. Most historians agree on the accuracy of Jackson's quote, though the more popular version holds that the president replied, "John Marshall has made his decision, now let him enforce it." Regardless of his actual words, subsequent federal actions made clear Jackson's policy to ignore the Supreme Court's holding. Finally, the literature on non-Indians divesting Indians of their land and resources in the nineteenth century is voluminous. Francis Paul Prucha provides the classic introduction to the many ways in which this was accomplished (Prucha, *Great Father*). For the more specific point of how non-Indians used the legal system

to erode tribal sovereignty, see Charles F. Wilkinson, *American Indians, Time, and the Law: Native Societies in a Modern Constitutional Democracy* (New Haven: Yale University Press, 1987), esp. 56–57; Sidney L. Harring, *Crow Dog's Case: American Indian Sovereignty, Tribal Law, and United States Law in the Nineteenth Century* (Cambridge: Cambridge University Press, 1994); David E. Wilkins, *American Indian Sovereignty and the U.S. Supreme Court: The Masking of Justice* (Austin: University of Texas Press, 1997), esp. chapter 3; and Lindsay Gordon Robertson, *Conquest by Law: How the Discovery of America Dispossessed Indigenous Peoples of Their Lands* (New York: Oxford University Press, 2005).

3. For early views and policies of European colonials and Americans toward American Indians, see Prucha, *Great Father*, esp. 5–9 and parts 1–2; Robert F. Berkhofer, *The White Man's Indian: Images of the American Indian from Columbus to the Present* (New York: Alfred A. Knopf, 1978); Brian W. Dippie, *The Vanishing American: White Attitudes and U.S. Indian Policy* (Middletown, CT: Wesleyan University Press, 1982), esp. parts 1–2; Bernard W. Sheehan, *Savagism and Civility: Indians and Englishmen in Colonial Virginia* (Cambridge: Cambridge University Press, 1980). For the mid-nineteenth-century emphasis on assimilation, and the later turn toward race as a marker of inferiority, see Frederick E. Hoxie, *A Final Promise: The Campaign to Assimilate the Indians, 1880–1920* (Lincoln: University of Nebraska Press, 1984). David Rich Lewis explains the prominent role of settled agriculture in the project to "civilize" Indian cultures. *Neither Wolf nor Dog: American Indians, Environment, and Agrarian Change* (New York: Oxford University Press, 1994), esp. 3–21.

4. The literature on Collier is extensive. A particularly helpful work explaining Collier's motivation to protect Indians' communal ethic is E. A. Schwartz, "Red Atlantis Revisited: Community and Culture in the Writings of John Collier," *American Indian Quarterly* 18, no. 4 (Autumn 1994): 507–31; see also Lawrence C. Kelly, *The Assault on Assimilation: John Collier and the Origins of Indian Policy Reform* (Albuquerque: University of New Mexico Press, 1983); Kenneth R. Philp, *John Collier's Crusade for Indian Reform, 1920–1954* (Tucson: University of Arizona Press, 1977); Elmer Rusco, *A Fateful Time: The Background and Legislative History of the Indian Reorganization Act* (Reno: University of Nevada Press, 2000); Graham D. Taylor, *The New Deal and American Indian Tribalism: The Administration of the Indian Reorganization Act, 1934–45* (Lincoln: University of Nebraska Press, 1980); and Stephen Kunitz, "The Social Philosophy of John Collier," *Ethnohistory* 18, no. 3 (Summer 1971): 213–29. For an explanation of how Collier's Office of Indian Affairs effectively retained control over Indian assets through its use of "technical assistance" to the tribes, see Thomas Biolsi, *Organizing the Lakota: The Political Economy of the New Deal on the Pine Ridge and Rosebud Reservations* (Tucson: University of Arizona Press, 1992), esp. chapter 6.

5. As I discuss in chapter 1, Felix Cohen's position stemmed from his normative vision of America as a legally pluralistic society with power decentralized to local authorities. For Cohen's concept of legal pluralism and his efforts to apply it to American Indian law, see Dalia Tsuk Mitchell, *Architect of Justice: Felix S. Cohen and the Founding of American Legal Pluralism* (Ithaca: Cornell University Press, 2007). For additional explanations of Cohen's approach to Indian law, particularly

how legal realism influenced his work, see Christian McMillen, *Making Indian Law: The Hualapai Land Case and the Birth of Ethnohistory* (New Haven: Yale University Press, 2007), 128–33; Jill Martin, "The Miner's Canary: Felix S. Cohen's Philosophy of Indian Rights," *American Indian Law Review* 23 (Summer 1999): 165–79; Martin P. Goldberg, "Realism and Functionalism in the Legal Thought of Felix S. Cohen," *Cornell Law Review* 66, no. 5 (1981): 1032–57; and Stephen M. Feldman, "Felix S. Cohen and His Jurisprudence: Reflections on Federal Indian Law," *Buffalo Law Review* 35, no. 2 (1986): 479–515. Chapter 1 also covers how the 1938 Indian Mineral Leasing Act provided a uniform mineral leasing system whereby tribes, through the Bureau of Indian Affairs, could solicit offers to extract reservation minerals, but they could not develop these resources themselves. Instead, the federal government would oversee the work of outside developers who "leased" Indian minerals for production. Indian Mineral Leasing Act, Public Law 75-506, 52 Stat. 347 (1938), codified as amended at 25 U.S.C. § 396a–f [2006]; Cohen, *Cohen's Handbook of Federal Indian Law,* 2005 ed., 1091.

6. Richard Nixon, "Special Message to Congress on Indian Affairs," July 8, 1970, The American Presidency Project, ed. Gerhard Peters and John T. Woolley, http://www.presidency.ucsb.edu/ws/index.php?pid=2573. For Nixon's Indian policy conforming to his New Federalism approach, see George Pierre Castile, *To Show Heart: Native American Self-Determination and Federal Indian Policy, 1960–1975* (Tucson: University of Arizona Press, 1998), 80–86. Nixon's self-determination policy actually continued a trend begun with President Lyndon Johnson's Office of Economic Opportunity to provide tribal governments direct control over reservation funds and resources. See Castile, *To Show Heart,* and Thomas Clarkin, *Federal Indian Policy in the Kennedy and Johnson Administrations, 1961–1969* (Albuquerque: University of New Mexico Press, 2001). As George Castile argues, "The rhetoric, the language of self-determination, had long been around; what was new [under the Johnson administration] was a practical mechanism to transfer authority to the tribes—the [Office of Economic Opportunity] system of compacting with local Indian community action agencies to carry out federal programs." George Pierre Castile, *Taking Charge: Native American Self-Determination and Federal Indian Policy, 1975–1993* (Tucson: University of Arizona Press, 2006), 14. According to Castile, Nixon simply carried forth this model and proposed new federal legislation that authorized the Bureau of Indian Affairs to transfer some of its responsibilities to tribal governments, again following the template already established by the Office of Economic Opportunity.

7. For a discussion of Nixon's original legislative proposals to effectuate his policy, how the Watergate scandal hampered the passage of these bills, and the Democratic Congress's embrace of the Indian Self-Determination and Education Act after Nixon's resignation, see Castile, *To Show Heart,* chapters 4 and 6–7. There is a robust and growing literature on Indian gaming. See, e.g., W. Dale Mason, *Indian Gaming: Tribal Sovereignty and American Politics* (Norman: University of Oklahoma Press, 2000); Angela Mullis and David Kamper, eds., *Indian Gaming: Who Wins?* (Los Angeles: UCLA American Indian Studies Center, 2000); Duane Champagne and Carol Goldberg, "Ramona Redeemed?: The Rise of Tribal Political Power in California," *Wicazo Sa Review* 17, no. 1 (2002): 43–63; Eve

Darian-Smith, *New Capitalists: Law, Politics, and Identity Surrounding Casino Gaming on Native American Land* (Belmont, CA: Thomson/Wadsworth, 2004); Steven Andrew Light and Kathryn Rand, *Indian Gaming and Tribal Sovereignty: The Casino Compromise* (Lawrence: University Press of Kansas, 2005); and Jessica R. Cattelino, *High Stakes: Florida Seminole Gaming and Sovereignty* (Durham: Duke University Press, 2008).

8. My notion of a "third area of sovereignty" is related to, but different from, Kevin Bruyneel's concept of a "third space of sovereignty." In *The Third Space of Sovereignty,* Bruyneel demonstrates how Euro-American legal institutions and cultural constructions continuously limited American Indians both to a place outside the American polity (spatial boundary) and to a time before the emergence of a modern American state (temporal boundary). However, while careful to note these limitations, Bruyneel also finds ambiguity in the application of these principles, stemming largely from the multifaceted nature of the American people and its state. The lack of uniformity in views and policies toward American Indians produces what Bruyneel calls "colonial ambivalence," creating a space within which American Indians could operate historically to exercise some sovereignty and extract benefits from the federal government. It is here, in this "third space of sovereignty," where American Indians are neither wholly within nor outside the American state, that Bruyneel finds Indian agency and the explanation for the continued resiliency of American Indian groups today. Kevin Bruyneel, *The Third Space of Sovereignty: The Postcolonial Politics of U.S.–Indigenous Relations* (Minneapolis: University of Minnesota Press, 2007), 1–25. While greatly influenced by Bruyneel's work, my use of the "third area of sovereignty" is less amorphous and stands simply for that area within federal jurisprudence where tribal governments, rather than federal or state governments, maintain primary authority.

9. Joseph F. Mulligan, *Introductory College Physics* (New York: McGraw-Hill, 1985), 138 and 157.

10. For Weber's understanding of social power, see H. H. Gerth and C. Wright Mills, eds., *From Max Weber: Essays in Sociology* (New York: Oxford University Press, 1962), 180. The literature on power from historians of technology and the environment has been reviewed recently by a group of scholars at the University of Virginia that includes myself, Edmund Russell, Thomas Finger, John K. Brown, Brian Balogh, and W. Bernard Carlson. The claims made here regarding the energetic basis of social power derive from that collective effort. See Edmund Russell et al., "The Nature of Power: Synthesizing the History of Technology and Environmental History," *Technology and Culture* 52, no. 2 (April 2011): 246–59. Latour's quote is in Bruno Latour, "The Powers of Association," in *Power, Action, and Belief: A New Sociology of Knowledge,* ed. John Law (Boston: Routledge and Keegan Paul, 1986), 273.

11. Immanuel Wallerstein's "world systems theory" provides the most influential analysis of these core-periphery relations. For a cogent summary of this theory, see Immanuel Maurice Wallerstein, *World-Systems Analysis: An Introduction* (Durham: Duke University Press, 2004). Representative examples of environmental histories that apply the theory to international development in the modern era include Richard P. Tucker, *Insatiable Appetite: The United States and the Ecologi-*

cal Degradation of the Tropical World (Berkeley: University of California Press, 2000), and John F. Richards, *The Unending Frontier: An Environmental History of the Early Modern World* (Berkeley: University of California Press, 2003). For studies of American development in this mold, see, e.g., Richard White, *The Roots of Dependency: Subsistence, Environment, and Social Change Among the Choctaws, Pawnees, and Navajos* (Lincoln: University of Nebraska Press, 1983); William Cronon, *Nature's Metropolis: Chicago and the Great West* (New York: W. W. Norton, 1991); and William G. Robbins, *Colony and Empire: The Capitalist Transformation of the American West* (Lawrence: University Press of Kansas, 1994). Influential anthropologies demonstrating the difficulties in applying universal ideologies in foreign, local contexts include James C. Scott, *Seeing Like a State: How Certain Schemes to Improve the Human Condition Have Failed* (New Haven: Yale University Press, 1998), and Anna Lowenhaupt Tsing, *Friction: An Ethnography of Global Connection* (Princeton: Princeton University Press, 2005).

12. A major exception to the statement that environmental histories have tended not to follow the trajectory of impacts outward from the periphery is Richard Grove's work, *Green Imperialism*. In it, Grove demonstrates how the incorporation of local knowledge of the natural world, generated in colonial peripheries, influenced scientific knowledge in the metropoles, leading ultimately to powerful scientific critiques of colonialism. Richard Grove, *Green Imperialism: Colonial Expansion, Tropical Island Edens, and the Origins of Environmentalism, 1600–1860* (New York: Cambridge University Press, 1995).

13. Arthur F. McEvoy, *The Fisherman's Problem: Ecology and Law in the California Fisheries, 1850–1980* (New York: Cambridge University Press, 1986), 13.

14. Studies that explain tribal factionalism in terms of resource conflicts include White, *Roots of Dependency*, esp. 109–17; Lewis, *Neither Wolf nor Dog*, esp. 41 and 154–55; Larry Nesper, *The Walleye War: The Struggle for Ojibwe Spearfishing and Treaty Rights* (Lincoln: University of Nebraska Press, 2002), chapter 8; and Paul C. Rosier, *Rebirth of the Blackfeet Nation* (Lincoln: University of Nebraska Press, 2001). Mitchell's quote is at Don Mitchell, *Cultural Geography: A Critical Introduction* (Malden, MA: Blackwell, 2000), 77.

PROLOGUE

1. According to the coal industry's leading trade journal, in 1972, Consolidation trailed only the Peabody Group in American coal production. "Top 15 Coal-Producing Groups in 1972," *Coal Age*, April 1973, 39. For details on Consolidation's proposal, see K. Ross Toole, *The Rape of the Great Plains: Northwest America, Cattle and Coal* (Boston: Little, Brown, 1976), 63–64; Marjane Ambler, *Breaking the Iron Bonds: Indian Control of Energy Development* (Lawrence: University Press of Kansas, 1990), 64–65; Michael Wenninger, "$1 Billion Coal Plant Discussed," *Billings Gazette,* November 29, 1972; and Michael Wenninger, "Battle Brews over Reservation's Coal," *Billings Gazette,* April 2, 1973.

2. Dell Adams to Northern Cheyenne Tribe, July 7, 1972 (quoted in Ziontz, Pirtle, Moresset, and Ernstoff, "Petition of the Northern Cheyenne Indian Tribe to Rogers C. B. Morton, Volume II: Appendix," January 7, 1974, A-142 to A-144,

K. Ross Toole Papers, series V, box 28, folder 2, Mansfield Library, University of Montana). For the Northern Cheyenne's average per capita income, see "Northern Cheyenne Highlights, Calendar Year 1969," 1970, 1, 8NN-75-92-206, box 14, folder "Evaluation of Ten Year Goals," National Archives, Denver, CO.

3. The few existing studies of Indian energy development generally portray tribal leaders as passive observers to a BIA-controlled system of exploitation. See Toole, *Rape of the Great Plains;* Ambler, *Breaking the Iron Bonds;* Donald Fixico, *The Invasion of Indian Country in the Twentieth Century American Capitalism and Tribal Natural Resources* (Niwot: University Press of Colorado, 1998); and Charles F Wilkinson, *Fire on the Plateau: Conflict and Endurance in the American Southwest* (Washington, DC: Island Press, 1999). A recent collection of essays, however, demonstrates how "from the beginning of energy development on Indian lands, Indian people have been actively engaged: as owners and lessees of resources, workers in the industries, consumers of electricity and gasoline, and developers of tribal energy companies, as well as environmentalists who sometimes challenge these enterprises." Sherry L. Smith and Brian Frehner, eds., *Indians and Energy: Exploitation and Opportunity in the American Southwest* (Santa Fe: SAR Press, 2010), 5. This work follows in the latter mold, explaining how through active engagement in energy development projects, tribal governments gained the knowledge and legal tools necessary to manage their own resources.

CHAPTER 1. THE TRIBAL LEASING REGIME

1. John Artichoker to James Canan, December 28, 1965 (quoted in Ziontz, Pirtle, Moresset, and Ernstoff, "Petition of the Northern Cheyenne Indian Tribe to Rogers C. B. Morton, Volume II: Appendix," January 7, 1974, A-1, K. Ross Toole Papers, series V, box 28, folder 2, Mansfield Library, University of Montana [hereafter Ziontz et al., "Northern Cheyenne Petition"]).

2. Ibid. To be clear, a small coal mine already existed on the reservation by the time Krueger submitted his proposal. This mine, however, supplied heating coal to reservation residents and did not export coal off reservation for industrial uses. Krueger's offer was the first proposal to develop Cheyenne coal in commercial quantities to be used for the industrial production of electricity. For the response from Billings BIA officials, see Ned O. Thompson, memo, January 7, 1966 (found in Ziontz et al., "Northern Cheyenne Petition," A-1 to A-2).

3. The quote describing the trustee duty as a cornerstone of Indian law comes from *Dept. of Interior v. Klamath Water Users Prot. Ass'n,* 532 U.S. 1, 11 (2001). In that opinion, the court merely affirmed the description of this duty as it appeared in Felix S. Cohen, *Cohen's Handbook of Federal Indian Law,* 2005 ed. (Newark: LexisNexis, 2005), 221. For further description of this trustee duty being akin to the common law duty of any fiduciary to responsibly manage a trust corpus for beneficiaries, see *United States v. Mitchell,* 463 U.S. 206, 225 (1983). John Marshall first acknowledged the United States' superior title to Indian lands in *Johnson v. M'Intosh,* reasoning the country's "discovery and conquest" of a new but inhabited land provided this right. Although he characterized the federal claim as an "absolute ultimate title," Marshall also admitted that Indians still possessed

the "legal as well as just" right of occupancy, which granted them certain sovereign rights within that territory. 21 U.S. 543, 592, 574 (1823). Later, in *Cherokee Nation v. Georgia,* Marshall elaborated that this unique indigenous land right did not create full sovereign Indian nations within the territory of the United States but instead made the tribes "domestic dependent nations . . . in a state of pupilage," likening their relationship to the United States as "that of a ward to his guardian." 30 U.S. 1, 17 (1831). This special status of Indian nations as "domestic dependent nations" forms the basis the United States' trustee duty to responsibly manage Indian land and resources. The last quote holding the federal government to the most exacting fiduciary standards comes from *Seminole Nation v. United States,* 187 U.S. 286, 297 (1942); see also Cohen, *Handbook of Federal Indian Law,* 2005 ed., 419–20, and Christian McMillen, *Making Indian Law: The Hualapai Land Case and the Birth of Ethnohistory* (New Haven: Yale University Press, 2007), 89–90.

4. Lyn Fisher, "Transcript of Notes of Conversation with J. Canan of the BIA Regarding the Northern Cheyenne Petition," June 15, 1979, 8, K. Ross Toole Papers, series V, box 28, folder 3, Mansfield Library, University of Montana.

5. Act of July 22, 1790, Public Law 1–33, § 4, 1 Stat. 137 (1790). The 1790 Non-Intercourse Act specifically prohibited the transfer of Indian land unless "duly executed at some public treaty, under the authority of the United States." As to major shifts in federal Indian policy, their justifications, and the impact on Indian land holdings, see notes 3–5 to introduction, above, and accompanying text.

6. As to John Collier's Indian New Deal, see generally notes 4–5 to introduction, above, and accompanying text.

7. E. A. Schwartz, "Red Atlantis Revisited: Community and Culture in the Writings of John Collier," *American Indian Quarterly* 18, no. 4 (Autumn 1994): 507–31. Schwartz argues that Collier's concept of a "Red Atlantis," which he developed after his first visit with the Taos Pueblo Indians in 1920, initially captured both the idea that Indians could offer lessons to white America on the values of group cohesion and also the recognition that this reservoir of knowledge required federal protection from capitalist attacks. Schwartz goes on to note, however, that Collier gradually subjugated the former concept to the latter, as he increasingly viewed his mission to slowly integrate—but not assimilate—Indians into American society and became less concerned with the direct transfer of Indian knowledge to whites. Other helpful works on Collier's life and his perception of American Indians include Lawrence C. Kelly, *The Assault on Assimilation: John Collier and the Origins of Indian Policy Reform* (Albuquerque: University of New Mexico Press, 1983); Kenneth R. Philp, *John Collier's Crusade for Indian Reform, 1920–1954* (Tucson: University of Arizona Press, 1977); Elmer Rusco, *A Fateful Time: The Background and Legislative History of the Indian Reorganization Act* (Reno: University of Nevada Press, 2000); Graham D. Taylor, *The New Deal and American Indian Tribalism: The Administration of the Indian Reorganization Act, 1934–45* (Lincoln: University of Nebraska Press, 1980); and Stephen Kunitz, "The Social Philosophy of John Collier," *Ethnohistory* 18, no. 3 (Summer 1971): 213–29.

8. For Collier's views on indirect administration, see Rusco, *Fateful Time,* 160–63 and 176. For a discussion of how, in practice, BIA's "technical assistance" could often preempt tribal decision making, see Thomas Biolsi, *Organizing the*

Lakota: The Political Economy of the New Deal on the Pine Ridge and Rosebud Reservations (Tucson: University of Arizona Press, 1998), 128–32.

9. Initially, two young attorneys, Cohen and Melvin Siegel, worked on the draft legislation. Little is known of Siegel, but Elmer Rusco reports that Lucy Cohen, Felix's wife, remembers Siegel remaining at the Department of the Interior for only a few months, and thus he could not have been a major contributor to Indian policy debates. Rusco, *Fateful Time,* 193. For the quotes describing Cohen's views on legal pluralism, see Dalia Tsuk Mitchell, *Architect of Justice: Felix S. Cohen and the Founding of American Legal Pluralism* (Ithaca: Cornell University Press, 2007), 57.

10. Mitchell, *Architect of Justice,* 82–90. The original bill's quotes are taken from ibid., at 83. It should be noted that Felix Cohen strongly opposed the BIA's position that the Indian Reorganization Act authorized only the federal government to issue corporate charters to Indian tribes. Cohen's stance, consistent with the argument he would make throughout his tenure, was that the right to incorporate was a fundamental right of any sovereign power. Because Congress had not explicitly extinguished this right for Indian tribes, they thus retained the authority to define their own powers through corporate charters. Felix Cohen to Frederic Kirgis, April 14, 1937, National Archives II, College Park, MD (hereafter NAII), RG 48, entry 809, box 12.

11. For the deliberations over Interior's bill, see Vine Deloria, Jr., and Clifford M. Lytle, *The Nations Within: The Past and Future of American Indian Sovereignty* (Austin: University of Texas Press, 1984), 66–79; Mitchell, *Architect of Justice,* 90–101; and Rusco, *Fateful Time,* 192–209. The final statute is at Indian Reorganization Act (IRA), Public Law 73-383, ch. 576, § 16 48 Stat. 984, 987 (1934), codified at 25 U.S.C. § 476 (2006). The quote from the Solicitor's Opinion is at Nathan Margold, U.S. Department of the Interior, "Powers of Indian Tribes," in *Opinions of the Solicitor: Indian Affairs* (Washington: Government Printing Office, 1946), 446. As to the novelty of Cohen's argument that tribal powers originated with the tribal sovereign, Charles Wilkinson demonstrates how this articulation of inherent sovereignty simply echoed sentiments expressed by Chief Justice John Marshall in *Worcester v. Georgia.* In that famous opinion, which Cohen cited liberally in his Solicitor's Opinion, Marshall stated that the "Indian nations had always been considered as distinct, independent, political communities, and the settled doctrine of the law of nations is that a weaker power does not surrender its independence—its right to self-government—by associating with a stronger, and taking its protection." 31 U.S. 515, 559 (1832). See also Charles F. Wilkinson, *American Indians, Time, and the Law* (New Haven: Yale University Press, 1987), 54–59. Marshall thus was first to advance the theory that tribes possessed all the powers of a sovereign, surrendering only their external sovereignty by virtue of Euro-American conquest, but Cohen resurrected this foundational principle after decades of its subjugation to the federal government's plenary power. See also David E. Wilkins, "The Era of Congressional Ascendancy over Tribes," in *American Indian Sovereignty and the U.S. Supreme Court* (Austin: University of Texas Press, 1997). Deloria's and Lytle's point about tribal powers is found at *Nations Within,* 159. These two authors also argue that when Congress slashed the Department of the Interior's original list

of tribal powers down to three it unwittingly expanded tribal sovereignty. They reason that although Interior's proposal included a long list of *potential* powers, these powers had to first be granted by the federal government in the form of a corporate charter tailor-made to the specific situation of each tribe. The final IRA, however, granted these three enumerated powers to any tribe organized under the statute, not to mention recognizing "all powers vested . . . by existing law." Thus, in the final law, although the BIA retained the right to approve tribes' organizing constitutions, once accepted it could not deny these powers. Deloria and Lytle, *Nations Within,* 142.

12. This premise of Indian powers mirrors the first principle Cohen would later articulate in his seminal work, *Handbook of Federal Indian Law.* Cohen, *Handbook of Federal Indian Law,* 2005 ed., 2. ("Nonetheless, there are some fundamental principles that underlie the entire field of federal Indian law. First, an Indian nation possesses in the first instance all of the powers of a sovereign state." Emphasis removed.) As to the debates within Interior, the Solicitor's Office itself was also divided over the proper interpretation of tribal powers. Within that office, the most prominent members of the divided camps were Assistant Solicitor Frederick Wiener and William Flannery, who invariably offered legal interpretations limiting tribal powers and affirming BIA's oversight role, versus Cohen, Solicitor Nathan Margold, and Charlotte Westwood, who offered consistently expansive interpretations of tribal sovereignty. On resolving inconsistencies between the Northern Cheyenne constitution and Interior's regulations relating to grazing leases, see William Flannery, memorandum to file, February 27, 1936, NAII, RG 48, entry 809, box 9; and Felix Cohen, memorandum to file, March 6, 1936, NAII, RG 48, entry 809, box 9. On disagreements over whether tribal governments can issue timber contracts, mineral leases, or agricultural leases to Indian cooperatives at a nominal sum, see William Flanery, memorandum to file, October 22, 1936, NAII, RG 48, entry 809, box 11; and William Flannery to Frederick Wiener, November 14, 1936, NAII, RG 48, entry 809, box 11. On whether a conflict of interest justifies the BIA's denial of a timber contract entered into by the Flathead Indians, see William Flanery to Frederick Wiener, December 1, 1936, NAII, RG 48, entry 809, box 11; and Charlotte Westwood to Frederick Wiener, December 1, 1936, NAII, RG 48, entry 809, box 9. On a dispute over whether the Paiute Indians of the Pyramid Lake Reservation can veto a mineral lease issued prior to the tribe's organization under the IRA, see Frederick Wiener to Nathan Margold, March 6, 1937, NAII, RG 48, entry 809, box 12; and unsigned memo to Assistant Secretary of the Interior, March 9, 1937, NAII, RG 48, entry 809, box 12.

13. The National Archives does not contain a copy of the BIA's initial proposal to streamline the process for developing Indian minerals, but it is referenced at Charles Fahy to the Geological Survey, August 8, 1933, NAII, RG 48, entry 809, box 2. No further action appears to have been taken on this proposal until 1935, when Felix Cohen drafted a memo on behalf of Solicitor Nathan Margold detailing the impacts of the proposed legislation. Nathan Margold to John Collier, February 6, 1935, NAII, RG 48, entry 809, box 6.

14. Cohen's "fiery retort" that was later amended to soften its tone can be found at Nathan Margold to John Collier, January 24, 1935, NAII, RG 48, entry 809,

box 6 (draft memorandum authored by Felix Cohen). Assistant Solicitor Rufus Poole's memo questioning the Solicitor's Office's role is at Assistant Solicitor Poole to Nathan Margold, January 28, 1935, NAII, RG 48, entry 809, box 6. Finally, as to Cohen's amendments, compare Nathan Margold to John Collier (draft memorandum authored by Felix Cohen), January 24, 1935, NAII, RG 48, entry 809, box 6 with Nathan Margold to John Collier, February 6, 1935, NAII, RG 48, entry 809, box 6. Cohen wrote in the margins of both the original draft and the memo from Poole, "revised as to form."

15. The final bill, along with Senate and House reports, can be found at S. 2638, H.R. 7681, 74th Cong. (1935). It is interesting to note the statutory language governing the secretary's veto authority is different for oil and gas leases than for other minerals. With respect to oil and gas, the final statute specified the secretary could reject bids for development "whenever in his judgment the interest of the Indians will be served by so doing." With other minerals, the statue authorized tribes to lease their interests only "with the approval of the Secretary of Interior." Compare 25 U.S.C. § 396(b) with § 396(a) (2006). For Interior's position that the 1938 IMLA controlled all transfers of Indian minerals, see Senate Select Committee on Indian Affairs, *Permitting Indian Tribes to Enter into Certain Agreements for the Disposition of Tribal Mineral Resources and for Other Purposes,* 97th Cong., 2d sess., June 10, 1982, 8–12; House Committee on Interior and Insular Affairs, *Permitting Indian Tribes to Enter into Certain Agreements for the Disposition of Tribal Mineral Resources and for Other Purposes,* 97th Cong., 2d sess., August 13, 1982, 9–13; and Senate Select Committee on Indian Affairs, *Hearings Before the Select Committee on Indian Affairs on S. 1894,* 97th Cong., 2d sess., 1982, 70–77.

16. Elmer Thomas's quote is found at S. 2638, 74th Cong., 1st sess., *Congressional Record* 79 (May 28, 1935): S8307. As for passage on the House's consent calendar, see H.R. 7626, S. 2689, 75th Cong., 3rd sess., *Congressional Record* 83 (May 2, 1938): H6057. Wiener's quotes are found at Frederick Wiener to Nathan Margold, March 5, 1936, NAII, RG 48, entry 809, box 9. Finally, the 1938 Indian Mineral Leasing Act is found at 25 U.S.C. § 396a–396g (2012). The act's implementing regulations in effect during the events detailed here are at 25 C.F.R. § 171.2 (1966).

17. Mining Act of 1866, 14 Stat. 251 (1866); Charles F. Wilkinson, *Crossing the Next Meridian: Land, Water, and the Future of the West* (Washington, DC: Island Press, 1992), 40–50; Samuel P. Hays, *Conservation and the Gospel of Efficiency: The Progressive Conservation Movement, 1890–1920* (New York: Atheneum, 1972), 67. For a discussion of the specific problems related to coal, see ibid., 82–83.

18. Hays, *Conservation and the Gospel of Efficiency,* 82–90; see also Wilkinson, *Crossing the Next Meridian,* 50–54. The 1920 Mineral Leasing Act is found at Mineral Leasing Act of 1920, Public Law 93–153, 41 Stat. 438 (1920), codified at 30 U.S.C. § 181 et seq. (2006).

19. Charles Fahy to the Geological Survey, August 8, 1933, NAII, RG 48, entry 809, box 2. The 1938 Indian Mineral Leasing Act is codified at 25 U.S.C. § 396a–g (2006), and the controlling regulations at the time of the Northern Cheyenne coal sales are at 25 C.F.R. § 171 (1966).

20. Richard White, *"It's Your Misfortune and None of My Own": A New History of the American West* (Norman: University of Oklahoma Press, 1991), 399.

21. James S. Cannon and Mary Jean Haley, *Leased and Lost: A Study of Public and Indian Coal Leasing in the West* (New York: Council on Economic Priorities, 1974), 21–23. Chapter 2, below, provides much greater detail of public officials' failure to carry out the mandates of the 1920 Mineral Leasing Act. See chapter 2, notes 7–12 and accompanying text.

22. The 1938 act's public bidding requirement for oil and gas is at 25 U.S.C. § 396b (2006). Nowhere in the act does it require bidding for minerals other than oil and gas, yet the controlling regulations requiring that all Indian minerals be "advertised for bids" are at 25 C.F.R. § 171.2 (1966).

23. The tribal resolution is at Northern Cheyenne Tribal Resolution No. 9 (66), February 10, 1966 (found in Ziontz et al., "Northern Cheyenne Petition, A-1 to A-2). Thompson's communication to BIA headquarters is located at Ned O. Thompson to Commissioner of Indian Affairs, April 2, 1966, Central Classified Files, 1958–75, Northern Cheyenne, decimal #332, box 21, RG 75, National Archives, Washington, DC. It is also described at Ziontz et al., "Northern Cheyenne Petition," A-3; and Toole, *Rape of the Great Plains*, 62.

24. The fixed royalty rate was provided in Charles Corke to James Canan, March 15, 1966 (found in Ziontz et al., "Northern Cheyenne Petition," A-4).

25. Interior put in place an acreage limit for Indian coal leases to prevent mining firms from securing a mineral development monopoly on any given reservation. The limitation, however, could be waived if a "larger acreage is in the interest of the [tribe] and is necessary to permit the establishment or construction of a thermal electric power plant or other industrial facilities on or near the reservation." 25 C.F.R. 171.9(b). For the rationale behind the acreage limitation, see Myron E. Saltmarsh, "Acting Area Realty Officer to Area Director," March 12, 1974, K. Ross Toole Papers, series V, box 28, folder 3, Mansfield Library, University of Montana. Washington officials actually authorized such a waiver for Northern Cheyenne development on numerous occasions. Fryer to James F. Canan, May 11, 1966, Central Classified Files, 1958–75, Northern Cheyenne, decimal #332, box 21, RG 75, National Archives, Washington, DC; and Ziontz et al., "Northern Cheyenne Petition," A-4. For further description of the acreage limit waiver and the reduction in royalties for coal burned on reservation, see Ziontz et al., "Northern Cheyenne Petition," A-4 to A-9.

26. The life of John Woodenlegs's famed grandfather is detailed in Wooden Leg and Thomas Bailey Marquis, *Wooden Leg: A Warrior Who Fought Custer* (Lincoln: University of Nebraska Press, 1962). Both the *Lincoln Star*'s editorial and Woodenlegs's reply ("From the President") were reprinted in the March 18, 1966, edition of the Northern Cheyenne newsletter, the *Morning Star News* (in author's possession). For Metcalf's introduction of Woodenlegs's letter on the Senate floor, see *Progress on the Northern Cheyenne Reservation*, 89th Cong., 2d sess., *Congressional Record* (February 21, 1966): S3391–92. Jim Canan describes his meeting with John Woodenlegs and reservation superintendent John Artichoker at the Billings, Montana, Northern Hotel to hear their strong support for coal development. Fisher, "Transcript of Notes of Conversation with J. Canan of the BIA Regarding

the Northern Cheyenne Petition," 2. Thompson's additional request for immediate action on the Cheyenne coal auction is found at Ned O. Thompson to Commissioner of Indian Affairs, May 6, 1966, Central Classified Files, 1958–75, Northern Cheyenne, decimal #332, box 21, RG 75, National Archives, Washington, DC. For a general description of Cheyenne actions to move along the process, from the Cheyenne's own attorneys, see Ziontz et al., "Northern Cheyenne Petition," A-5.

27. Steven H. Chestnut, "Coal Development on the Northern Cheyenne Reservation," in Commission on Civil Rights, *Energy Resource Development: Implications for Women and Minorities in the Intermountain West* (Washington, DC: Commission on Civil Rights, 1979), 162–63.

CHAPTER 2. POSTWAR ENERGY DEMANDS AND THE SOUTHWESTERN EXPERIENCE

1. For the tripling of American oil consumption from 1948 to 1972, see Daniel Yergin, *The Prize: The Epic Quest for Oil, Money, and Power* (New York: Simon and Schuster, 1991), 541.

2. As to the post–World War II deals that brought Middle Eastern oil to the world, see ibid., chapter 21. For the broad societal impacts of cheap oil, see ibid., 541–60; and Rudi Volti, *Cars and Culture: The Life Story of a Technology* (Westport, CT: Greenwood Press, 2004), 105–13.

3. Ivan Given, "Toward Energy Entity," *Coal Age*, November 1966; "The Coal Industry Makes a Dramatic Comeback," *Business Week*, November 4, 1972, 52–53; James S. Cannon and Mary Jean Haley, *Leased and Lost: A Study of Public and Indian Coal Leasing in the West* (New York: Council on Economic Priorities, 1974), 3 and 9–11; Bureau of Competition and Bureau of Economics, *Staff Report to the Federal Trade Commission on the Structure of the Nation's Coal Industry, 1964–1974* (Washington, DC: Federal Trade Commission, 1978), 159–61; and Peter Galuszka, "1911–1986: Coal's Rise and Fall and Rise," *Coal Age*, June 1986, 52–53.

4. "The Coal Industry's Controversial Move West," *Business Week*, May 11, 1974; Cannon and Haley, *Leased and Lost*, 3–6; and Bureau of Competition and Bureau of Economics, *Staff Report to the Federal Trade Commission*, 37–39, 156.

5. Alfred E. Flowers, "Energy and Security," *Coal Age*, August 1968, 59. The Clean Air Acts of 1963 and 1967 were the first statutes to focus on controlling air emissions, though they established a research regime to determine the best pollution control techniques, rather than setting specific air emission limits. Clean Air Act of 1963, Public Law 88–206, 77 Stat. 392 (1963); Air Quality Act of 1967, Public Law 90–148, 81 Stat. 48 (1967). The 1970 Clean Air Act, however, greatly expanded the federal government's role in regulating air pollution by establishing emission limits for both stationary and mobile sources. Clean Air Act of 1970, Public Law 91–604, 84 Stat. 1676 (1970); see also Office of Air and Radiation, Environmental Protection Agency, "History of the Clean Air Act," http://epa.gov/air/caa/caa_history.html (accessed April 2, 2013). For the federal government's increasing concern over sulfur emissions and industry's response, see "HEW Slaps Low Sulfur Limits on Fuel," *Coal Age*, January 1967; Alfred E. Flowers, "Cleaning the Air," *Coal Age*, November 1967; "Keys to Big Markets for Coal: Research and

Pollution Control," *Coal Age,* November 1967; and Alfred E. Flowers, "The Sulfur Question," *Coal Age,* April 1968. For the impacts of the 1967 oil embargo and 1970 Clean Air Act on promoting western coal, see "Western Coal Is Booming, but Serious Problems Lie Ahead," *Coal Age,* September 1971; "The Challenges and Opportunities in Mining Western Coal," *Coal Age,* April 1973; "Western Coal . . . Important Element in National Energy Outlook," *Coal Age,* April 1973; and "The Coal Industry's Controversial Move West," *Business Week,* May 11, 1974.

6. The figure noting that 80 percent of western coal underlies federal or tribal land comes from Cannon and Haley, *Leased and Lost,* 2. For more detailed description of the existing legal regime, and the wasteful practices it replaced, see, above, chapter 1, notes 17–18 and accompanying text.

7. Bennethum's quote is found in Cannon and Haley, *Leased and Lost,* 22. The historical data on the mineral leasing program are ibid., 4, and the figures on coal's average market value are ibid., 27. In 1975, the Federal Trade Commission issued a report on Indian mineral leasing that confirmed the general pattern of industry-led development, though it noted the Navajo tribe had nominated its own tracts of land for energy development. Federal Trade Commission, *Staff Report on Mineral Leasing on Indian Lands* (Washington, DC: Federal Trade Commission, October 1975), 20–23.

8. Cannon and Haley, *Leased and Lost,* 2–3.

9. Ibid., 4–6. As to coal lease concentration among large oil companies, see ibid., 9–11.

10. The quotes from both the General Accounting Office and the Council for Economic Priorities are found at Canon and Haley, *Leased and Lost,* 22.

11. Details of the moratoriums are found ibid., 24; and Sally Jacobsen, "The Great Montana Coal Rush," *Bulletin of the Atomic Scientists* 29, no. 4 (April 1973): 41. As to Interior's decision to lift the moratorium and impose new policies and procedures, see Thomas Kleppe, "Press Release: New Federal Coal Leasing Policy to Be Implemented under Controlled Conditions" (Department of the Interior, January 26, 1976), series 6: NCAI Committees and Special Issues, box 234, "Coal Regs. [II]," National Congress of American Indians Collection, National Museum of American Indians Archive Center, Suitland, MD (hereafter NCAI Collection).

12. Thomas Clarkin, *Federal Indian Policy in the Kennedy and Johnson Administrations, 1961–1969* (Albuquerque: University of New Mexico Press, 2001), 2–3; and Harvard Project on American Indian Economic Development, *The State of the Native Nations: Conditions under U.S. Policies of Self-Determination* (New York: Oxford University Press, 2008), 114–15. American Indian income levels are taken from Alan Sorkin, "Trends in Employment and Earnings of American Indians," in *Toward Economic Development for Native American Communities: A Compendium of Papers Submitted to the Subcommittee on Economy in Government of the Joint Economic Committee, Congress of the United States* (Washington, DC: Government Printing Office, 1969), 107, 109, 111, and 114–15. Educational statistics can be found at Margaret Connell Szasz, *Education and the American Indian: The Road to Self-Determination* (Albuquerque: University of New Mexico, 1999), 134. Mortality rates are located in Helen Johnson, "American Indians in Rural

Poverty," in *Toward Economic Development for Native American Communities*, 21–22. Some experts placed the life expectancy rate for reservation Indians even lower, at an astonishing forty-two years. House Committee on Interior and Insular Affairs, Subcommittee on Indian Affairs, *A Review of the Indian Health Program: Hearing Before the House Committee on Interior and Insular Affairs, Subcommittee on Indian Affairs*, 88th Cong., 1st sess., 1945, 21.

13. The BIA's assessment of tribal coal possessions is found at Federal Trade Commission, *Staff Report on Mineral Leasing on Indian Lands*, 6. The Geological Survey's estimate is found at Comptroller General of the United States, *Indian Natural Resources: Part 2, Coal, Oil, and Gas: Better Management Can Improve Development and Increase Indian Income and Employment: Report to the Senate Committee on Interior and Insular Affairs* (Washington DC: Government Printing Office, March 31, 1976), 2. Tribal assessments can be found in Joseph Jorgensen, ed., *Native Americans and Energy Development II* (Boston: Anthropology Resource Center and Seventh Generation Fund, 1984), 6; and Joseph Jorgensen, ed., *Native Americans and Energy Development* (Cambridge, MA: Anthropology Resource Center, 1978), 6.

14. Oil, gas, and uranium figures can be found in Comptroller General of the United States, *Indian Natural Resources: Part 2, Coal, Oil, and Gas*, 1–2; Federal Trade Commission, *Staff Report on Mineral Leasing on Indian Lands*, 8; and Marjane Ambler, *Breaking the Iron Bonds: Indian Control of Energy Development* (Lawrence: University Press of Kansas, 1990), 94, n. 8. The Harris quote is found in Ambler, *Breaking the Iron Bonds*, 94.

15. American Indian Policy Review Commission, *American Indian Policy Review Commission Final Report Submitted to Congress May 17, 1977*, vol. 1 (Washington, DC: Government Printing Office, 1977), 7.

16. For the Navajo's and Hopi's long knowledge of their energy minerals and how such knowledge influenced the formation of their tribal governments, see Peter Iverson, *Diné: A History of the Navajos* (Albuquerque: University of New Mexico Press, 2002), 133–36; Lawrence C Kelly, *The Navajo Indians and Federal Indian Policy, 1900–1935* (Tucson: University of Arizona Press, 1968); Kathleen P. Chamberlain, *Under Sacred Ground: A History of Navajo Oil, 1922–1982* (Albuquerque: University of New Mexico, 2009); and Charles F Wilkinson, *Blood Struggle: The Rise of Modern Indian Nations* (New York: Island Press, 2005), 284–87. As to the rapid growth of the American West after World War II, see Lisa McGirr, *Suburban Warriors: The Origins of the New American Right* (Princeton: Princeton University Press, 2001), esp. 25–29. For World War II and the effect of the Cold War on the American West generally, see Gerald D. Nash, *The American West Transformed: The Impact of the Second World War* (Bloomington: Indiana University Press, 1985); and Gerald D. Nash, *World War II and the West: Reshaping the Economy* (Lincoln: University of Nebraska Press, 1990).

17. The numbers on postwar energy demand in the American Southwest come from Brian Morton, "Coal Leasing in the Fourth World: Hopi and Navajo Coal Leasing, 1954–1977" (PhD diss., University of California, Berkeley, 1985), 49. Alexander's quote is found in Alvin M. Josephy, Jr., "The Murder of the Southwest," *Audubon*, July 1971, 54.

18. Peter Iverson covers Navajo oil and uranium mining in *The Navajo Nation* (Westport, CT: Greenwood Press, 1981), 77–80; and Iverson, *Diné,* 220. Benally's quote is found at Iverson, *Diné,* 219. For uranium mining impacts to the Navajo, see also Judy Pasternak, *Yellow Dirt: An American Story of a Poisoned Land and a People Betrayed* (New York: Free Press, 2010); Doug Brugge, Timothy Benally, and Esther Yazzie-Lewis, *The Navajo People and Uranium Mining* (Albuquerque: University of New Mexico Press, 2007); Peter Eichstaedt, *If You Poison Us: Uranium and Native Americans* (Santa Fe: Red Crane Books, 1994); and Ward Churchill and Winona LaDuke, "Native America: The Economics of Radioactive Colonization," in *Review of Radical Political Economics* 15 (Fall 1983): 9–19.

19. Jones's 1956 quote is found in Morton, "Coal Leasing in the Fourth World," 189. The 1959 quote is at Peter Iverson and Monty Roessel, eds., *For Our Navajo People: Diné Letters, Speeches and Petitions, 1900–1960* (Albuquerque: University of New Mexico Press, 2002), 253.

20. Todd Andrew Needham, "Power Lines: Urban Space, Energy Development and the Making of the Modern Southwest" (PhD diss., University of Michigan, 2006), 145–46.

21. Andrew Needham and Allen Dieterich-Ward, "Beyond the Metropolis: Metropolitan Growth and Regional Transformation in Postwar America," *Journal of Urban History* 35, no. 7 (2009): 950–51. For background on the Four Corners Plant and the Navajo Mine, see Iverson, *Navajo Nation,* 79–80; Morton, "Coal Leasing in the Fourth World," 7–8; and Josephy, "Murder of the Southwest," 55. To be clear, Utah International obtained its coal mining lease prior to entering an agreement to supply coal to the Four Corners Plant. As Andrew Needham demonstrates, however, from at least 1957 onwards, the power plant intended to use Navajo coal as its fuel source. Needham, "Power Lines," 219–20.

22. Information on WEST's Grand Plan is provided in Josephy, "Murder of the Southwest," 62–64; and Charles F. Wilkinson, *Fire on the Plateau: Conflict and Endurance in the American Southwest* (Washington, DC: Island Press, 1999), 220–22. The WEST official's quote is found in Wilkinson, *Fire on the Plateau,* 212. While Wilkinson does not provide a source for this quote, the same statistics on the size of this regional project appear in other contemporary accounts, e.g., Josephy, "Murder of the Southwest," 61; and "Power: WESTward Ho!," *Time* (October 2, 1964).

23. The decision to combine private and federal systems is covered in Needham, "Power Lines," 245–56. Needham also explains in great detail the environmental opposition to more federal dams in the Southwest and thus Udall's move to interconnect federal hydroelectric and irrigation systems with the WEST network. Ibid., chapter 7. Udall's first quote comes from John Redhouse, *Geopolitics of the Navajo Hopi Land Dispute* (Albuquerque: Redhouse/Wright Prod., 1985), 16 (quoting Suzanne Gordon, *Black Mesa: The Angel of Death* (New York: John Day, 1973)). His second quote is at "Udall Pledges Cooperation with Utilities: Prophecies Great Future," *Arizona Republic,* June 24, 1965.

24. Morton, "Coal Leasing in the Fourth World," 7–12.

25. Ibid., chapter 5. Morton blames the suboptimal leases on an overriding federal policy to develop the nation's coal at all cost. I question whether he confuses

policy goals with executive agency actions, as a close reading of his analysis reveals that federal agents simply failed to uphold the intent of mineral leasing legislation, which was to thoughtfully and systematically develop the nation's resources so as to avoid waste, prevent monopolies, and regulate mining in the public interest. For Morton, this failure to perform indicates that the 1920 Mineral Leasing Act and the 1938 Indian Mineral Leasing Act did not substantially alter nineteenth-century policies that encouraged, and failed to regulate, private exploitation of public and Indian resources. My view is different, as these Progressive reforms were intended to curtail many of the excesses of Gilded Age mining, but the federal agencies tasked with carrying out these directives simply were not provided the tools and resources for doing so. Still, we both arrive at the same conclusion: that the federal regime failed to efficiently develop western resources for the good of public and Indian owners. See Morton, "Coal Leasing in the Fourth World," chapter 7.

26. Lynn A. Robbins, "Energy Development and the Navajo Nation," in Jorgensen, *Native Americans and Energy Development*, 43. Smith's quote is found in Josephy, "Murder of the Southwest," 64.

27. Josephy, "Murder of the Southwest," 67.

28. Lynn A. Robbins, "Energy Development and the Navajo Nation," in Jorgensen, *Native Americans and Energy Development*, 43.

29. Josephy, "Murder of the Southwest," 64; Federal Trade Commission, *Staff Report on Mineral Leasing on Indian Lands*, 22–23.

30. For detailed accounts of Hopi villagers' struggle to prevent Black Mesa mining, see Wilkinson, *Fire on the Plateau;* Josephy, "Murder of the Southwest," 64–67; and Richard O. Clemmer, "Black Mesa and the Hopi," in Jorgensen, *Native Americans and Energy Development*. At the time the Black Mesa lease was issued, only six of the eighteen Hopi Tribal Council slots were filled validly. Josephy, "Murder of the Southwest," 66; Jorgensen, *Native Americans and Energy Development*, 26–27. Alvin Josephy's quote is found at Josephy, "Murder of the Southwest," 66. Charles Wilkinson uncovered John Boyden's clear conflict of interest. See Wilkinson, *Fire on the Plateau*, 169–71. The quote from the Hopi leader is found in Clemmer, "Black Mesa and the Hopi," in Jorgensen, *Native Americans and Energy Development*, 30.

31. Comptroller General of the United States, *Indian Natural Resources*, 11. Federal Trade Commission, *Staff Report on Mineral Leasing on Indian Lands*, 21 and 95.

32. Redhouse, *Geopolitics of the Navajo Hopi Land Dispute*, 16. The Peabody permit revoked by the tribal council was designed to provide coal to the proposed Mohave Generating Station, owned by the WEST-affiliated Southern California Edison Company.

33. Redhouse, *Geopolitics of the Navajo Hopi Land Dispute*, 16–17. Udall's quote is found in "News about Navajo Country," *Navajo Times*, July 29, 1965 (quoted in Redhouse, *Geopolitics of the Navajo Hopi Land Dispute*, 16). Littell's first quote comes from "Norman M. Littell Makes Statement," *Navajo Times*, November 18, 1965. The second quote is found in "Norman M. Littell, General Counsel for the Navajo Tribe, Makes Statement on Conflicting Claims of Navajo and Hopi Tribes," *Navajo Times*, January 6, 1966 (both are quoted in Redhouse, *Geopolitics of the Navajo Hopi Land Dispute*, 17).

34. Iverson, *Navajo Nation*, 105.

35. For environmental opposition to Grand Canyon dams and thus need to construct the Navajo Generating Station, see Needham, "Power Lines," chapter 7.

36. Wilkinson, *Blood Struggle*, 303–4; Josephy, "Murder of the Southwest," 62–64; and Redhouse, *Geopolitics of the Navajo Hopi Land Dispute*, 18–22. In 1948, the states of Wyoming, Colorado, Utah, New Mexico, and Arizona signed the Colorado River Compact to allocate water rights to this valuable western water source. Arizona received 50,000 acre-feet, but no provision was made for Navajo rights even though the majority of state land adjoining the river was on the reservation. Although these specific Navajo water rights had not been determined, the 1908 Supreme Court *Winters v. United States* decision held that the creation of Indian reservations implied a reserved right to the water flowing through or adjacent to them in order to fulfill the purpose of the reservation system, which was to provide a self-sufficient homeland to transform Indians from "wild" hunters and gatherers to "civilized" agricultural and pastoral people. 207 U.S. 564 (1908); and Cohen, *Federal Indian Law*, § 19.02 (2005). Under the *Winters* doctrine, the Navajo thus had a strong legal claim to a majority of Arizona's allocated Colorado River water. The deal orchestrated by the Department of the Interior and WEST, however, required the Navajo to give up this legal claim to 34,100 acre-feet of water, plus an additional 3,000 acre-feet for the town of Page, Arizona, where the Navajo Generating Station would be built.

37. Josephy's quote is found at Josephy, "Murder of the Southwest," 64. For more on the unfairness of the deal to supply water and coal to the Navajo Generating Station, see Philip Reno, "High, Dry, and Penniless," *The Nation* (March 29, 1975), and Wilkinson, *Fire on the Plateau*, 212–23. Josephy's presidential report, commissioned by President Nixon's chief of staff Bob Haldeman, is found at "The American Indian and the Bureau of Indian Affairs: A Study with Recommendations, February 11,1969," in *Red Power: The American Indians Fight for Freedom*, ed. Alvin Josephy, Jr. (New York: McGraw-Hill, 1971). As George Pierre Castile shows, Haldeman's memo requesting this report conveyed Nixon's desire to "show more heart, and that we care about people, and [Nixon] thinks the Indian problem is a good area for us to work in." Castile, *To Show Heart*; Thomas Clarkin, *Federal Indian Policy in the Kennedy and Johnson Administrations, 1961–1969* (Albuquerque: University of New Mexico Press, 2001), 76.

38. For the Navajo's Committee to Save Black Mesa, see Josephy, "Murder of the Southwest," 64. The quote from Hopi elders is found at Clemmer, "Black Mesa and the Hopi," in Jorgensen, *Native Americans and Energy Development*, 29. Clemmer's assessment of the Senate hearings is at Clemmer, "Black Mesa and the Hopi," in Jorgensen, *Native Americans and Energy Development*, 30.

39. For discussions on the rampant news coverage of Navajo and Hopi coal development, see Needham, "Power Lines," 312; and Clemmer, "Black Mesa and the Hopi," in Jorgensen, *Native Americans and Energy Development*, 28. The *New York Times* quote is found at Stan Steiner, "The Navajo vs. the Bulldozer," *New York Times*, March 20, 1971.

40. For Peter MacDonald's efforts to tap into rising nationalist sentiment among younger Navajo and his actions to control, not suspend, energy development, see Needham, "Power Lines," 309–39; and Andrew Needham, "'A Piece of the

Action': Navajo Nationalism, Energy Development, and Metropolitan Inequality," in Sheri L. Smith and Brian Frehner, *Indians and Energy: Exploitation and Opportunity in the American Southwest* (Santa Fe: School for Advanced Research Press, 2010), 210–14. The anticolonial quote comes from "Candidates for Chairman," *Navajo Times,* October 19, 1970, and the quote about reclaiming Navajo control of their resources is mentioned in Josephy, "Murder of the Southwest," 64.

41. Andrew Needham is especially helpful in understanding MacDonald's new approach to reservation development. As he explains, "By the time the tribe began questioning the electrical development on their land, most of the projects needed to generate electricity—strip mines, railroads, slurry pipes, power plants, and transmission lines—were already in place. As fixed capital, this geography resisted change imposed from the outside, leading Navajos to pursue regulatory instead of transformative change." Needham, "Power Lines," 261.

CHAPTER 3. "THE BEST SITUATION IN THEIR HISTORY"

1. Federal Trade Commission, *Staff Report on Mineral Leasing on Indian Lands* (Washington, DC: Federal Trade Commission, 1975), 41–43.

2. Ibid., 5; and James S. Cannon and Mary Jean Haley, *Leased and Lost: A Study of Public and Indian Coal Leasing in the West* (New York: Council on Economic Priorities, 1974), 31. To reiterate, these lease acreages represented only a tiny fraction of Indian lands actually opened to energy companies because the prospecting permits that led to leases gave mining firms access to much larger areas of the reservation to drill and explore. Once locating particularly desirable deposits, the coal companies then held exclusive rights to convert the large prospecting permit into a smaller lease, which authorized the actual removal of coal. As we will see in chapters 4 and 5, for American Indians, the presence of outside energy developers scouring their reservations for precious minerals was often as disturbing as the actual mining activities.

3. The lease royalty figures come from Cannon and Haley, *Leased and Lost,* 4; and Federal Trade Commission, *Staff Report on Mineral Leasing on Indian Lands,* 83–84. The Montana coal excise tax is discussed at K. Ross Toole, *The Rape of the Great Plains: Northwest America, Cattle and Coal* (Boston: Little, Brown 1976), 62–64. Ultimately, the Ninth Circuit Court of Appeals found Montana's taxation of tribal mineral revenues to be an unlawful infringement on tribal sovereignty. *Crow Tribe v. Montana,* 819 F.2d 895, 903 (9th Cir. 1987). The Supreme Court later clarified, however, that Montana's excise tax was unlawful not because states lacked the authority to tax non-Indian development of reservation resources but because Montana's tax was "extraordinarily high" and unfairly discriminated against the tribe's ability to market their coal. *Cotton Petroleum Corp. v. New Mexico,* 490 U.S. 163, 186–87, n. 17 (1989); for further clarification see also *Montana v. Crow Tribe,* 523 U.S. 696, 715 (1998) ("Montana, *Cotton Petroleum* thus indicates, had the power to tax Crow coal, but not at an exorbitant rate."). The Supreme Court thus left open the possibility of states imposing reasonable taxes on non-Indian operators extracting minerals from Indian reservations.

4. Charles P. Corke to William G. Lavell, November 3, 1966, Central Classified Files, 1958–75, Northern Cheyenne, decimal #332, box 21, RG 75, National Archives, Washington, DC; F. F. DuBray, Realty Officer to Realty Files, July 14, 1966 (found in Ziontz, Pirtle, Moresset, and Ernstoff, "Petition of the Northern Cheyenne Indian Tribe to Rogers C. B. Morton, Volume II: Appendix," January 7, 1974, A-9, K. Ross Toole Papers, series V, box 28, folder 2, Mansfield Library, University of Montana [hereafter Ziontz et al., "Northern Cheyenne Petition"]).

5. John R. White to Area Office Realty Files, May 9, 1973, 3, K. Ross Toole Papers, series V, box 28, folder 3, Mansfield Library, University of Montana; John Woodenlegs, "Statement Presented by John Woodenlegs, President, Northern Cheyenne to Conference called by Robert L. Bennett," October 5, 1966, Lee Metcalf Papers, General Correspondence, Collection No. 172, box 237, folder 237-1, Montana Historical Society, Digital Library and Archives.

6. Ziontz et al., "Northern Cheyenne Petition," A-11 to A-14. The first document that directly discusses Peabody's takeover of Sentry's interests is a May 18, 1967, letter from the coal company's attorneys to the BIA's Northern Cheyenne office. But several other documents make it clear that discussions for this takeover were ongoing between Peabody and the Northern Cheyenne since the end of 1966. For instance, on December 17, 1966, Tribal President John Woodenlegs told President Lyndon Johnson's National Advisory Committee on Rural Poverty that his tribe had recently "advertise[d] for coal prospecting, resulting in a very hopeful negotiation with the largest coal mining company in America." Similarly, early in 1967, Peabody Vice President Richard Miller wrote Senator Lee Metcalf of Montana to thank him and fellow Montana Senator Mike Mansfield, for their "offer to assist us with federal departments and agencies that may be helpful in the development of [Northern Cheyenne coal]." Metcalf's subsequent correspondence makes clear that the parties involved understood that Peabody's goals included the construction of a power plant on or near the reservation. John Woodenlegs, "Statement Presented to President's Johnson's National Advisory Committee on Rural Poverty," December 17, 1966, Lee Metcalf Papers, General Correspondence, Collection No. 172, box 237, folder 237-1, Montana Historical Society, Digital Library and Archives; Richard Miller to Lee Metcalf, February 15, 1967, Lee Metcalf Papers, General Correspondence, Collection No. 172, box 237, folder 237-1, Montana Historical Society, Digital Library and Archives; Lee Metcalf to Oakley Coffee, February 25, 1967, Lee Metcalf Papers, General Correspondence, Collection No. 172, box 237, folder 237-1, Montana Historical Society, Digital Library and Archives. The Northern Cheyenne's approval of the permit expansion is found at John Woodenlegs, "Resolution No. 70 (67)," October 16, 1967, Central Classified Files, 1958–75, Northern Cheyenne, decimal #332, box 21, RG 75, National Archives, Washington, DC. John White's quote is found in Ziontz et al., "Northern Cheyenne Petition," A-20.

7. James Canan to Commissioner of Indian Affairs, November 9, 1967, Central Classified Files, 1958–75, Northern Cheyenne, decimal #332, box 21, RG 75, National Archives, Washington, DC; Charles Corke to James Canan, November 16, 1967, Central Classified Files, 1958–75, Northern Cheyenne, decimal #332,

box 21, RG 75, National Archives, Washington, DC; A. F. Czarnowsky, memo, November 16, 1967 (found in Ziontz et al., "Northern Cheyenne Petition," A-21).

8. John R. White to Area Office Realty Files, 3. For a thorough description of the Peabody extension negotiations, see Ziontz et al., "Northern Cheyenne Petition," A-14 to A-23.

9. For the tribal council taking the initiative to offer more land for mining and Rowland's leadership in opening the entire reservation, see John R. White to Area Office Realty Files, 4. ("It is my belief that no one in the Bureau up to that point [of the Northern Cheyenne resolution] had suggested that another coal sale be held.") The actual tribal resolution authorizing the reservation-wide lease sale is found at John Woodenlegs, "Resolution No. 37 (68)," April 22, 1968, Central Classified Files, 1958–75, Northern Cheyenne, decimal #332, box 21, RG 75, National Archives, Washington, DC.

10. Reinholt Brust, memo, May 6, 1968 (found in Ziontz et al., "Northern Cheyenne Petition," A-55, n. 165); A. F. Czarnowsky, handwritten note, April 30, 1968 (found ibid., A-57).

11. Ziontz et al., "Northern Cheyenne Petition," A-63 to A-64. Rowland's quote is found in Toole, *Rape of the Great Plains*, 52.

12. A. F. Czarnowsky to Superintendent, Northern Cheyenne Agency, August 1, 1969 (found in Ziontz et al., "Northern Cheyenne Petition," A-80).

13. As to Peabody pressure, see "Northern Cheyenne Highlights, Calendar Year 1969," 1–2; and Ziontz et al., "Northern Cheyenne Petition," A-30 to A-31, A-82. At the same meeting where the tribal council considered Peabody's second bid, company executive J. H. Hobbs announced that his firm planned to exercise the lease option on its first permit and extract coal, but only if the tribe allowed Peabody to construct a railroad line to the coal fields. No doubt the implied assertion was that Peabody's willingness to continue the entire project also hung on the council approving Peabody's second bid. Tribal council actions to accept Peabody's second bid, issue a lease on the first coal permit, and negotiate for transportation infrastructure across the reservation can be found at Northern Cheyenne Tribal Resolution No. 20 (70), August 18, 1969 (found in Ziontz et al., "Northern Cheyenne Petition," A-81); Northern Cheyenne Tribal Council Resolution No. 10 (71), July 20, 1970 (found in Ziontz et al., "Northern Cheyenne Petition," A-35); and Northern Cheyenne Tribal Council Resolution No. 24 (70), August 31, 1970 (found in Ziontz et al., "Northern Cheyenne Petition," A-43).

14. W. H. Oestreicher to Allen Rowland, June 1, 1970, Central Classified Files, 1958–75, Northern Cheyenne, decimal #332, box 21, RG 75, National Archives, Washington, DC. For tribal council efforts to renegotiate royalty terms, see Ziontz et al., "Northern Cheyenne Petition," A-38 to A-44. The original August 1970 deal terms included minimum royalty payments that would commence in the third year of the contract to insure Peabody actively pursued production rather than simply sitting on the coal deposits until the market improved. The tribal council successfully negotiated an increase in these minimum royalty terms and secured a promise from Peabody to start paying them in the contract's first, not third, year. The BIA official assisting the tribe in these negotiations was Donald Maynard, and his quote regarding immediate tribal needs is found at Donald Maynard to Acting

Director, Economic Development, September 28, 1970, Central Classified Files, 1958–75, Northern Cheyenne, decimal #332, box 21, RG 75, National Archives, Washington, DC. There were also numerous other incidents where the Northern Cheyenne pushed back against Peabody and demanded amendments to their existing contracts, with the BIA's blessing. For instance, when Peabody's second permit came up for renewal in fall 1971 and it became clear the coal company needed Cheyenne water to fully develop the coal resources, the two sides hammered out an agreement where the tribe promised certain water rights in exchange for more advanced royalties. Ziontz et al., "Northern Cheyenne Petition," A-50 to A-55, A-84 to A-87. The new BIA superintendent Alonzo Spang—himself, an enrolled member of the tribe—encouraged the tribe's hard negotiating tactics, writing to President Rowland, "The Tribal Council has every right and power to request that leases be re-negotiated. Our [BIA] action would be required once negotiations are complete. We are in full agreement with the Council's request to have Peabody Coal Company become involved in a re-negotiation of the cited leases." Alonzo T. Spang to Allen Rowland, November 26, 1971 (found in Ziontz et al., "Northern Cheyenne Petition," A-85).

15. Maurice W. Babby to A. F. Czarnowsky, February 3, 1971 (found in Ziontz et al., "Northern Cheyenne Petition," A-89 to A-90). As to interest generated for Northern Cheyenne coal, see Allen Rowland to John R. White, October 1, 1970 (found in Ziontz et al., "Northern Cheyenne Petition," A-103).

16. Allen Rowland to John R. White, October 1, 1970 (found in Ziontz et al., "Northern Cheyenne Petition," A-103); Allen Rowland to John R. White, December 4, 1970 (found in Ziontz et al., "Northern Cheyenne Petition," A-105).

17. Ziontz et al., "Northern Cheyenne Petition," A-111 to A-113, A-121 to A-123.

18. Compare Regional Mining Supervisor to Superintendent, Northern Cheyenne Agency, April 28, 1971 (found in Ziontz et al., "Northern Cheyenne Petition," A-123) with John J. V. Pereau to Allen Rowland, April 30, 1971; and Office of Area Director to Superintendent, Northern Cheyenne Agency, May 18, 1971 (both found in Ziontz et al., "Northern Cheyenne Petition," A-123 to A-124). Final contract figures come from Rogers Morton, "Decision on Northern Cheyenne Petition," June 4, 1974, 2, Eloise Whitebear Pease Collection, 10:31, Little Bighorn College Archives, Crow Agency, MT; Ziontz et al., "Northern Cheyenne Petition," A-124 to A-127, A-136; and Alvin M. Josephy, Jr., "Agony of the Northern Plains," *Audubon* 75, no. 4 (July 1973): 92. These numbers include the previous Peabody permits.

19. Ziontz et al., "Northern Cheyenne Petition," A-126.

20. Ibid., A-137 to A-139. For further details of Consolidation's proposal, see chapter 1, above, notes 1–2 and accompanying text. Toole's quote is found at Toole, *Rape of the Great Plains,* 49.

CHAPTER 4. "THE MOST IMPORTANT TRIBE IN AMERICA"

1. U.S. Department of the Interior, *North Central Power Study* (Billings, MT: Bureau of Reclamation, 1971), 5; see also K. Ross Toole, *The Rape of the Great*

Plains: Northwest America, Cattle and Coal (Boston: Little, Brown, 1976), 19–20; and Marjane Ambler, *Breaking the Iron Bonds: Indian Control of Energy Development* (Lawrence: University Press of Kansas, 1990), 67–68. As for analyses of the projects' potential impacts, see Alvin M. Josephy, Jr., "Agony of the Northern Plains," *Audubon* 75, no. 4 (July 1973); Alvin M. Josephy, Jr., "Plundered West: Coal Is the Prize," *Washington Post,* August 26, 1973; and Lynton R. Hayes, *Energy, Economic Growth, and Regionalism in the West* (Albuquerque: University of New Mexico Press, 1980), 24. The National Academy of Sciences first articulated the concept of a "national sacrifice area" to meet the nation's energy needs in their 1974 report, *Rehabilitation Potential of Western Coal Lands.* Examining the coal industry's recent trend to locate mines on public and tribal lands in the western United States, this report noted vast difficulties in reclaiming strip mines in arid regions. Concluding that restoration of such lands to their previous ecological state "is not possible anywhere," the report suggested bluntly that the United States declare certain regions "National Sacrifice Areas," where reclamation would not even be attempted. James S. Cannon and Mary Jean Haley, *Leased and Lost: A Study of Public and Indian Coal Leasing in the West* (New York: Council on Economic Priorities, 1974), 7–8. Two years later, K. Ross Toole first applied the label of "national sacrifice area" to the Northern Plains. Toole, *Rape of the Great Plains,* 4.

2. Toole, *Rape of the Great Plains,* 52.

3. The letter is quoted in both Ambler, *Breaking the Iron Bonds,* 65; and Josephy, "Agony of the Northern Plains," 96.

4. This portion of the letter is quoted at Ziontz, Pirtle, Moresset, and Ernstoff, "Petition of the Northern Cheyenne Indian Tribe to Rogers C. B. Morton, Volume II: Appendix," January 7, 1974, A-144 to A-146, K. Ross Toole Papers, series V, box 28, folder 2, Mansfield Library, University of Montana (hereafter Ziontz et al., "Northern Cheyenne Petition").

5. Bert W. Kronmiller to Don Maynard, July 26, 1972 (found in Ziontz et al., "Northern Cheyenne Petition," A-126).

6. Interview with William L. Bryan, Jr., June 13, 2011, Bozeman, MT, in author's possession; and William L. Bryan, Jr., "Report on the July 1972 Activities of William L. Bryan, Jr., Northern Rocky Mountain Environmental Advocate," July 1972, in author's possession. Bryan's dissertation is found at William LaFrentz Bryan, Jr., "An Identification and Analysis of Power-Coercive Change Strategies and Techniques Utilized by Selected Environmental Change Agents" (PhD diss., University of Michigan, 1971).

7. Toole, *Rape of the Great Plains,* 52.

8. Bryan's first quote is from William L. Bryan, Jr., "The Northern Rocky Mountain Environmental Advocate," September 1, 1972, 3, in author's possession. His second quote and Gordon's warning come from William L. Bryan, Jr., "Report on the August 1972 Activities of William L. Bryan, Jr., Northern Rocky Mountain Environmental Advocate," August 1972, 4, in author's possession.

9. Interview with William L. Bryan, Jr., August 15, 2008, Bozeman, MT, in author's possession; William L. Bryan, Jr., "September Report on the Activities of William L. Bryan, Jr., Northern Rocky Mountain Environmental Advocate," September 1972, 1, in author's possession.

10. Interview with Marie Brady Sanchez, August 24, 2009, Lame Deer, MT, in author's possession; National Park Service, "Sand Creek Massacre Project, Volume 1: Site Location Study," 2000, 268–69, home.nps.gov/sand/parkmgmt/upload/site-location-study_volume-1-2.pdf (accessed December 30, 2014). Allotment came late to the Northern Cheyenne Reservation, and as a result the tribe retained a sizeable portion of their reservation in communal ownership. The 1926 Northern Cheyenne Allotment Act authorized allotment, but tribal rolls were not completed and the reservation was not fully surveyed until the early 1930s. At that time, there were only 1,457 qualified allottees, meaning 234,732.56 acres were apportioned to these individuals in lots of 160 acres or less, leaving 209,791.90 acres in tribal ownership. The 1934 Indian Reorganization Act ended the practice of allotment, and subsequent opening of "surplus" land to white settlers, before this additional land could be distributed. Over time, the tribal government reacquired 46,781 allotted acres, giving the tribe 62 percent ownership by the 1970s. Of the remaining 38 percent, much of it had not been granted to the allottees in outright fee, thus the BIA retained trust oversight over this allotted land. See Testimony of Bert W. Kronmiller, Tribal Attorney, "To Grant Minerals, Including Oil, Gas, and Other Natural Deposits, on Certain Lands in the Northern Cheyenne Indian Reservation, Montana, to Certain Indians," Hearings Before the House Subcommittee on Indian Affairs, Committee on Interior and Insular Affairs, March 28, 1968, 11–12, folder "Northern Cheyenne 14," box 257, no. 1 (reel 167), Native America: A Primary Record, series 2: Assn. on American Indian Affairs Archives, General and Tribal Files, 1851–1983, microfilm collection published by Primary Source Media, filmed from the holdings of the Seeley G. Mudd Library, Princeton University (hereafter Assn. on American Indian Affairs Archives); Petition of Writ of Certiorari at 8, n. 5, *Northern Cheyenne v. Hollowbreast*, 425 U.S. 649 (1976) (No. 75-145).

11. Interview with Marie Brady Sanchez, August 24, 2009, Lame Deer, MT, in author's possession.

12. For a concise discussion of federal funding increases for Indian programs during the 1960s, including Indian higher education, and its contribution to increased Indian activism, see Joane Nagel, *American Indian Ethnic Renewal: Red Power and the Resurgence of Identity and Culture* (New York: Oxford University Press, 1996), 122–30. Nagel also provides an apt description of AIM's strategic shift, ibid., 166–68. Marie Sanchez's meeting with Russell Means is detailed in Michael Parfit, *Last Stand at Rosebud Creek: Coal, Power, and People* (New York: E. P. Dutton, 1980), 85–86.

13. Bryan, "September Report on the Activities of William L. Bryan, Jr.," 2.

14. Parfit, *Last Stand at Rosebud Creek,* chapters 20–21 and 23–24.

15. Josephy, "Agony of the Northern Plains"; David Earley, "Group Forms to Battle Strip Mining," *Billings Gazette,* April 27, 1972. Charter's quote is found at Calvin Kentfield, "New Showdown in the West," *New York Times,* January 28, 1973.

16. Earley, "Group Forms to Battle Strip Mining"; see also Northern Plains Resource Council website, "History," http://www.northernplains.org/about/history. McRae's quote is at Parfit, *Last Stand at Rosebud Creek,* 96.

17. Denise Curran, "Voice of Land Speaks Up," *Billings Gazette,* November 16, 1972.

18. Northern Plains Resource Council, "Newsletter," Billings, MT, June–July 1972, in author's possession; Northern Plains Resource Council, "Newsletter," Billings, MT, October–November 1972, in author's possession; Curran, "Voice of Land Speaks Up"; Parfit, *Last Stand at Rosebud Creek,* 91; Bryan, "September Report on the Activities of William L. Bryan, Jr."; Glenn Fowler, "Harry M. Caudill, 68, Who Told of Appalachian Poverty," December 1, 1990, *New York Times.*

19. Northern Plains Resource Council, "Newsletter," Billings, MT, October–November 1972; Northern Plains Resource Council, "Newsletter," Billings, MT, December–January 1972, 1973; interview with William L. Bryan, Jr., June 13, 2011, Bozeman, MT, in author's possession; and William L. Bryan, Jr., "October Activities of William L. Bryan, Jr.," October 1972, in author's possession.

20. Mining firms with prospecting crews active on the Northern Cheyenne Reservation in fall 1972 included Peabody, Consolidation, Chevron, and AMAX, as well as local speculators Bruce Ennis and Norsworthy & Reger, Inc. As to damages caused by some of these companies, see Ziontz et al., "Northern Cheyenne Petition," A-131 to A-134 and A-143. For the actual formation of the NCLA, see Bryan, "October Activities of William L. Bryan, Jr.," 3.

21. Bill Bryan notes how the AIM caravan's arrival disrupted the first attempt to organize the NCLA. Bryan, Jr., "October Activities of William L. Bryan, Jr.," 2. Organized by several Indian activist groups but led by AIM, the Trail of Broken Treaties was part of AIM's transition away from focusing on the civil rights of urban Indians and toward a broader message of enforcing tribal treaty rights. Ward Churchill and James Vander Wall, *Agents of Repression: The FBI's Secret Wars against the Black Panther Party and the American Indian Movement* (Boston: South End Press, 1990), 121–22. For more on the Trail of Broken Treaties and AIM's leadership, see Vine Deloria, *Behind the Trail of Broken Treaties: An Indian Declaration of Independence* (New York: Dell Publishing, 1974); Paul Chaat Smith and Robert Allen Warrior, *Like a Hurricane: The Indian Movement from Alcatraz to Wounded Knee* (New York: New Press, 1996), part 2; and Charles F. Wilkinson, *Blood Struggle: The Rise of Modern Indian Nations* (New York: Island Press, 2005), 139–43. For a history of the Red Power Movement that began before AIM's ascendance, see Bradley Shreve, *Red Power Rising: The National Indian Youth Council and the Origins of Native Activism* (Norman: University of Oklahoma Press, 2011).

22. Rising Sun's first quote and Bixby's response are found at Nagel, *American Indian Ethnic Renewal,* 169. For a discussion of generational differences between American Indians' reactions to the Trail of Broken Treaties, see ibid., at 136–37. Rising Sun's second quote is ibid., 41–42. For the Northern Cheyenne's condemnation of the BIA takeover, see Allen Rowland, "Northern Cheyenne Resolution No. 64 (73)," November 14, 1972, John Melcher Papers, series 1, box 115, folder 5, Mansfield Library, University of Montana. Two years after this condemnation, dozens of AIM members returned to the Northern Cheyenne Reservation after the organization's armed standoff with federal agents at Wounded Knee, South Dakota. AIM members declared that their mission was only to establish a legal aid center and

perhaps organize a Lame Deer chapter, but once again Cheyenne residents harassed the activists. This time, federal agents had to be called in to protect the peace. Jim Crane, "AIM to Aid in Opposing Coal Development," November 24, 1974 *Missoulian* (Missoula, MT); "AIM Organizing at Lame Deer," August 15, 1974, *Missoulian;* and "Most AIM Backers Leave Lame Deer," August 25, 1974, *Missoulian*. Interestingly, the visiting AIM activists camped at the home of Marie and Chuck Sanchez, who participated in the protest at Wounded Knee and then hosted Russell Means, Leonard Peltier, and about thirty other AIM members after the event. Marie Sanchez dismissed the publicity this second visit generated, explaining, "They [local reporters] just wanted to sell papers." In her recollection, AIM's presence on the reservation was a non-event and its contribution to the anti-coal cause minimal. Interview with Marie Brady Sanchez, August 24, 2009, Lame Deer, MT, in author's possession.

23. Results from the Northern Cheyenne Research Project and the tribal members' quotes are found at Jean Nordstrom et al., *The Northern Cheyenne Tribe and Energy Development in Southeastern Montana* (Lame Deer, MT: Northern Cheyenne Research Project, 1977), 174–75.

24. Ibid. Woodenlegs's statement is at "Proceedings of the Native American, Environmentalist, and Agriculturalist Workshop" (Northern Rockies Action Group, December 10, 1975), 14, in author's possession.

25. Tribal quotes regarding disruptions to the community are found at Nordstrom et al., *Northern Cheyenne Tribe and Energy Development,* 166, 164, and 161, respectively. For comparison sake, only 9 percent listed environmental impacts as coal mining's worst possible effect; another 7 percent feared most the loss of land and water that could be used for other industrial development. Rising Sun's and Sootkis's quotes come from George Wilson, "Indian Coal Fight Tests U.S. Policies," *Washington Post,* June 11, 1973.

26. For years, George Bird Grinnell's tome provided the primary account of the Northern Cheyenne's flight from Indian Territory back to Montana. *The Fighting Cheyennes* (New York: Scribner's, 1915), 383–411. Recently, James Leiker and Ramon Powers have supplied a much-needed update to this dramatic tale that includes recollections of the event and its contested meaning along the Great Plains. This work is especially instructive for understanding how the Northern Cheyenne's collective memory of this nineteenth-century ordeal serves to unite the tribe. *The Northern Cheyenne Exodus in History and Memory* (Norman: University of Oklahoma Press, 2011), esp. 183–195. Several other books relay the events as remembered by the participants. Edger Beecher Bronson, *Reminiscences of a Ranchman* (New York: McClure, 1908) 139–97; E. A. Brininstool, *Dull Knife: A Cheyenne Napoleon* (Hollywood: E. A. Brininstool, 1935); Thomas Marquis, trans., *Wooden Leg: A Warrior Who Fought Custer* (Lincoln: University of Nebraska Press, 1957), 321; and John Stands in Timber and Margot Liberty, *Cheyenne Memories,* (New Haven: Yale University Press, 1998), 232–37. Other secondary works dedicate substantial focus to the flight, including Stan Hoig, *Perilous Pursuit: The U.S. Cavalry and the Northern Cheyenne* (Boulder: University Press of Colorado, 2002); John H. Monnet, *Tell Them We Are Going Home: The Odyssey of the Northern Cheyennes* (Norman: University of Oklahoma Press, 2001); Orlan J. Svingen, *The*

Northern Cheyenne Indian Reservation, 1877–1900 (Niwot: University Press of Colorado, 1993), 19–24; Tom Weist, *A History of the Cheyenne People* (Billings, MT: Montana Council for Indian Education, 1977), 80–87; and Verne Dusenberry, "The Northern Cheyenne: All They Have Asked Is to Live in Montana," *Montana: The Magazine of Western History* 5 (Winter 1955): 28–30. For an alternative account arguing the Northern Cheyenne were awarded a reservation due to the tribe's selective adoption of settled agriculture, see James Allison, "Beyond the Violence: Indian Agriculture, White Removal, and the Unlikely Construction of the Northern Cheyenne Reservation, 1876–1900," *Great Plains Quarterly* 32, no. 2 (Spring 2012): 91–111.

27. Bill Parker's quote is found in "Proceedings of the Native American, Environmentalist, and Agriculturalist Workshop," 9–10. The tribe's comments opposing the Colstrip Power Plant are at Tom Scheuneman, "Statement of the Northern Cheyenne Tribe before the State of Montana Department of Natural Resources and Conservation," December 30, 1974, 3–4, Montana Energy Division Records, 1972–1990, record series 328, box 15, DNRC Public Hearings on Colstrip 3 and 4, Montana Historical Society, Digital Library and Archives (emphasis removed). Tribal comments related to air shed redesignation are at the Northern Cheyenne Research Project, "The Northern Cheyenne Air Quality Redesignation Request and Report," December 11, 1976, 3–10, in author's possession. Text on the tribe's official stationery is noted at Ambler, *Breaking the Iron Bonds*, 8. And finally, the last quote from the young tribal member comes from Nordstrom et al., *Northern Cheyenne Tribe and Energy Development in Southeastern Montana*, 174.

28. The text from Bill Bryan's pamphlet is found at Michael Wenninger, "$1 Billion Coal Plant Discussed," *Billings Gazette*, November 29, 1972; and William L. Bryan, Jr., "Northern Rocky Mountain Environmental Advocate, November Activities of William L. Bryan, Jr.," November 1972, 2, in author's possession. Bill Bryan provided the "Coal: Black Death" poster, and it is in the author's possession.

29. Unfortunately, Toole cites no sources for this meeting between Dahle and Crossland, and subsequent accounts simply cite Toole. Thus it is difficult to verify the meeting took place or assess its impact on tribal leaders. Toole, *Rape of the Great Plains*, 53–55; and Ambler, *Breaking the Iron Bonds*, 65. For the subsequent NCLA meetings and Rowland's and Spang's support, see Wenninger, "$1 Billion Coal Plant Discussed"; Michael Wenninger, "Cheyennes Eye Coal Proposal," *Billings Gazette*, November 30, 1972; Michael Wenninger, "Indians Mull Coal Referendum," *Billings Gazette*, December 1, 1972; and Bryan, "November Activities of William L. Bryan, Jr."

30. Attendees at this December 7 meeting are detailed in William L. Bryan, Jr., "Northern Rocky Mountain Environmental Advocate, December Activities of William L. Bryan, Jr.," December 1972, in author's possession; and Betty Clark to William Byler, December 1972, folder "Northern Cheyenne 16," box 257, no. 1 (reel 167), Native America: A Primary Record, series 2: Assn. on American Indian Affairs Archives, General and Tribal Files, 1851–1983. For NARF's founding and experience defending southwestern Indians, see Native American Rights Fund, *Announcements* 1, no. 1 (June 1972), 3–4 and 13. Brecher's personal involvement

with NARF is detailed in Michael Wenninger, "Northern Cheyenne to Fight Coal Complex," *Billings Gazette,* January 27, 1973.

31. Wenninger, "Northern Cheyenne to Fight Coal Complex."

32. For the suspension of drilling activities, see Ziontz et al., "Northern Cheyenne Petition," A-177. Rowland's and Dahle's quotes come from Wilson, "Indian Coal Fight Tests U.S. Policies." Gardner's quote is at Ben Franklin, "Indian Tribe in Montana Weighs Major Offer to Strip Mine Coal as Profitable but Perilous," *New York Times,* February 5, 1973.

33. As to Joseph Brecher's alienating style, see interview with William L. Bryan, Jr., June 13, 2011, Bozeman, MT, in author's possession. For tribal council efforts to draft tax and reclamation codes, see Franklin, "Indian Tribe in Montana Weighs Major Offer to Strip Mine Coal as Profitable but Perilous." The resolution canceling all existing coal deals is at Allen Rowland, "Resolution No. 132 (73): A Resolution of the Northern Cheyenne Tribal Council Relating to the Cancellation and Termination of All Existing Coal Permits and Leases on the Northern Cheyenne Reservation," March 5, 1973, Eloise Whitebear Pease Collection, 10:31, Little Bighorn College Archives, Crow Agency, MT.

34. To be clear, the Northern Cheyenne's initial grounds for terminating its leases rested on the BIA violating 25 C.F.R.§ 177.4, but once the tribe hired the Seattle law firm of Ziontz, Pirtle, Moresset, and Ernstoff, it greatly expanded its legal arguments. Filed on January 7, 1974, the official petition listed thirty-six violations of the law, each of which the tribe argued provided grounds to void the coal contracts. Steven Chestnutt, "Coal Development on the Northern Cheyenne Reservation," in Commission on Civil Rights, *Energy Resource Development: Implications for Women and Minorities in the Intermountain West* (Washington, DC: Government Printing Office, 1979), 165–71. Rowland's comparison of the Northern Cheyenne's situation to the Navajo and Hopi tribes is found in Allen Rowland to James Canan, March 9, 1973, 3, Lee Metcalf Papers, General Correspondence, Collection No. 172, box 219, folder 219–3, Montana Historical Society, Digital Library and Archives. Dahle's quote is in Nancy Cardwell, "Cheyenne's Last Stand?: Indians Fight New Battle in Montana, To Limit Coal Mining on Reservation," *Wall Street Journal,* September 10, 1975.

35. 25 C.F.R. § 177.4(a)(1) (1970); National Environmental Policy Act, Public Law 91–190, § 102, 83 Stat. 853, 854 (1970) (codified at 42 U.S.C. § 4332 (2006)). In 1972, the comptroller general failed to find documentation of the required "technical examinations" for any Indian mineral leases previously approved by the BIA. United States General Accounting Office, *Administration of Regulations for Surface Exploration, Mining, and Reclamation of Public and Indian Coal Lands* (Washington, DC: Government Printing Office, 1972), 13. In response, the BIA took the position that staff need not physically perform the technical examination as long as this requirement could be fulfilled by the "data available in the offices of the USGS and BIA plus the familiarity of the field offices employees with the land." John Crow to BIA Area Directors, November 17, 1972, Lee Metcalf Papers, General Correspondence, Collection No. 172, box 219, Montana Historical Society, Digital Library and Archives. Only after offering this post hoc rationale did the

Billings area office direct the Northern Cheyenne and Crow reservation superintendents to document how they fulfilled the technical examination requirements for leases and permits already issued. Maurice Babby to Superintendents, Crow and Northern Cheyenne Agencies, December 12, 1972, Lee Metcalf Papers, General Correspondence, Collection No. 172, box 219, folder 219–3, Montana Historical Society, Digital Library and Archives. K. Ross Toole argues this was "a blatant attempt, *ex post facto,* to doctor the files." Toole, *Rape of the Great Plains,* 59. For the Department of the Interior's position that NEPA did not apply to agency actions for Indian assets, see United States General Accounting Office, *Administration of Regulations for Surface Exploration, Mining, and Reclamation of Public and Indian Coal Lands;* and Harrison Loesch to John Dingell, November 12, 1971, folder "Natural Resources," box 147, no. 4 (reel 71), Native America: A Primary Record, series 2: Assn. on American Indian Affairs Archives, General and Tribal Files, 1851–1983. In 1975, the Ninth Circuit Court of Appeals rejected this argument, making clear NEPA applied to federal actions managing Indian resources. Further, although no federal court has determined whether compliance with the "technical examination" of 25 C.F.R. part 177 satisfies NEPA's procedural requirements for an environmental review of any major federal action, the Ninth Circuit held that BIA's compliance with NEPA's requirements renders the requirements of part 177 moot. *Davis v. Morton,* 469 F.2d 593 (10th Cir. 1972). Ambler's quote comes from Ambler, *Breaking the Iron Bonds,* 69.

36. Richard Nixon, "Special Message to Congress on Indian Affairs," July 8, 1970, The American Presidency Project, ed. Gerhard Peters and John T. Woolley, http://www.presidency.ucsb.edu/ws/index.php?pid=2573. For Nixon's message as just a continuation of the previous administrations' Indian policy, see Thomas Clarkin, *Federal Indian Policy in the Kennedy and Johnson Administrations, 1961–1969* (Albuquerque: University of New Mexico Press, 2001); and George Pierre Castile, *To Show Heart: Native American Self-Determination and Federal Indian Policy, 1960–1975* (Tucson: University of Arizona Press, 1998), chapters 1–3. In fact, Lyndon Johnson provided his own message to Congress two years earlier, which contained some of the same policy language: "I propose a new goal for our Indian programs: A goal that ends the old debate about 'termination' of Indian programs and stresses self-determination; a goal that erases old attitudes of paternalism and promotes partnership self-help." Lyndon B. Johnson, "Special Message to the Congress on the Problems of the American Indian: 'The Forgotten American,'" March 6, 1968, The American Presidency Project, ed. Gerhard Peters and John T. Woolley, http://www.presidency.ucsb.edu/ws/index.php?pid=28709#axzz1ckaZdTec.

37. Rogers Morton, "Decision on Northern Cheyenne Petition," June 4, 1974, Eloise Whitebear Pease Collection, 10:31, Little Bighorn College Archives, Crow Agency, MT. Morton actually denied most of the Northern Cheyenne's claims but did find that the BIA violated acreage limitations placed on the size of mineral leases and that the agency had not yet conducted the proper environmental analyses required by NEPA. On the original question of whether the BIA conducted the proper technical examination, Morton punted, requesting more information on agency actions to fulfill this requirement. The point, however, was moot since Morton already demanded a NEPA-style environmental analysis before mining could

commence. Rowland is quoted in John J. Fialka, "The Indians, the Royalties, and the BIA," *Civil Rights Digest* (Winter 1978): 29.

38. Ambler, *Breaking the Iron Bonds,* 69. For Northern Cheyenne meeting with Montana's congressional delegation, see Roger, "Memo on the Meeting on Northern Cheyenne Coal Lease," August 1, 1973, Lee Metcalf Papers, General Correspondence, Collection No. 172, box 218, folder 218-4, Montana Historical Society, Digital Library and Archives; Dorothy Tenenbaum, "Memo to File," September 7, 1973, Lee Metcalf Papers, General Correspondence, Collection No. 172, box 218, folder 218-4, Montana Historical Society, Digital Library and Archives; and Mike Mansfield and Lee Metcalf to Roy E. Huffman, September 12, 1973, Lee Metcalf Papers, General Correspondence, Collection No. 172, box 218, folder 218-4, Montana Historical Society, Digital Library and Archives. For tribal efforts to develop a mining enterprise business plan, see Alonzo Spang to Allen Rowland, August 28, 1973, 8NN-75-92-206, box 14, folder "Comprehensive Plan for the Northern Cheyenne Res.," National Archives, Denver; and Northern Cheyenne Tribal Council, "A Proposal to Develop a Preliminary Business Plan for the Development of Coal Reserves and Related Industry on Tribally Owned and Controlled Lands on the Northern Cheyenne Reservation," February 1974, Bradley H. Patterson Files, box 4, Northern Cheyenne-Coal, Gerald R. Ford Library, Ann Arbor, MI. The tribal council's tour of Peabody facilities is detailed in Fialka, "Indians, the Royalties, and the BIA," 22.

39. Northern Cheyenne Tribal Council, "A Proposal to Develop a Preliminary Business Plan for the Development of Coal Reserves and Related Industry on Tribally Owned and Controlled Lands on the Northern Cheyenne Reservation," 2.

CHAPTER 5. DETERMINING THE SELF

Epigraph. Washington Irving, *The Adventures of Captain Bonneville* (New York: John B. Alden, 1886), 138–39.

1. H. J. Armstrong to Commissioner of Indian Affairs, March 24, 1882, 6491, Letters Received—Office of Indian Affairs, RG 75, National Archives (quoted in Frederick Hoxie, *Parading through History: The Making of the Crow Nation in America, 1805–1935* [New York: Cambridge University Press, 1995], 21).

2. The quotes come from Hoxie, *Parading through History,* 29. Hoxie's coverage of the Sword Bearer incident is found ibid., 154–64. Other accounts of this incident are summarized in Colin Calloway, "Sword Bearer and the 'Crow Outbreak' of 1887," *Montana: The Magazine of Western History* 36, no. 4 (Autumn 1986): 38–51.

3. Patrick Stands Over Bull, "Statement from the Crow Tribal Chairman, Patrick Stands," August 29, 1975, 1, Joseph Medicine Crow Collection, 24:12, Little Bighorn College Archives, Crow Agency, MT (hereafter LBC Archives).

4. Ibid., 6.

5. Crow Coal, Inc.'s proposal is at Joseph Rawlins to Crow Industrial Development Commission, May 10, 1966, Eloise Whitebear Pease Collection, 16:54, LBC Archives. For background on the company and its formation, see "Articles of Incorporation of Crow Coal, Inc.," January 7, 1966, Eloise Whitebear Pease

Collection, 16:54, LBC Archives; Joseph Rawlins to Eloise Pease, October 6, 1966, Eloise Whitebear Pease Collection, 16:54, LBC Archives; and A. F. Czarnowsky, Deputy Regional Mining Supervisor, to Superintendent, Northern Cheyenne Reservation, February 4, 1965, 8NN-075-91-008, box 8, folder "Coal Leasing and Permit (Sene and Scott)," National Archives, Denver.

6. The federal government's 1910 assessment of Crow Reservation land and resources is found in House Committee on Indian Affairs, *Sale of Certain Land, etc. within the Diminished Crow Reservation, Mont.*, 61st Cong., 2d sess., 1910, H. Rep. 1495, 2. Yellowtail is quoted in Megan Benson, "The Fight for Crow Water: Part 1, The Early Reservation Years through the New Deal," *Montana: The Magazine of Western History* 57, no. 4 (Winter 2007): 36. The Crow Allotment Act is at Act of June 4, 1920, Public Law 66-239, 41 Stat. 751 (1920).

7. For oil and gas activity on the Crow Reservation, see Superintendent, Crow Indian Agency, to Area Director et al., Re: The Ten Year Goals of the Crow Reservation, July 13, 1964, 2–3, 8NN-75-92-206, box 9, folder "Res. Programs—Crow Res.," National Archives, Denver; and John Cummins and Otto Weaver, "Application to Lease Tribal Lands for Oil and Gas Purposes," May 17, 1963, 8NS-075-97-341, box 11, folder "Confidential Crow Requests for Oil and Gas Lease Sale," National Archives, Denver. As of 1967, the Department of the Interior reported the tribe had received only $3,665,000 in mineral revenue since 1920, with 40 percent of this coming over the previous five years. Senate Committee on Interior and Insular Affairs, *Granting Minerals, Including Oil and Gas, on Certain Lands in the Crow Reservation, Mont., to Certain Indians, and for Other Purposes,* 90th Cong., 1st sess., 1967, S. Rep. 690, 3. The law transferring reservation minerals to the Crow in perpetuity is at *An Act to Grant Minerals, Including Oil and Gas, on Certain Lands in the Crow Indian Reservation, Montana, to Certain Indians, and for other Purposes,* Public Law 90-308, 82 Stat. 123 (1968). In passing this law, Congress thwarted the expectation of individual allottees and surface owners who, under the 1920 Allotment Act, would have received mineral rights at the conclusion of the fifty-year period reserving these rights to the tribe. Despite this sudden change in future ownership, no widespread opposition seems to have materialized on the Crow Reservation. On the neighboring Northern Cheyenne Reservation, however, allottees challenged a similar law passed the same year transferring their minerals to tribal ownership. As discussed in chapter 7, the Supreme Court ultimately upheld the law, affirming that all reservation minerals belonged to the Northern Cheyenne, and by implication, the Crow as well. *Northern Cheyenne v. Hollowbreast,* 425 U.S. 649 (1976); see chapter 7, note 6 and accompanying text.

8. As to tribal governance under the 1948 constitution, see Crow Tribe, *Crow Tribal Report, Presented to the American Indian Policy Review Commission* (Crow Agency, MT: Crow Tribal Council, 1976), 77–78 and 86–87. For how this "open council" form of government led to Crow factionalism, see ibid., 76–87, and Hoxie, *Parading through History,* chapter 8.

9. The resolution creating the Oil and Gas Committee is at Fred Froze, "Resolution," November 13, 1952, Eloise Whitebear Pease Collection, 16:54, LBC Archives. Subsequent clarification of this committee's powers is found at John Cummins, "Resolution No. 64-09, Resolution of the Crow Tribal Council Granting

Power to the Oil and Gas Committee to Transact Business and for Other Purposes," July 13, 1963, Eloise Whitebear Pease Collection, 16:54, LBC Archives; and James Torske to Westmoreland Resources, February 18, 1972, Eloise Whitebear Pease Collection, 16:54, LBC Archives.

10. For local media coverage of the emerging demand for Crow coal, see "Indians Could Be Big Winners in Coal Boom," *Billings Gazette,* September 14, 1967. The resolution conferring unilateral powers to the tribal chairman is at Edison Real Bird, "Resolution No. 68–2: A Resolution of the Crow Tribal Council Authorizing the Crow Tribal Council Chairman to Issue Prospecting Permits and to Grant Mining Leases of Coal Resources of the Crow Tribe of Indians and for Other Purposes," October 31, 1967, Eloise Whitebear Pease Collection, 16:20, LBC Archives.

11. Thomas Kleppe, "Decision of the Secretary of the Interior Relating to Crow Tribe v. Kleppe, Et Al.," January 17, 1977, 1–3, Eloise Whitebear Pease Collection, 14:37, LBC Archives. Peabody's bonus was $1.00 an acre, Gulf's was approximately $3.50, and Shell paid $12.00 per acre. These figures are not insignificant, but as we well see, none of the companies ever developed their coal rights and thus never provided a steady, lucrative revenue stream to the Crow tribe.

12. The act transferring Crow land in the Ceded Strip to the federal government is at Act of April 27, 1904, Public Law 58–183, 33 Stat. 352 (1904). Although negotiated in 1899, this transaction was not formalized until several years later, when Congress unilaterally adjusted the payment terms. For the negotiations leading to the land cession and Congress's alteration of the terms, see Hoxie, *Parading through History,* 233–39. The act transferring mineral rights back to the Crow is at Act of May 19, 1958, Public Law 85–420, 72 Stat. 121 (1958). For a helpful review of the Ceded Strip's convoluted history, see *Crow Tribe of Indians v. U.S.,* 657 F. Supp. 573 (D. Mont., 1985), 575–78. To be clear, though the tribe owned mineral rights in the Ceded Strip and the federal government acted as a trustee over these subsurface rights, the surface area was not part of the reservation. See *Crow Tribe v. Montana,* 650 F.2d 1104, 1107 (9th Cir. 1981) (noting the opinion in *Little Light v. Crist,* 649 F.2d 682, 685 [9th Cir. 1981]) that "the ceded area is not a part of the reservation").

13. For the negotiations between Norsworthy & Reger, the Crow tribe, and the BIA that resulted in an oral auction for Crow coal rights, see Jase Norsworthy to J. O. Jackson, September 5, 1969, Central Classified Files, 1958–75, Crow, decimal #323, box 38, RG 75, National Archives, Washington, DC; Office of Area Director to Commissioner of Indian Affairs, September 29, 1969, Central Classified Files, 1958–75, Crow, decimal #323, box 38, RG 75, National Archives, Denver; A. F. Czarnowsky, Regional Mining Supervisor, to Area Realty Officer, September 30, 1969, Central Classified Files, 1958–75, Crow, decimal #323, box 38, RG 75, National Archives, Washington, DC; and George Hubley, Commissioner of Indian Affairs to Area Director, Billings Area, October 20, 1969, Central Classified Files, 1958–75, Crow, decimal #323, box 38, RG 75, National Archives, Washington, DC. To be clear, oral bidding was available only to firms that had first submitted sealed, written bids. Bruce Ennis to Louis R. Bruce, July 17, 1970, Central Classified Files, 1958–75, Crow, decimal #323, box 38, RG 75, National Archives, Washington, DC. Recall that the following month, in October 1970, Northern

Cheyenne Tribal President Allen Rowland demanded the same oral auction procedure for his tribe's third, final, and most lucrative coal sale. See chapter 3, note 16 and accompanying text. The results of the Crow's third coal sale are at Bureau of Indian Affairs, "Abstract of Sealed and Oral Bids on Coal Sale #3," September 16, 1970, Central Classified Files, 1958–75, Crow, decimal #323, box 38, RG 75, National Archives, Washington, DC; and BIA Regional Office to Commissioner of Indian Affairs, September 22, 1970, Central Classified Files, 1958–75, Crow, decimal #323, box 38, RG 75, National Archives, Washington, DC.

14. For the various per cap distributions following the Crow's coal sales, see Edison Real Bird, "Resolution No. 68–21: A Resolution Providing for the Appropriation of Tribal Funds for Social and Economic Purposes," April 13, 1968, Eloise Whitebear Pease Collection, 16:20, LBC Archives; Edison Real Bird, "Resolution 68–31: A Resolution of the Crow Tribal Council Providing for the Appropriation of Tribal Funds for Social and Economic Purposes," April 26, 1968, Eloise Whitebear Pease Collection, 16:4, LBC Archives; and James Canan to Edison Real Bird, October 16, 1970, John Melcher Papers, series 1, box 113, folder 12, Mansfield Library, University of Montana.

15. For Westmoreland's acquisition of Norsworthy & Reger coal rights and Crow water rights, see A. E. Bielefeld to Norsworthy & Reger, May 19, 1971, Westmoreland Coal Company Records, Acc. #1765, "Sarpy Creek, Land Questions, 8–71–6-73, WE3FEB2," box 830, Hagley Museum and Library, Wilmington, DE (hereafter Hagley Museum); United States Bureau of Reclamation, "Contract among the United States, Norsworthy & Reger, and Westmoreland Resources to Assist Contract No. 14–06–600–329A for Furnishing Water for Industrial Use," July 22, 1971, Westmoreland Coal Company Records, Acc. #1765, "Sarpy Creek, Land Questions, 8–71–6-73, WE3FEB2," box 830, Hagley Museum; R. L Freeman to Charles Stewart, October 22, 1971, Eloise Whitebear Pease Collection, 17:8, LBC Archives; Lucille Cooke to Walter Fenney, November 16, 1971, Eloise Whitebear Pease Collection, 17:8, LBC Archives; and Clarence Stewart, "Resolution of the Crow Tribal Mineral Committee," January 25, 1972, Eloise Whitebear Pease Collection, 17:8, LBC Archives. For constructing a railroad line to the Ceded Strip and unifying Westmorland's leases, see Eloise Pease, "Annual Overall Economic Development Program Progress Report (For the Calendar Year 1971)," 1972, 4, Eloise Whitebear Pease Collection, 7:7, LBC Archives; Eloise Pease, "Meeting of Mineral Committee [Handwritten] Minutes," February 4, 1972, Eloise Whitebear Pease Collection, 16:57, LBC Archives; Ralph E. Moore to Mineral Committee, June 2, 1972, Westmoreland Coal Company Records, Acc. #1765, "Misc. Correspondence, 1974–76," box 837, Hagley Museum; and United States Bureau of Indian Affairs, "Coal Mining Lease Indian Lands, Contract No. 14–20–0252–3863," June 6, 1972, Eloise Whitebear Pease Collection, 16:66, LBC Archives. For coverage of the royalty negotiations and the tribe's rejection of the amended terms, see Pease, "Meeting of Mineral Committee [Handwritten] Minutes"; Minturn Wright to Pemberton Hutchinson, May 8, 1972, Westmoreland Coal Company Records, Acc. #1765, "Sarpy Creek, Land Questions, 8–71–6-73, WE3FEB2," box 830, Hagley Museum; Theodore Voorhees to Louis R. Bruce, May 9, 1972, Westmoreland Coal Company Records, Acc. #1765, "Sarpy Creek, Land Questions, 8–71–6-73, WE3FEB2," box 830, Hagley Museum; and "Memorandum:

Westmoreland Resources," October 22, 1972, Westmoreland Coal Company Records, Acc. #1765, "Land Questions, 7–73 to 3–75, WR3FEB2," box 830, Hagley Museum. To be clear, Westmoreland was not the only energy company that elected to transform its prospecting permit into a lease. Shell and AMAX also decided to "go to lease" in summer 1972, but these companies were much further away from beginning actual mining operations. With their prospecting permits set to expire, it appears AMAX and Shell determined to take leases and simply pay the Crow penalties under their contracts' minimum production requirements in lieu of forfeiting all rights to Crow coal. United States Bureau of Indian Affairs, "Coal Mining Lease Indian Lands, Contract No. 14–20–0252," June 5, 1972, Eloise Whitebear Pease Collection, 17:26, LBC Archives; United States Bureau of Indian Affairs, "Coal Mining Lease Indian Lands, Contract No. 14–20–0252–3863"; and United States Bureau of Indian Affairs, "Coal Mining Lease Indian Lands, Contract No. 14–20–0252–3917," September 12, 1972, Eloise Whitebear Pease Collection, 16:66, LBC Archives.

16. Internal Westmoreland correspondence documents this dispute within the tribe over the terms of their deal. According to Westmoreland officials, the BIA was especially wary of approving any lease terms that might contradict the desires of a large portion of the Crow tribe, thus Westmoreland executives expended considerable efforts to demonstrate to the BIA why the amendments to their coal contract were necessary to make their projects viable and that the Crow tribe was fully informed and supported these changes. Minturn Wright to Pemberton Hutchinson, May 4, 1972, Westmoreland Coal Company Records, Acc. #1765, "Sarpy Creek, Land Questions, 8–71–6–73, WE3FEB2," box 830, Hagley Museum; Minturn Wright to Pemberton Hutchinson, May 8, 1972; and Theodore Voorhees to Louis R. Bruce, May 9, 1972. David Stewart's new list of demands to Westmoreland are detailed at "Memorandum: Westmoreland Resources," October 22, 1972, Westmoreland Coal Company Records, Acc. #1765, "Land Questions, 7–73 to 3–75, WR3FEB2," box 830, Hagley Museum.

17. In *Davis v. Morton*, the Tenth Circuit Court of Appeals rejected the BIA's stance that the National Environmental Policy Act did not apply to the issuance of Indian mineral leases. 469 F.2d 593 (10th Cir. 1972). Westmoreland communication with BIA officials, who then were tasked with preparing the required environmental analyses, makes clear that the BIA was prepared to delay its report due to Crow dissatisfaction with the current royalty. Theodore Voorhees to Pemberton Hutchinson, March 15, 1973, 2 and 6, Westmoreland Coal Company Records, Acc. #1765, "Legal Correspondence, 1974–76," box 836, Hagley Museum. As for Crow intervention into the Sierra Club suit, Westmoreland's payment of attorney's fees, and Crow demands for advanced royalties, see Charles Brinley, "Westmoreland Resources Meeting Minutes," September 13, 1973, Westmoreland Coal Company Records, Acc. #1765, "Directors' Meetings, 1–71 to 9–81, #58.04," box 831, Hagley Museum; Pemberton Hutchinson to Evalyn Carson, September 21, 1973, Westmoreland Coal Company Records, Acc. #1765, "Sierra Club v. Morton, et al., 9/73–1/76, #350.10" box 832, Hagley Museum; and Pemberton Hutchinson to Partners, September 21, 1973, Westmoreland Coal Company Records, Acc. #1765, "Sierra Club v. Morton, et al., 9/73–1/76, #350.10," box 832, Hagley Museum. Hutchinson's comment about not wanting the Crow to develop Cheyenne

attitudes is at Pemberton Hutchinson to Partners, June 18, 1973, 2, Westmoreland Coal Company Records, Acc. #1765, "Land Questions, 7–73 to 3–75, WR3FEB2," box 830, Hagley Museum; see also Charles Brinley, "Westmoreland Resources Meeting Minutes," May 17, 1973, 3, Westmoreland Coal Company Records, Acc. #1765, "Directors' Meetings, 1–71 to 9–81, #58.04," box 831, Hagley Museum. Additional correspondence making clear tribal support for the Ceded Strip's environmental impact statement depended on securing higher royalties is at Daniel Israel to Pemberton Hutchinson, January 30, 1974, Westmoreland Coal Company Records, Acc. #1765, "Land Questions, 7–73 to 3–75, WR3FEB2," box 830, Hagley Museum; Charles Brinley to Partners, February 1, 1974, Westmoreland Coal Company Records, Acc. #1765, "Land Questions, 7–73 to 3–75, WR3FEB2," box 830, Hagley Museum; Pemberton Hutchinson to Daniel Israel, February 14, 1974, Westmoreland Coal Company Records, Acc. #1765, "Land Questions, 7–73 to 3–75, WR3FEB2," box 830, Hagley Museum; and Charles Brinley, "Westmoreland Resources Meeting Minutes," March 13, 1974, Westmoreland Coal Company Records, Acc. #1765, "Misc. Correspondence, 1974–76," box 837, Hagley Museum. This correspondence also makes clear that the federal government was withholding final issuance of the environmental analysis until the tribe secured satisfactory royalties.

18. "Coal (Crow) Agency," October 1973, 1, Joseph Medicine Crow Collection, 24:12, LBC Archives.

19. Crow Tribe Community Action Program, "Crow Coal Survey and Preliminary Social Impact Report," October 1973, 2–3, Eloise Whitebear Pease Collection, 16:52, LBC Archives.

20. David Stewart, "Resolution No. 74–09: A Resolution of the Crow Tribal Council Providing for the Election of a Mineral Committee of the Crow Tribe, Defining the Powers and Duties of Said Mineral Committee, Rescinding and Repealing Any and All Resolutions Heretofore Passed and Adopted by the Crow Tribal Council Which Are in Conflict with the Provisions of This Resolution, and for Other Purposes," October 13, 1973, 2, Eloise Whitebear Pease Collection, 22c:3:1, LBC Archives. Although the enacting resolution unambiguously charged the Minerals Committee with handling all mineral development, a subsequent resolution gave the committee more specific directions for negotiating with Westmoreland. Tribal attorney Thomas Lynaugh later argued that this subsequent resolution limited the Minerals Committee's authority to dealing only with the Westmoreland lease. "Resolution No. 74–17: A Resolution of the Crow Tribal Council Authorizing the Mineral Committee of the Crow Tribe to Take Certain Actions, and for Other Purposes," January 12, 1974, Eloise Whitebear Pease Collection, LBC Archives; and Thomas Lynaugh to Bud Lozar, November 8, 1976, Eloise Whitebear Pease Collection, 16:19, LBC Archives.

21. Israel's first meeting with the Mineral Committee is documented in Eloise Pease, "Mineral Committee Meeting [Handwritten] Minutes," December 4, 1973, 1, Eloise Whitebear Pease Collection, 16:52, LBC Archives. As to Israel's coordination with the Crow's community action program, see Daniel Israel to Ken Toineeta, December 13, 1973, Eloise Whitebear Pease Collection, 16:57, LBC Archives. In July 1973, the Crow had received a $125,000 grant from the Department of Health,

Education, and Welfare to study the best method for managing their coal resources. Caspar Weinberger to Lee Metcalf, January 23, 1974, Eloise Whitebear Pease Collection, 16:52, LBC Archives. The hired consultants' assessment of past deals and their advice to the Crow is at Daniel Israel, "Memorandum: Meeting with Carmel Patton on November 28, 1973," November 29, 1973, 1, Eloise Whitebear Pease Collection, 16:57, LBC Archives.

22. For the Crow's strategy to focus on the Westmoreland deal and use it as the basis for subsequent negotiations, see Daniel Israel to Crow Mineral Committee, December 20, 1973, Eloise Whitebear Pease Collection, 16:57, LBC Archives. For the actual negotiations, see Daniel Israel to Pemberton Hutchinson, February 8, 1974, Westmoreland Coal Company Records, Acc. #1765, "Land Questions, 7–73 to 3–75, WR3FEB2," box 830, Hagley Museum; Pemberton Hutchinson to Partners, February 8, 1974, Westmoreland Coal Company Records, Acc. #1765, "Land Questions, 7–73 to 3–75, WR3FEB2," box 830, Hagley Museum; Pemberton Hutchinson to Daniel Israel, February 14, 1974; Pemberton Hutchinson to Partners, March 1, 1974, Westmoreland Coal Company Records, Acc. #1765, "Land Questions, 7–73 to 3–75, WR3FEB2," box 830, Hagley Museum; Pemberton Hutchinson to Dan Israel, March 11, 1974, Eloise Whitebear Pease Collection, 16:54, LBC Archives; and Eloise Pease and Pemberton Hutchinson, "Memorandum of Understanding," March 13, 1974, Eloise Whitebear Pease Collection, 16:35, LBC Archives. Israel's quote is at Dan Israel and Dale Emling to Crow Mineral Committee and Crow Tribal Leaders, May 20, 1974, Westmoreland Coal Company Records, Acc. #1765, "Land Questions, 7–73 to 3–75, WR3FEB2," box 830, Hagley Museum. For tribal meetings that resulted in postponing a decision on the Westmoreland amended contract, see Pemberton Hutchinson to Partners, March 25, 1974, Westmoreland Coal Company Records, Acc. #1765, "Land Questions, 7–73 to 3–75, WR3FEB2," box 830, Hagley Museum; and Pemberton Hutchinson to Partners, April 9, 1974, Westmoreland Coal Company Records, Acc. #1765, "Land Questions, 7–73 to 3–75, WR3FEB2," box 830, Hagley Museum. For additional consultants advising the Mineral Committee and Crow candidates, see P. J. Stevens to Robert Howe, April 10, 1974, Westmoreland Coal Company Records, Acc. #1765, "Misc. Correspondence, 1974–76," box 837, Hagley Museum; Charles Beasley to Alex Birdinground, April 16, 1974, Eloise Whitebear Pease Collection, 16:48, LBC Archives; Pemberton Hutchinson to Partners, April 18, 1974, Westmoreland Coal Company Records, Acc. #1765, "Land Questions, 7–73 to 3–75, WR3FEB2," box 830, Hagley Museum; Charles Brinley to Partners, May 2, 1974, Westmoreland Coal Company Records, Acc. #1765, "Land Questions, 7–73 to 3–75, WR3FEB2," box 830, Hagley Museum; and Dan Israel and Dale Emling to Crow Mineral Committee and Crow Tribal Leaders, May 20, 1974. The decision to postpone any vote on Westmoreland's deal until after tribal elections is at Eloise Pease to Crow Tribal Members, May 3, 1974, Eloise Whitebear Pease Collection, 16:54, LBC Archives. Finally, Howard Frey's bloody tomahawk is found in Pemberton Hutchinson to Partners, April 9, 1974.

23. For the May 1974 election turnout, see Eloise Pease to Members of the Crow Tribe, May 14, 1974, Westmoreland Coal Company Records, Acc. #1765, "Land Questions, 7–73 to 3–75, WR3FEB2," box 830, Hagley Museum. Stands Over

Bull's quote is in Donald Fixico, *The Invasion of Indian Country in the Twentieth Century: American Capitalism and Tribal Natural Resources* (Boulder: University of Colorado Press, 1998), 146. The mining moratorium resolution is at Patrick Stands Over Bull, "Resolution No. 75–06A: A Resolution Providing General Direction on Matters Concerning Pending Coal Development on Tribally Owned Coal Resources and on All Coal Resources within the Boundaries of the Crow Indian Reservation," July 13, 1974, Apsaalooke Nation Council and District Records, Crow Tribal Government Building, Crow Agency, MT. For Stands Over Bull's private negotiations with Westmoreland, see Pemberton Hutchinson to Partners, July 8, 1974, Westmoreland Coal Company Records, Acc. #1765, "Misc. Correspondence, 1974–76," box 837, Hagley Museum; and Patrick Stands Over Bull, "Resolution No. 75–12: A Resolution Authorizing a Delegation of the Crow Tribal Council to Negotiate Specific Matters in Order to Obtain a Final Agreement on Tracts 2 and 3," October 12, 1974, Apsaalooke Nation Council and District Records, Crow Tribal Government Building, Crow Agency, MT.

24. For the amended agreement's terms, see Crow Delegation to Crow Tribal Council, November 3, 1974, Joseph Medicine Crow Collection, 24:12, LBC Archives; Charles Brinley to Partners, November 4, 1974, Westmoreland Coal Company Records, Acc. #1765, "Legal Correspondence, 1974–76," box 836, Hagley Museum; and Patrick Stands Over Bull, "Resolution No. 75–17: A Resolution Approving a Final Agreement between the Crow Tribe of Indians and Westmoreland Resources with Respect to Coal Leases on Tracts 2 and 3," November 23, 1974, Apsaalooke Nation Council and District Records, Crow Tribal Government Building, Crow Agency, MT. The actual tribal council vote was 343 for the amended Westmoreland deal versus 33 opposed.

25. Daniel Israel, "Report on the Shell Coal Lease," December 4, 1974, 2–3, 21–22, Eloise Whitebear Pease Collection, 17:13, LBC Archives (emphasis in original).

26. The tribal poll is at "Crow Tribal Coal Survey, 1975," *Hardin Herald,* April 6, 1975, 1.

27. For Shell's reliance on Crow coal, see Israel, "Report on the Shell Coal Lease," 23–24. Shell's letter to tribal members is at N. J. Isto to Joe Medicine Crow, June 30, 1975, Joseph Medicine Crow Collection, 24:12, LBC Archives; see also Richard H. Geissler, "Crows Criticize 'Fraudulent' Offer," *Billings Gazette,* July 9, 1975.

28. The Coal Office's mandates are at "Crow Tribal Coal Survey, 1975," 1. Examples of information sheets can be found at Office of Coal Research, "Information Sheet #1–75," February 17, 1975, Eloise Whitebear Pease Collection, 17:13, LBC Archives; Office of Coal Research, "Information Sheet #2–75," April 25, 1975, Eloise Whitebear Pease Collection, 16:49, LBC Archives; and Office of Coal Research, "Information Sheet #3–75," June 25, 1975, Eloise Whitebear Pease Collection, 16:1, LBC Archives.

29. Angela Russell to Joe Medicine Crow, August 22, 1975, Joseph Medicine Crow Collection, 24:12, LBC Archives. The participants' survey is at Office of Coal Research, "Black Mesa Site Visit," November 8, 1975, 6–10, Joseph Medicine Crow Collection, 24:12, LBC Archives.

30. Edmund Littlelight, Jr., to *Hardin Herald* Editor, December 17, 1975, Eloise Whitebear Pease Collection, 22c:3:1, LBC Archives.

31. Stands Over Bull's first quote comes from Patrick Stands Over Bull to N. J. Isto, July 3, 1975, Lee Metcalf Papers, General Correspondence, Collection No. 172, box 161, folder 161–5, Montana Historical Society, Digital Library and Archives, Helena, MT. The chairman's public statement is at Patrick Stands Over Bull, "Statement of Patrick Stands Over Bull, Chairman Crow Tribal Council," September 19, 1975, 3, Eloise Whitebear Pease Collection, 16:11, LBC Archives; see also Patrick Stands Over Bull, "Statement from the Crow Tribal Chairman, Patrick Stands," August 29, 1975, 1, Joseph Medicine Crow Collection, 24:12, LBC Archives; and Patrick Stands Over Bull, Tyrone Ten Bear, Jiggs Yellowtail, and Oliver Hugs to Crow Tribal Members, September 19, 1975, Joseph Medicine Crow Collection, 24:12, LBC Archives. For helpful reviews of the tribal ordinances enacted to control coal mining, as well as interpretations of their legality, see Kent Frizzell to Patrick Stands Over Bull, March 22, 1976, Eloise Whitebear Pease Collection, 16:11, LBC Archives; and Department of the Interior Solicitor, "Solicitor to Secretary," October 13, 1976, Joseph Medicine Crow Collection, 4:31, LBC Archives. Stands Over Bull's preconditions for further agreements are found in Patrick Stands Over Bull to Keith Doig, March 12, 1976, Eloise Whitebear Pease Collection, 16:11, LBC Archives; and Patrick Stands Over Bull to Amax Coal Company, March 19, 1976, Eloise Whitebear Pease Collection, 16:11, LBC Archives.

32. Formal protests lodged against the October 1975 Mineral Committee election show that tribal members disputed whether Stands Over Bull properly noticed the special election or instead simply forced through his preferred candidates. "Crow Tribal Response to Protest of the October Quarterly Council Meeting Filed by Robert Howe, Jr.," October 1975, Eloise Whitebear Pease Collection, 22d:1:2, LBC Archives.

33. In spring 1976, Stands Over Bull was negotiating with at least four different coal companies: Westmoreland, Shell, AMAX, and Gulf. See Keith Doig to Pat Stands Over Bull, February 12, 1976, Eloise Whitebear Pease Collection, 17:26, LBC Archives; Patrick Stands Over Bull to AMAX Coal Company, March 19, 1977; R. B. Crowl to Patrick Stands Over Bull, March 24, 1976, Eloise Whitebear Pease Collection, 16:11, LBC Archives; Patrick Stands Over Bull to Charles Brinley, March 25, 1976, Eloise Whitebear Pease Collection, 16:11, LBC Archives; Keith Doig to Patrick Stands Over Bull, March 29, 1976, Eloise Whitebear Pease Collection, 16:11, LBC Archives; Charles Brinley to Patrick Stands Over Bull, March 30, 1976, Eloise Whitebear Pease Collection, 16:11, LBC Archives; and R. J. Gocken to Patrick Stands Over Bull, March 30, 1976, Eloise Whitebear Pease Collection, 16:11, LBC Archives. For tribal members complaining at the spring council meeting about these on-reservation mining negotiations, see "Public Hearing at Crow Tribal Building," March 16, 1976, Eloise Whitebear Pease Collection, 16:11, LBC Archives. As for attacks on Stands Over Bull's coal policy and allegations of public drunkenness, see John Pretty On Top, "So the People May Know!," May 1976, Joseph Medicine Crow Collection, 4:16, LBC Archives. The four candidates opposed to reservation mining were Sargie Howe, Andy Russell, John Pretty On Top, and Jiggs Yellowtail, the last being Stands Over Bull's vice chairman. Joseph Medicine

Crow, "May 8, 1976 Tribal Election Results [handwritten]," May 8, 1976, Joseph Medicine Crow Collection, 4:16, LBC Archives.

34. For a complete history of the fight over the Bighorn River dam, see Megan Benson, "The Fight for Crow Water: Part 1, The Early Reservation Years through the New Deal," *Montana: The Magazine of Western History* 57, no. 4 (Winter 2007): 24–42; and Megan Benson, "The Fight for Crow Water: Part 2, Damming the Bighorn," *Montana: The Magazine of Western History* 58, no. 1 (Spring 2008): 3–23. Ultimately, neither side could claim victory; the tribe decided to sell the land for a dam but never received the full agreed-upon payment. Meanwhile, Northsider leader Robert Yellowtail suffered the indignity of having the dam he opposed named after him. As for pre-reservation Crow divisions, see Hoxie, *Parading through History,* chapter 2. The third major group was a subgroup of the Mountain Crow, known as the Kicked In the Bellies. For the division between and characteristics of the River Crow/Southsiders versus Mountain Crow/Northsiders, see Timothy P. McCleary, "An Ethnohistory of Pentecostalism among the Crow Indians of Montana," *Wicazo Sa Review* 15, no. 1 (Spring 2000): 123; and Mardell H. Plainfeather, "Factionalism among Contemporary Crow Indians," n.d., unpub. manuscript, Little Bighorn College Library, Lame Deer, MT.

35. For Sonny Yellowtail's vote against his father, see Constance J. Poten, "Robert Yellowtail, the New Warrior," *Montana: The Magazine of Western History* 39, no. 3 (July 1, 1989): 40.

36. Frederick Hoxie also argues that generational differences greatly influenced Crow positions on reservation allotment during the early twentieth century. According to Hoxie, older, "long hairs" generally opposed the breakup of communal land, while younger, "short hairs" were more comfortable with individual plots and believed allotment to be the only way to preserve Indian land. Hoxie, *Parading through History,* 260–63. Kindness's quote is found in National Congress of American Indians, *Proceedings from the National Congress of American Indians, Indian Energy Conference, Billings, Montana, August 28–29, 1974,* August 28, 1974, folder "Natural Resources," box 147, no. 4 (reel 71), 30, Native America: A Primary Record, series 2: Assn. on American Indian Affairs Archives, General and Tribal Files, 1851–1983.

37. Kindness's quote is at National Congress of American Indians, *Proceedings from the National Congress of American Indians, Indian Energy Conference,* 29.

38. For details on this protest and quotes of the participants, see Bryce Nelson, "Custer Relative Has No Role in Helping Mark 100th Anniversary of 'Last Stand,'" *Los Angeles Times,* June 26, 1976; Bryce Nelson, "Indians Stalk Custer Ghost: After 100 Years Wounds of Bighorn Still Festering," *Los Angeles Times,* June 25, 1976; and *Akwesasne Notes,* August 1976, 21. For a discussion of the changing and various meanings attached to the Battle of the Little Bighorn site, see Edward Tabor Linenthal, "Ritual Drama at the Little Big Horn: The Persistence and Transformation of a National Symbol," *Journal of the American Academy of Religion* 51, no. 2 (June 1, 1983): 267–81.

39. Lipton's recommendation to establish a Crow operating company is at Charles Lipton to Patrick Stands Over Bull, October 1, 1976, Eloise Whitebear Pease Collection, 16:8, LBC Archives. The Coal Authority's enacting resolution is

at Patrick Stands Over Bull, "Resolution 77–08: A Resolution Setting Forth Terms for Discussions with Off Reservation Energy Companies: Establishing a Crow Coal Authority, Setting Qualifications and Duties for Said Authority: Protecting the Crow Reservation: And Providing for a Per Capita Distribution," October 9, 1976, Apsaalooke Nation Council and District Records, Crow Tribal Government Building.

40. Eloise Pease to Stephen Lozar, October 19, 1976, 3, Eloise Whitebear Pease Collection, 22c:4, LBC Archives; see also Patrick Stands Over Bull to Stephen Lozar, November 12, 1976, Eloise Whitebear Pease Collection, 16:38, LBC Archives. As to the competing bodies negotiating with different mining firms, see Stephen Lozar to Eloise Pease, October 29, 1976, Eloise Whitebear Pease Collection, 22c:4:4, LBC Archives; Thomas Lynaugh to Bud Lozar, November 8, 1976, Eloise Whitebear Pease Collection, 16:19, LBC Archives; and Thomas J. Lynaugh to Crow Tribal Officers, Members of Executive and Minerals Committees, December 13, 1976, Eloise Whitebear Pease Collection, 16:44, LBC Archives. Varying accounts of the violent December 22 meeting are found in Phillip White Clay, "Crow Tribal Special Council Meeting Minutes," December 22, 1976, Eloise Whitebear Pease Collection, 16:43, LBC Archives; Eloise Pease, "Statement of Eloise Pease, Parliamentarian at the Council of December 22, 1976," Eloise Whitebear Pease Collection, 14:15, LBC Archives; and Urban Bear Don't Walk to Ben Reifel, January 24, 1977, 8, Eloise Whitebear Pease Collection, 14:15, LBC Archives. This special council meeting was called after Stands Over Bull's supporters gathered a petition to create yet another minerals committee to conclude negotiations with Shell. At the December 13 executive council meeting that considered the petition, however, anti-coal opponents countered with their own petition to suspend Stands Over Bull. "Executive Committee Meeting Minutes," December 13, 1976, Eloise Whitebear Pease Collection, 14:15, LBC Archives. As to Stands Over Bull's actions to adjourn and leave the meeting, see Patrick Stands Over Bull to Stephen Lozar, December 27, 1976, Eloise Whitebear Pease Collection, 22c:4:4, LBC Archives.

41. The BIA order invalidating Stands Over Bull's suspension is at *Patrick Stands Over Bull and Urban J. Bear Don't Walk v. Billings Area Director, BIA*, 6 IBIA 98 (June 6, 1977), 110. In a clear nod to tribal sovereignty, the Board of Indian Appeals held that the question of Stands Over Bull's suspension was a parliamentary issue that only the tribe could resolve. Because the tribal council never affirmed this action and, in fact, voted down a subsequent suspension resolution on January 8, 1977, the appeals board found the suspension ineffective. The January and April meetings' minutes are at Phillip White Clay, "Quarterly Crow Tribal Council Meeting Minutes," January 8, 1977, Eloise Whitebear Pease Collection, 2c:4:4, LBC Archives; and Phillip White Clay, "Crow Tribal Council Minutes, April 9, 1977," April 9, 1977, Eloise Whitebear Pease Collection, 2c:4:1, LBC Archives. Pease's quote comes from the January meeting, at 2.

42. *Patrick Stands Over Bull and Urban J. Bear Don't Walk v. Billings Area Director, BIA*, 6 IBIA 98 (June 6, 1977), 109.

43. Philip Whiteclay, "Crow Tribal Council Meeting Minutes," July 9, 1977, 2–4, 8, 9, 11, 12, and 17, Eloise Whitebear Pease Collection, 2c:4:2, LBC Archives. The opposition argued the popular practice of walking "through the line" to support

a resolution pressured individuals to follow clan lines rather than vote their conscious, which was at odds with their conception of sovereignty emanating from the free will of the people.

44. Ibid., 15.

CHAPTER 6. TAKING THE FIGHT NATIONAL

1. Department of the Interior News Release (October 3, 1972) (found in *Kleppe v. Sierra Club*, 427 U.S. 390 [1976], Appendix, 132 and 134). For a concise description of the overall project, see *Kleppe*, 427 U.S. at 396–97.

2. Morton's quote is located in Department of the Interior News Release (October 3, 1972) (found in *Kleppe*, 427 U.S. at Appendix, 133). Nixon's April energy address can be accessed at Richard Nixon, "Special Message to Congress on Energy Policy," April 18, 1973, The American Presidency Project, ed. Gerhard Peters and John T. Woolley, http://www.presidency.ucsb.edu/ws/?pid=3817. In his first energy message to Congress, on June 4, 1971, the president called for an increased supply of domestic, "clean" energy. In 1973, the president repeated this call for increased domestic production in dozens of addresses, though the emphasis on clean energy had conspicuously disappeared. The most significant of these 1973 messages were delivered on April 18, June 29, November 7, and November 25. These speeches and remarks are available online at The American Presidency Project, ed. Gerhard Peters and John T. Woolley, www.presidency.ucsb.edu.

3. Native American Rights Fund, "An Unfinished Drama: The Declaration of Indian Independence," *Announcements* 3, no. 2, part 1 (April–June 1975): 28; Native American Natural Resource Development Federation, "Native American Natural Resources Management Program: A Proposal to Provide Management-Development Plans to the Member Tribes of the Native American Natural Resource Development Federation," April 1, 1975, 2–3, series 6: NCAI Committees and Special Issues, box 236, "Energy (General) 1975 [1 of 2]," National Congress of American Indians Collection, National Museum of American Indians Archive Center, Suitland, MD (hereafter NCAI Collection).

4. Native American Rights Fund, "Unfinished Drama," 28–31.

5. Ibid.; Native American Natural Resource Development Federation, "Native American Natural Resources Management Program," 2–5. For Burnette's involvement with the NCAI and his own tribal political career, see Thomas W. Cowger, *The National Congress of American Indians: The Founding Years* (Lincoln: University of Nebraska Press, 1999), 141–48. As for Burnette being the first to conceive of the Trail of Broken Treaties, see Robert Burnette and John Koster, *The Road to Wounded Knee* (New York: Bantam Books, 1974), 195–98; and Paul Chaat Smith and Robert Allen Warrior, *Like a Hurricane: The Indian Movement from Alcatraz to Wounded Knee* (New York: New Press, 1996), 139. For more on the Trail of Broken Treaties and its influence, or lack thereof, on the Northern Cheyenne's protest against energy development, see chapter 4, notes 21–22 and accompanying text.

6. Native American Rights Fund, "Unfinished Drama," 9–35; Native American Natural Resources Development Federation "A Declaration of Indian Rights to the Natural Resources in the Northern Great Plains," quoted ibid., 29.

7. Native American Natural Resource Development Federation, "Native American Natural Resources Management Program," 5.

8. George Crossland to Stuart Jamieson, February 13, 1974, series 6: NCAI Committees and Special Issues, box 238, "Surface Mining Legislation, etc. (Strip Mining) 1974," NCAI Collection; George Crossland to Chuck Trimble, March 25, 1974, 4 and 9, series 6: NCAI Committees and Special Issues, box 235, "Energy (General) 1974 [1 of 2]," NCAI Collection.

9. For the NCAI's founding and early tactics, see generally Cowger, *National Congress of American Indians*. For NCAI's moderate approach in the early 1960s, see ibid., 146–49; and Bradley Shreve, *Red Power Rising: The National Indian Youth Council and the Origins of Native Activism* (Norman: University of Oklahoma Press, 2011), 119 and 208. For a discussion of how the 1964 election of Vine Deloria, Jr., as NCAI's executive director reenergized and redirected the organization toward a more activist bent, see Charles F. Wilkinson, *Blood Struggle: The Rise of Modern Indian Nations* (New York: Island Press, 2005), 106–12. To be clear, even though the NCAI consistently disavowed direct action protests, it was instrumental in forging the Red Power Movement, most specifically by organizing the American Indian Chicago Conference that launched the National Indian Youth Council. Cowger, *National Congress of American Indians*, 133–41; and Shreve, *Red Power Rising*, 89–93. The NCAI's own description of its "industrial show" type approach is at National Congress of American Indians, "A Proposal to the Office of Native American Programs and the Economic Development Administration to Develop and Implement a National Indian Economic Development Program," April 15, 1974, 3, series 6: NCAI Committees and Special Issues, box 235, "Energy Resources Seminar—NCAI," NCAI Collection.

10. National Congress of American Indians, "Proposal to the Office of Native American Programs and the Economic Development Administration," 1–5. NCAI Executive Director Chuck Trimble repeated this explanation for his organization's change in reservation development strategy at the first Indian Energy Conference held in Billings, Montana, on August 28, 1974. National Congress of American Indians, *Proceedings from the National Congress of American Indians, Indian Energy Conference, Billings, Montana, August 28–29, 1974,* August 28, 1974, 7, folder "Natural Resources," box 147, no. 4 (reel 71), Native America: A Primary Record, series 2: Assn. on American Indian Affairs Archives, General and Tribal Files, 1851–1983.

11. Dan Israel and Tom Fredericks to Stu Jamieson, July 19, 1974, series 6: NCAI Committees and Special Issues, box 235, "Energy—Energy Seminar, Billings, Mont., August 28–29, 1974," NCAI Collection; and Dan Israel and Tom Fredericks to Stu Jamieson, July 24, 1974, series 6: NCAI Committees and Special Issues, box 235, "Energy—Energy Seminar, Billings, Mont., August 28–29, 1974," NCAI Collection. As to NARF's influence on the Indian Energy Conference's agenda, compare Dan Israel and Tom Fredericks to Stu Jamieson, July 24, 1974, with "NCAI Sponsors National Indian Energy Resources Conference," *Sentinel: National Congress of American Indians Bulletin* (July–August 1974).

12. National Congress of American Indians, *Proceedings from the National Congress of American Indians, Indian Energy Conference,* 6 and 29.

13. Ford Foundation, Energy Policy Project, *A Time to Choose: America's Energy Future* (Cambridge, MA: Ballinger, 1974), 325. Specifically, the report concluded that, among a host of possible alternatives, "a conservation oriented energy policy provides benefits in every major area of concern—avoiding shortages, protecting the environment, avoiding problems with other nations, and keeping real social costs as low as possible."

14. National Congress of American Indians, *Proceedings from the National Congress of American Indians, Indian Energy Conference*, 8.

15. Ibid., 10–11.

16. Ibid., 16.

17. Ibid., 128.

18. As for the creation of the Federal Energy Office, see Executive Order No. 11748 (December 4, 1973); and Richard Nixon, "Remarks Announcing Establishment of the Federal Energy Office," December 4, 1973, The American Presidency Project, ed. Gerhard Peters and John T. Woolley, http://www.presidency.ucsb.edu/ws/index.php?pid=4060. For the Federal Energy Administration's creation and its duties, see Federal Energy Administration Act of 1974, Public Law 93–275, 88 Stat. 96 (1974); and Executive Order No. 11790 (June 25, 1974), The American Presidency Project, ed. Gerhard Peters and John T. Woolley, http://www.presidency.ucsb.edu/ws/index.php?pid=59130. For background on these and other 1970s energy agencies, see Jack M Holl, *The United States Department of Energy: A History* (Washington, DC: Department of Energy, 1982). As Holl explains, the Energy Reorganization Act of 1974 redefined the roles of several energy agencies and created another entity, the Energy Research and Development Administration, to coordinate federal support of energy research and development. However, despite the seeming transfer of research and development responsibility to this new institution, the FEA continued to support nonfederal efforts to expand domestic production, particularly those taken by energy tribes.

19. Old Coyote's quote is at National Congress of American Indians, *Proceedings from the National Congress of American Indians, Indian Energy Conference*, 129.

20. Trimble's quote is found ibid., 131. Mahkijani's quote is found in National Congress of American Indians, *Proceedings from the 31st Annual Convention of National Congress of American Indians, Workshop Five: Tribal Natural Resources*, October 23, 1974, 9, folder "Natural Resources," box 147, no. 4 (reel 71), Native America: A Primary Record, series 2: Assn. on American Indian Affairs Archives, General and Tribal Files, 1851–1983. Crossland's comments are ibid., 4 and 19.

21. The meetings in Washington, DC, and the letter to President Ford is described in Bob Hanfling, "Final Edition of the Indian Position Paper for John Hill," May 8, 1975, 1, series 6: NCAI Committees and Special Issues, box 236, "Energy (General) 1975 [1 of 2]," NCAI Collection. The request to Zarb is described in Wilkinson, Cragun and Barker, "General Memorandum No. 75–36," April 30, 1975, 1, series 6: NCAI Committees and Special Issues, box 236, "Energy (General) 1975 [2 of 2]," NCAI Collection.

22. The Indian Caucus, "Position Paper of the Indian Caucus, The Federal Energy Administration Consumer Workshop," April 22, 1975, 2, series 6: NCAI Committees and Special Issues, box 238, "FEA [Federal Energy Administration] Energy Meeting 1975," NCAI Collection. The Washington, DC, meeting with Zarb is described in Hazel Rollins to [numerous recipients], June 1975, series 6: NCAI Committees and Special Issues, box 238, "FEA [Federal Energy Administration] Energy Meeting 1975," NCAI Collection; Wilkinson, Cragun and Barker, "General Memorandum No. 75–36"; and Hanfling, "Final Edition of the Indian Position Paper for John Hill," 2.

23. Hazel Rollins to [numerous recipients], June 1975; Wilkinson, Cragun and Barker, "General Memorandum No. 75–36"; "Indian Energy Task Force Forms," *Sentinel: National Congress of American Indians Bulletin* (July 1975); and Hanfling, "Final Edition of the Indian Position Paper for John Hill," 1–3.

24. The Council of Energy Resource Tribes to Frank G. Zarb, September 16, 1975, series 6: NCAI Committees and Special Issues, box 236, "Energy Meeting—Billings, Montana (Ramada Inn) 10/13–14, 1975 I," NCAI Collection; "Indian Energy Tribes Task Force Meeting," September 16, 1975, series 6: NCAI Committees and Special Issues, box 236, "Energy Meeting—Billings, Montana (Ramada Inn) 10/13–14, 1975 II," NCAI Collection; Wilkinson, Cragun and Barker, "General Memorandum No. 75–50," September 24, 1975, series 6: NCAI Committees and Special Issues, box 239, "Task Force on Indian Resource Development and FEA," NCAI Collection; and Marjane Ambler, *Breaking the Iron Bonds: Indian Control of Energy Development* (Lawrence: University Press of Kansas, 1990), 91–94. Lohah's quote is ibid., 91.

25. Compare Council of Energy Resource Tribes, "Organization Charter of Council of Energy Resource Tribes (CERT)," September 16, 1975, 1, series 6: NCAI Committees and Special Issues, box 236, "Energy Meeting—Billings, Montana (Ramada Inn) 10/13–14, 1975 I," NCAI Collection with the Council of Energy Resource Tribes to Frank G. Zarb, September 17, 1975, 1–2. For a brief description of the two separate documents, see also Wilkinson, Cragun and Barker, "General Memorandum No. 75–50." The FEA's influential role in organizing CERT is further evidenced by the fact that agency officials took responsibility for gathering final versions of these foundational documents and circulating them to the energy tribes for final approval. Hazel Rollins to Participants of the September 16 Indian Energy Tribes Task Force Meeting, September 24, 1975, series 6: NCAI Committees and Special Issues, box 236, "Energy Meeting—Billings, Montana (Ramada Inn) 10/13–14, 1975 I," NCAI Collection.

26. Allen Rowland to Charles E. Trimble, September 23, 1975, series 6: NCAI Committees and Special Issues, box 236, "Energy Meeting—Billings, Montana (Ramada Inn) 10/13–14, 1975 I," NCAI Collection.

27. "National Congress of American Indians, Energy Meeting, Billings, Montana, October 13–14, 1975," October 13, 1975, 19, 33, 35, 37, series 6: NCAI Committees and Special Issues, box 236, "Energy Meeting—Billings, Montana (Ramada Inn) 10/13–14, 1975 II," NCAI Collection. Frederick's line-by-line analysis is found ibid., 29–41. This conversation continues in part 2 of the proceedings,

and a marked-up copy indicating the changes is attached as a "supplement." All documents are found in the same location in the archives.

28. Ambler, *Breaking the Iron Bonds,* 95–96. CERT initially requested $1 million in federal funds for its resource inventory but received only $200,000. As we will see, the reluctance of the federal government to fully fund CERT's endeavors pushed the organization to look elsewhere—including to OPEC—for additional support.

29. For Carter's emphasis on energy policy during his first ninety days in office, see Daniel Yergin, *The Prize: The Epic Quest for Oil, Money, and Power* (New York: Simon and Schuster, 1991), 661–64. For MacDonald's frustration with the lack of federal support and the conflict between FEA and BIA, see Ambler, *Breaking the Iron Bonds,* 95; Bill Strabala, ""Indian Tribes Seek to Form OPEC-Style Energy Cartel" *Denver Post,* July 10, 1977; "U.S. Indians Ask OPEC, Third World Nations to Help in Developing Resources," *Washington Post,* July 10, 1977; and William Greider, "Indians Organize Own Energy Combine: Patterned after OPEC," *Washington Post,* July 17, 1977. According to Ambler, the BIA argued it was already conducting an inventory of Indian resources and that such an action was not within the FEA's mandate. Ultimately, the FEA would provide $250,000 for this initial resource inventory, and the BIA reluctantly offered an additional $200,000 for establishing an "energy information clearinghouse." MacDonald's quotes are at Strabala, "Indian 'OPEC' Formed; Navajo Leader Tells Why," *Denver Post,* July 10, 1977.

30. The full text of Carter's April 1977 address can be found at Jimmy Carter, "Address to the Nation on Energy," April 18, 1977, The American Presidency Project, ed. Gerhard Peters and John T. Woolley, http://www.presidency.ucsb.edu/ws/?pid=7369. The CERT statement is at Council of Energy Resource Tribes, "Statement of the Council of Energy Resource Tribes (CERT)," April 8, 1977, series 6: NCAI Committees and Special Issues, box 239, "Energy Meeting—White House, 4/8/77 and Related Energy Material," NCAI Collection.

31. Numerous reputable newspapers reported on the CERT-OPEC meetings, though it is unclear whether MacDonald was their only source. Bill Strabala, "Indian Tribes Seek to Form OPEC-Style Energy Cartel" *Denver Post,* July 10, 1977; "U.S. Indians Asks OPEC, Third World Nations to Help in Developing Resources," *Washington Post,* July 10, 1977; William Greider, "Indians Organize Own Energy Combine: Patterned after OPEC," *Washington Post,* July 17, 1977; and William Endicott, "Indians Seek Help from OPEC: Ask for Advice on Development of Energy Resources," *Los Angeles Times,* October 16, 1977. Winona LaDuke later questioned whether these meetings ever took place or whether rumors of the meetings were spread by MacDonald as part of his grand strategy to gain federal support. Winona LaDuke, "The Council of Energy Resource Tribes," in Joseph Jorgensen, *Native Americans and Energy Development II* (Boston: Anthropology Resource Center and Seventh Generation Fund, 1984), 59. MacDonald's quote on "federal red tape and foot dragging" comes from Endicott, "Indians Seek Help from OPEC." MacDonald's insistence on seeking long-range technical help comes from "U.S. Indians Asks OPEC," *Washington Post,* July 10, 1977, wherein MacDonald also noted: "We've found how (energy) companies have dealt with [OPEC nations]

in the past—bad leases and one-sided operations. We wanted to see if they could give us some technical assistance we can't get from the United States government." For MacDonald's use of anticolonial rhetoric to bolster his support on the Navajo Reservation, see Todd Andrew Needham, "Power Lines: Urban Space, Energy Development and the Making of the Modern Southwest" (PhD diss., University of Michigan, 2006), 326–30; see also chapter 2, notes 40–41 and accompanying text. MacDonald's quote to the *Navajo Times* is at Jim Benally, "Navajos, Arab-Style, to Cash in on Resources," *Navajo Times,* March 13, 1974 (quoted in Needham, "Power Lines," 335).

32. For the public backlash against CERT generally, see Ambler, *Breaking the Iron Bonds,* 96–99. For the various causes and impacts of this Second Energy Crisis, see Yergin, *Prize,* 674–98.

33. For CERT's 1978 financial requests to the federal government, see Gaylord Shaw, "Tribes Put Off on Bid for Resource Aid: Indians May Go Back to OPEC," *Los Angeles Times,* February 15, 1978; see also "Tribes Seek Fuel-Catalog Grant," *Arizona Republic,* November 20, 1978. As to CERT's 1979 requests, reports differ whether the organization sought $700 million over ten years or $60 million per year. Compare Council of Energy Resource Tribes, "$24 Million," *CERT Report* 2, no. 5 (March 17, 1980): 3, with Mark Potts, "Tribes Mining Independence: Energy Resource Bring Change," *Chicago Tribune,* February 3, 1980. The *Denver Post* editorial is at "Indians in OPEC?" *Denver Post,* August 13, 1979.

34. Carter's full address is at Jimmy Carter, "Address to the Nation on Energy and National Goals: 'The Malaise Speech,'" July 15, 1979, The American Presidency Project, ed. Gerhard Peters and John T. Woolley, http://www.presidency.ucsb .edu/ws/?pid=32596. Peter MacDonald's correspondence is at Peter MacDonald to President Carter, July 20, 1979 (quoted in Ambler, *Breaking the Iron Bonds,* 100).

35. Ambler, *Breaking the Iron Bonds,* 100–101; and Council of Energy Resource Tribes, "$24 Million," *CERT Report* 2, no. 5 (March 17, 1980): 3. CERT and others quickly pointed out that not all the $24 million represented new federal commitments and that much of this money was simply redirected from other Indian programs. Still, earmarking these funds specifically for Indian energy development represented a major coup for the energy tribes.

36. Ambler's quote is at Ambler, *Breaking the Iron Bonds,* 102. LaDuke's description of disgruntled Navajo tribal members is in Winona LaDuke, "The Council of Energy Resource Tribes," in Jorgensen, *Native Americans and Energy Development II,* 60. Gabriel's quote is at Ambler, *Breaking the Iron Bonds,* 101.

37. CERT's statement that federal funds would flow directly to tribes is at Council of Energy Resource Tribes, "$24 Million." For CERT's shifting tactics to focus on technical assistance, including moving staff to the Denver office, and their success in obtaining funds, see Marjane Ambler, "Uncertainty in CERT," in Jorgensen, *Native Americans and Energy Development II,* 71–74. Stone's quote also comes from ibid., at 74.

38. Even though CERT helped obtain the funding and feasibility studies for several Indian energy projects, many, like the Crow's synthetic fuel facility, were never constructed. Council of Energy Resource Tribes, "Synfuels Awards," *CERT Report* 2, no. 13 (July 18, 1980): 4–5; Dan Jackson and Charlene McGrady, "Mine

Development on U.S. Indian Lands," *Engineering and Mining Journal* (January 1980); and Ambler, "Uncertainty in CERT," in Jorgensen, *Native Americans and Energy Development II,* 75–76.

39. Winona LaDuke, "The Council of Energy Resource Tribes," in Jorgensen, *Native Americans and Energy Development II,* 62–63.

40. Gabriel's comments and Baker's quote are in Ambler, "Uncertainty in CERT," in Jorgensen, *Native Americans and Energy Development II,* 73, and 76–77.

CHAPTER 7. RECOGNIZING TRIBAL SOVEREIGNTY

1. For putting the federal grant money to work, see Daniel Israel, "New Opportunities for Energy Development on Indian Reservations," *Mining Engineering* (June 1980): 652. The 1980 proposed regulations are found at Indian Mineral Development Regulations, 45 Fed. Reg. 53164 (proposed August 11, 1980) (to be 25 C.F.R. § 171.4 and § 182.9), 53166 and 53175. To be clear, these proposed regulations did not include a section on coal mining on Indian lands, as the DOI determined to separate out this mineral for regulation under a separate provision. The agency, however, did not issue proposed new regulations for coal until after the passage of the 1982 Indian Mineral Development Act, when the entire regulatory structure was amended to comply with new tribal powers afforded by that act. Council of Energy Resource Tribes, "BIA Indian Minerals Rules," *CERT Report* 2, no. 14 (August 29, 1980): 1–2; and Mining Regulations, 48 Fed. Reg. 31978 (proposed July 12, 1983) (to be codified at 25 C.F.R. § 211).

2. Council of Energy Resource Tribes, "CERT Board Meeting," *CERT Report* 2, no. 17 (September 12, 1980): 1 and 3–4.

3. Wilfred Scott's quote comes from ibid., at 1. As for Interior's position on the Northern Cheyenne/ARCO agreement, see Council of Energy Resource Tribes, "ARCO–N. Cheyenne," *CERT Report* 2, no. 18 (September 26, 1980): 2–3.

4. For Martz's qualifications and standing as a leader in natural resource law, see Senate Committee on Energy and Natural Resources, *Clyde O. Martz Nomination,* 96th Cong., 2d sess., May 12, 1980; University of Colorado–Boulder Law School, "Clyde Martz Passes," http://lawweb.colorado.edu/news/showArticle.jsp?id=606 (accessed July 7, 2014); and "Clyde Martz Was Natural-Resources Expert, Who Served Two Presidents," *Denver Post,* June 7, 2010. Martz's statement on the legality of alternative contracts is at Council of Energy Resource Tribes, "Alternative Minerals Contracts Disputed," *CERT Report* 2, no. 18 (September 26, 1980): 1–2.

5. MacDonald's statement is at Council of Energy Resource Tribes, "Alternative Minerals Contracts Disputed," at 2.

6. The 1926 Northern Cheyenne Allotment Act reserved to the tribe all "timber, coal or other minerals, including oil, gas, and other natural deposits" found on the reservation, but provided that after fifty years, these resources "shall become the property of the respective allottees or their heirs." Northern Cheyenne Allotment Act of June 3, 1926, 44 Stat. 690, 691 (1926). As to the 1968 law, see Public Law 90–424, 82 Stat. 424 (1968); Senate Committee on Interior and Insular Affairs, *Granting Minerals, Including Oil, Gas and Other Natural Deposits, on Certain*

Lands in the Northern Cheyenne Indian Reservation, Mont., to Certain Indians, 90th Cong., 2d sess., 1968, S. Rep. 1145, esp. 4–5. For the Supreme Court decision, see *Northern Cheyenne Tribe v. Hollowbreast,* 425 U.S. 649 (1976), esp. 655–56.

7. Compare Alvin M. Josephy, Jr., "Agony of the Northern Plains," *Audubon* 75, no. 4 (July 1973): 87, with Alvin M. Josephy, Jr., "The Murder of the Southwest," *Audubon,* July 1971, 55.

8. The 1970 Clean Air Act's initial implementing regulations are at 40 C.F.R. § 52.21(c)(3)(i), 39 Fed. Reg. 42509 (December 5, 1974). For an explanation of these regulations' impact to tribal governments, see Wilkinson, Cragun and Barker, "General Memorandum No. 74-59," December 27, 1974, series 6: NCAI Committees and Special Issues, box 235, "Energy (General) 1974 [1 of 2]," National Congress of American Indians Collection, National Museum of American Indians Archive Center, Suitland, MD (hereafter NCAI Collection). For Montana's approval of the Colstrip expansion, see Grace Lichtenstein, "Montana Ruling Won by Utilities: 2 Plants Using Strip-Mine Coal Are Approved," *New York Times,* November 22, 1975; and *New York Times,* "Montana Allows 2 Power Plants," June 26, 1976. Allen Rowland's announcement that the Northern Cheyenne intended to reclassify the reservation to Class I standards is at Allen Rowland to Department of Intergovernmental Relations, July 2, 1976, Montana Air Quality Bureau Records, Subject Files, record series 38, box 4, Tribal Assistance Northern Cheyenne Reservation: Prevention of Significant Deterioration (PSD) redesignation (1976–1981), Montana Historical Society, Digital Library and Archives.

9. As to the Northern Cheyenne being the first land manager to request an upgrade in air shed status, see Marjane Ambler, "Northern Cheyenne Ask for Class 1 Air," *High Country News,* August 1976. For the Northern Cheyenne's title of "Environmentalist of the Year," see Elliot Rockler, "Environmentalists of the Year," *Borrowed Times,* January 1977. Transcripts of tribal members testifying in opposition to Colstrip's expansion can be found in the Montana Energy Division Records, 1972–1990, record series 328, box 18, vol. 38, Montana Historical Society, Digital Library and Archives; see also David Robinson, "Northern Cheyenne Landowners Association Statement to the Montana Department of Natural Resources and Conservation Concerning the Proposed Generating Plants, Colstrip 3 and 4," December 14, 1974, 2, Montana Energy Division Records, 1972–1990, record series 328, box 15, Public Hearing File: Colstrip 3 and 4 Proposal—Ashland, Montana Historical Society, Digital Library and Archives. The tribe's official comments are at Tom Scheuneman, "Statement of the Northern Cheyenne Tribe before the State of Montana Department of Natural Resources and Conservation," December 30, 1974, Montana Energy Division Records, 1972–1990, record series 328, box 15, DNRC Public Hearings on Colstrip 3 and 4, Montana Historical Society, Digital Library and Archives (quotes at 3 and 4, emphasis in original). Rowland's quote is found in Northern Cheyenne Research Project and Richard Monteau, *The Northern Cheyenne Air Quality Redesignation Report and Request,* December 11, 1976, in author's possession (emphasis in original).

10. For EPA's denial of Colstrip's expansion permit, see Alan Merson to William H. Coldiron, September 30, 1977, Montana Energy Division Records, 1972–1990, record series 38, box 28, Colstrip Units 3 and 4—Federal Corresp.,

Environmental Protection Agency, Montana Historical Society, Digital Library and Archives; Bill Richards, "Indians Block Electric Plant in Montana," *Washington Post,* June 13, 1978; and "Cheyenne Indians Block Construction of 2 Power Plants," *New York Times,* June 13, 1978.

11. For the Northern Cheyenne's lawsuit and negotiations with Colstrip's owners, see Patrick Dawson, "Is Cheyenne Air for Sale?," *Billings Gazette,* October 1979. Gabriel's comment is at Ed Gabriel, "News and Views," *News and Views* 1, no. 4 (May 5, 1980), folder "Council of Energy Resource Tribes," box 85, no. 11 (reel 26), Native America: A Primary Record, series 2: Assn. on American Indian Affairs Archives, General and Tribal Files, 1851–1983. Dahle's first quote is in Council of Energy Resource Tribes, "Northern Cheyenne," *CERT Report* 2, no. 8 (April 28, 1980): 3. Dahle's second quote comes from Clara Caufield, "Northern Cheyenne Tribe Saw Victories on Energy," *Indianz.com,* April 9, 2014, at http://www.indianz.com/News/2014/013181.asp.

12. For the 1978 shift in the Cheyenne's approach to energy development, see James Boggs, "The Challenge of Reservation Resource Development: A Northern Cheyenne Instance," in Joseph Jorgensen, ed., *Native Americans and Energy Development II* (Boston: Anthropology Resource Center and Seventh Generation Fund, 1984), 221–23. Rowland's quote is in Steve Jessen, "Northern Cheyenne Tribe Fights Mines, Woos Drillers," *Billings Gazette,* September 21, 1980.

13. For the 1978 orientation program, see *Tsistsistas Press* (Lame Deer, MT), September 1978; "Official Agenda: Orientation for the New Tribal Council," September 13, 1978, series 7: U.E.T. (United Effort Trust), box 9, "UET Northern Cheyenne," NCAI Collection. For the background and objectives of the Northern Cheyenne Research Project, see Northern Cheyenne Research Project and Robert Bailey, *Northern Cheyenne Research Project: Life Support Systems, First Annual Report* (Lame Deer, MT: Northern Cheyenne Research Project, 1974), esp. 31–32; and Joe Lamson, *Northern Cheyenne Research Project: Second Annual Report* (Busby, MT: Northern Cheyenne Research Project, 1975), esp. 3–5.

14. Boggs, "Challenge of Reservation Resource Development," in Jorgensen, *Native Americans and Energy Development II,* 221–22.

15. Ibid., 221–23. Little Coyote's quote comes from Len Ackland, "Mineral Wealth Gives Indians a Bargaining Tool to Shape the Future," *Chicago Tribune,* February 22, 1981.

16. Boggs, "Challenge of Reservation Resource Development," in Jorgensen, *Native Americans and Energy Development II,* 223–27.

17. As to Northern Cheyenne advertising for development partners, the response received, and the request for BIA technical assistance, see Allen Rowland to James Badura, February 27, 1980, Select Committee on Indian Affairs, 97th Congress, Legislative Files, box 97-2, Records of the United States Senate, RG 46, National Archives, Washington, DC. For the Northern Cheyenne using its own expertise to evaluate these proposals, see Allen Rowland to Members of the Northern Cheyenne Tribe, December 5, 1980, Select Committee on Indian Affairs, 97th Congress, Legislative Files, box 97-2, Records of the United States Senate, RG 46, National Archives, Washington, DC. As to disputes whether the loss of the NCRP left the tribe with adequate expertise to evaluate proposals, see Boggs, "The

Challenge of Reservation Resource Development," in Jorgensen, *Native Americans and Energy Development II*, 227–29; Ackland, "Mineral Wealth Gives Indians a Bargaining Tool to Shape the Future"; and Len Ackland, "U.S. Lets Indians Make Their Own Deals," *Chicago Tribune*, March 4, 1981. The details of the ARCO deal can be found at Boggs, "Challenge of Reservation Resource Development," 206–8; and Council of Energy Resource Tribes, "ARCO—N. Cheyenne," *CERT Report* 2, no. 18 (September 26, 1980): 2–3. As to the duties of the tribal Oil and Gas Office to monitor ARCO's activities, see Allen Rowland to Bill Benjamin, November 25, 1980, Select Committee on Indian Affairs, 97th Congress, Legislative Files, box 97–2, Records of the United States Senate, RG 46, National Archives, Washington, DC.

18. As to the two referenda, see Senate Select Committee on Indian Affairs, *Hearings on S. 1894*, 97th Cong., 2d sess. (Washington DC: Government Printing Office, February 12, 1982), 86–89; and Council of Energy Resource Tribes, "ARCO—N. Cheyenne," 3. Rowland's and Little Coyote's statements are in Steve Jessen, "Northern Cheyenne Tribe Fights Mines, Woos Drillers," *Billings Gazette*, September 21, 1980. Interior's environmental assessment is summarized in Council of Energy Resource Tribes, "Northern Cheyenne," *CERT Report* 2, no. 19 (October 10, 1980): 5.

19. For a review of the various federally approved alternative contracts since 1975, see Senate Select Committee on Indian Affairs, *Hearings on S. 1894*, 1982, 72; see also Council of Energy Resource Tribes, "Energy Agreements Affected by Joint Venture Bill," *CERT Report* 4, no. 11 (September 13, 1982): 19–20. For details on the Navajo and Blackfeet deals, and the BIA quote, see "Indians Want a Bigger Share of Their Wealth," *Business Week*, May 3, 1976, 100. Black is quoted in Molly Ivins, "Indians' Tribal Chairmen's Group Demanding a Voice in Energy Policy," *New York Times*, August 4, 1979.

20. Senate Select Committee on Indian Affairs, *Hearings on S. 1894*, 70–77. At these spring 1982 hearings, Interior officials identified six negotiated agreements that had been approved under various legal theories. These involved energy projects on the Navajo, Jicarilla Apache, Blackfeet, Crow, and Wind River Reservations and included four oil and gas agreements, one coal contract, and one uranium project. Later that fall, however, CERT identified fifteen negotiated agreements between western tribes and energy companies, eight of which the Department of the Interior had approved, and seven that were being held up until Congress clarified tribal authority to negotiate energy contracts. As opposed to Interior's list of approved contracts, CERT noted that the Crow's 1980 negotiated coal agreement with Shell Oil was never formally approved. Council of Energy Resource Tribes, "Energy Agreements Affected by Joint Venture Bill."

21. Senate Select Committee on Indian Affairs, *Hearings on S. 1894*, 87 and 92; Council of Energy Resource Tribes, "ARCO—N. Cheyenne," 3; and Ackland, "U.S. Lets Indians Make Their Own Deals."

22. For Martz's view on the legality of the Northern Cheyenne-ARCO deal, see Ambler, *Breaking Iron Bonds*, 87. Ambler actually interviewed Martz shortly after his decision. Hiwalker's quote is at Senate Select Committee on Indian Affairs, *Hearings on S. 1894*, 87. As to the process that produced the legislative solution,

see Council of Energy Resource Tribes, "'Alternative Agreements' Bill Passes Both Houses, Awaits Final Actions," *CERT Report* 4, no. 11 (September 13, 1982): 17. Although both the Department of the Interior and Senator Melcher drafted their own versions of the proposed legislation, the two sides shared draft bills and worked cooperatively. See Tim Vollman to Ginny Boylan, May 5, 1981, Select Committee on Indian Affairs, 97th Congress, Legislative Files, box 97–2, Records of the United States Senate, RG 46, National Archives, Washington, DC; Senate Select Committee on Indian Affairs, *Hearings on S. 1894*, 87; and Ambler, *Breaking the Iron Bond*, 88.

23. For Reagan's views on Indian Policy, see George Pierre Castile, *Taking Charge: Native American Self-Determination and Federal Indian Policy, 1975– 1993* (Tucson: University of Arizona Press, 2006), esp. 50–52. After pledging to support the Indian self-determination policy as a candidate, President Reagan did not issue a formal Indian policy statement until 1983. In that message Reagan confirmed his commitment to Indian self-determination, though he noted that "there has been more rhetoric than action." "To reverse this trend," the statement continued, the president would "remov[e] the obstacles to self-government by creating a more favorable environment for the development of healthy reservation economies." In other words, Reagan viewed free markets as the key to self-determination. Ronald Reagan, "Statement on Indian Policy," January 24, 1983, The American Presidency Project, ed. Gerhard Peters and John T. Woolley, http://www.presidency. ucsb.edu/ws/?pid=41665. For Reagan's cuts to federal Indian programs, see Council of Energy Resource Tribes, "Indian Programs Hit Hard in Proposed Budget Cuts," *CERT Report* 3, no. 5 (April 3, 1981): 1–3. These cuts extended beyond agencies typically charged with administering Indian programs, like the BIA and the Indian Health Service, and included deep cuts at the Department of Energy that would remove support for Indian energy projects. See Council of Energy Resource Tribes, "Planned Energy Department Cuts Hit Tribes Hard," *CERT Report* 3, no. 6 (April 24, 1981): 3–4.

24. The Energy Department's cuts and MacDonald's quote are covered in Council of Energy Resource Tribes, "Planned Energy Department Cuts Hit Tribes Hard," 3. For James Watt's recent work with the Mountain States Legal Foundation, see Council of Energy Resource Tribes, "Interior Secretary," *CERT Report* 2, no. 22 (December 19, 1980): 4–5; and Council of Energy Resource Tribes, "Watt Approved as Interior Secretary," *CERT Report* 3, no. 1 (January 23, 1981): 1–2. The case for which Watt filed the amicus brief involved the Jicarilla Apache tribe's authority to tax oil and gas companies operating on their reservation. In a landmark decision for tribal sovereignty, the Supreme Court held that tribal authority to tax "is an essential attribute of Indian sovereignty because it is a necessary instrument of self-government and territorial management." *Merrion v. Jicarilla Apache Indian Tribe*, 455 U.S. 130 (1982), 130.

25. For energy tribes' fight against Reagan's proposed cuts, see Council of Energy Resource Tribes, "Indian Programs Hit Hard in Proposed Budget Cuts"; Council of Energy Resource Tribes, "Planned Energy Department Cuts Hit Tribes Hard"; Council of Energy Resource Tribes, "House Panel Proposes to Restore Indian Budget," *CERT Report* 3, no. 6 (April 24, 1981): 1–2; and Council of Energy

Resource Tribes, "Tribal Leaders Angry over Budget Cuts," *CERT Report* 3, no. 7 (May 26, 1981): 1–2. For tribal reaction to Reagan's proposed reduction in federal Indian programs generally, see Castile, *Taking Charge,* 51–56. For the percentage of CERT's budget tied to federal support, see Ambler, *Breaking the Iron Bonds,* 106. Gabriel's letter is at Ed Gabriel, "Open Letter from Ed Gabriel," September 1981, series 5: Records of Indian Interest Organizations, box 149, "C.E.R.T.," NCAI Collection.

26. Peter MacDonald, "Statement, CERT 1981 Annual Meeting," October 26, 1981, 4 and 9, folder "Council of Energy Resource Tribes," box 85, no. 11 (reel 26), Native America: A Primary Record, series 2: Assn. on American Indian Affairs Archives, General and Tribal Files, 1851–1983. At this gathering, MacDonald also addressed the recent cuts in federal spending. A staunch Republican, Reagan supporter, and proponent of free market principles, the CERT chairman did not oppose the transition from federal to private support for Indian energy development, but he feared the drastic reduction in federal funding could so damage tribal communities as to shake Indians' faith in the private sector. Thus, MacDonald tacitly supported some budgetary "belt-tightening," but he argued for "a little bit of realism, a little bit of political pragmatism with the [free market] ideology that all of us were willing to try out." "I buy the ideology of the private sector and am prepared to back governmental efforts to apply that ideology," MacDonald explained, but "there comes a point when the disparity between reality and ideology is so great that people throw out the baby with the bath water." Ibid., at 4. For other speakers at the CERT annual conference and Halbouty's quote, see Council of Energy Resource Tribes, "It's Time the Private Sector Discovered Indian America, Speakers Tell Tribal Leaders at 1981 CERT Annual Meeting," October 26, 1981, folder "Council of Energy Resource Tribes," box 85, no. 11 (reel 26), Native America: A Primary Record, series 2: Assn. on American Indian Affairs Archives, General and Tribal Files, 1851–1983; and Lynn A. Robbins, "'Doing Business with Indian Tribes': The 1981 Annual Meeting of the Council of Energy Resource Tribes," in Jorgensen, *Native Americans and Energy Development II,* 52–57.

27. MacDonald, "Statement, CERT 1981 Annual Meeting," 1. For more on tribal leaders' improving knowledge of the energy industry and their desire to employ this expertise in private-tribal projects, see Jim Hendon, "Indian Tribes Hope for More Energy Flexibility," *Rocky Mountain News,* October 25, 1981.

28. For coverage of the concluding resolutions and MacDonald's statement, see Council of Energy Resource Tribes, "CERT Board of Directors Calls for an End to Economic Dependence for Indian Tribes," October 28, 1981, folder "Council of Energy Resource Tribes," box 85, no. 11 (reel 26), Native America: A Primary Record, series 2: Assn. on American Indian Affairs Archives, General and Tribal Files, 1851–1983. NARF's opinion regarding tribes' existing authority to enter into alternative contracts is at Richard B. Collins to Council of Energy Resource Tribes, October 13, 1981, Select Committee on Indian Affairs, 97th Congress, Legislative Files, box 97–2, Records of the United States Senate, RG 46, National Archives, Washington, DC. The resolution opposing Melcher's and Interior's bills is at Council of Energy Resource Tribes, "Resolution No. 81–10, Amendment of the 1938 Indian Mineral Leasing Act," October 28, 1981, Select Committee on Indian Affairs,

97th Congress, Legislative Files, box 97–2, Records of the United States Senate, RG 46, National Archives, Washington, DC.

29. In contrast to CERT's and Melcher's proposals, Interior proposed a convoluted process for approving alternative contracts. The agency's bill authorized tribes to negotiate deals, but before they could be approved, the federal government would have to determine whether an agreement conveyed an interest in land. If it did, under Interior's approach, the old 1938 Leasing Act would determine the deal's validity. If, however, Interior found the agreement was not a lease—meaning it did not convey a property interest—then the agency would follow the new law's procedures to determine whether to approve the negotiated contract. Compare Tim Vollman to Ginny Boylan (Interior's draft) with "Senator Melcher of Montana," *Congressional Record* (November 30, 1981): S14127–28 (Melcher's draft), and Richard B. Collins to Council of Energy Resource Tribes, October 13, 1981 (CERT/NARF's draft). The Department of Justice's endorsement is at Robert McConnell to David Stockman, October 20, 1981, 2, Select Committee on Indian Affairs, 97th Congress, Legislative Files, box 97–2, Records of the United States Senate, RG 46, National Archives, Washington, DC. For further details of Melcher's bill, see "Senator Melcher of Montana," *Congressional Record* (November 30, 1981): S14127–28; Council of Energy Resource Tribes, "Sen. Melcher Introduces 'Alternative Agreements' Bill for Tribal Minerals," *CERT Report* 3, no. 16 (December 21, 1981): 1–2; and Association on American Indian Affairs, Inc., "Memorandum No. 81–36, Proposed Tribal Mineral Rights Legislation," December 30, 1981, folder "Legislative and Administrative Memoranda, 1976–1982," box 293, no. 1–6 (reel 3), Native America: A Primary Record, series 3: Assn. on American Indian Affairs Archives, Publications, Programs and Organizational Files, 1851–1983.

30. Harrison's and Burton's quotes are at Senate Select Committee on Indian Affairs, *Hearings on S. 1894,* 34 and 10, respectively. For additional corporate support, see ibid., at 106, 111, and 162.

31. Ibid., 57. For additional opposition to Melcher's bill based on the fear that uneducated Indians would be taken advantage of, see ibid., 121–36; Paul Frye to Jennie Boylan, May 11, 1982, Select Committee on Indian Affairs, 97th Congress, Legislative Files, box 97–2, Records of the United States Senate, RG 46, National Archives, Washington, DC; and Paul Frye to Debby Brokenrope, May 25, 1982, Select Committee on Indian Affairs, 97th Congress, Legislative Files, box 97–2, Records of the United States Senate, RG 46, National Archives, Washington, DC. In addition to opposition based on this fear, other detractors of the bill included a minority faction of Northern Cheyenne opposed to all mineral development, an energy company seeking to ensure that federal courts, not tribal judges, retained jurisdiction over disputes arising from alternative contracts, and state officials seeking to clarify their ability to tax mineral proceeds generated by alternative agreements. Senate Select Committee on Indian Affairs, *Hearings on S. 1894,* 20–26 and 93–103; Terry O'Conner, "Testimony of Terry O'Conner, Director of Legal and Governmental Affairs, Rocky Mountain Division, Peabody Coal Company, on S. 1894," July 27, 1982, series 6: NCAI Committees and Special Issues, box 238, "Mineral Resources—S. 1894," NCAI Collection; Chris Farrand to John Melcher, August 27, 1982, Select Committee on Indian Affairs, 97th Congress, Legislative

Files, box 97–2, Records of the United States Senate, RG 46, National Archives, Washington, DC; and Ted Schwinden to John Melcher, June 15, 1982, Senate Select Committee on Indian Affairs, 97th Congress, 1st sess., Bill Files, box 17, Records of the United States Senate, RG 46, National Archives, Washington, DC. Further, the Northern Cheyenne tribal government opposed the retroactive authorization provision as written because they feared it could be interpreted to imply their ARCO agreement was invalid without congressional approval; or alternatively, the new law could preclude the Northern Cheyenne from later challenging certain provisions of its agreement. Senate Select Committee on Indian Affairs, *Hearings on S. 1894*, 17–19, 86–92; Allen Rowland to John Melcher, March 2, 1982, Senate Select Committee on Indian Affairs, 97th Congress, 1st sess., Bill Files, box 17, Records of the United States Senate, RG 46, National Archives, Washington, DC; and George Hiwalker, "Statement of George Hiwalker, Jr., Vice President, Northern Cheyenne Tribal Council," July 27, 1982, series 6: NCAI Committees and Special Issues, box 238, "Mineral Resources—S. 1894," NCAI Collection. For similar reasons, energy companies with previously executed alternative agreements also opposed the proposed retroactive authorization clause. See Mary Anne Sullivan to John Melcher, September 10, 1982, Select Committee on Indian Affairs, 97th Congress, Legislative Files, box 97–2, National Archives, Washington, DC; and Forest Gerard to William S. Cohen, October 20, 1982, Select Committee on Indian Affairs, 97th Congress, Legislative Files, box 97–2, Records of the United States Senate, RG 46, National Archives, Washington, DC. Ultimately, this provision was amended to establish a set of guidelines the Department of the Interior must use to evaluate past deals for approval, rather than simply providing blanket authorization for all existing alternative agreements. *Indian Mineral Development Act of 1982*, S. 1894, 97th Cong., 2d sess., *Congressional Record* (December 8, 1982): S14194–96; and *Permitting Tribal Agreements to Dispose of Mineral Resources*, S. 1894, 97th Cong., 2nd sess., *Congressional Record* (December 10, 1982): H9440–41.

32. Senate Select Committee on Indian Affairs, *Permitting Indian Tribes to Enter into Certain Agreements for the Disposition of Tribal Mineral Resources and for Other Purposes*, 97th Cong., 2d sess., 1982, S. Rep. 472, 7. Paradoxically, existing law arguably allowed "competent" allottees to negotiate their own mineral leases, even though this new bill would not authorize them to negotiate alternative agreements. Act of March 3, 1909, 35 Stat. 781 (1909), codified as amended at 25 U.S.C. § 396 (1980), implementing regulations at 25 C.F.R. § 172.1–172.33 (1980); see also Senate Select Committee on Indian Affairs, *Hearings on S. 1894*, 121–22 and 126–27.

33. Gabriel's testimony is at Senate Select Committee on Indian Affairs, *Hearings on S. 1894*, 84. The Department of the Interior's letters in support are at Ken Smith to William S. Cohen, March 15, 1982, 2–3, Select Committee on Indian Affairs, 97th Congress, Legislative Files, box 97–2, Records of the United States Senate, RG 46, National Archives, Washington, DC; and Roy H. Sampsel to Morris K. Udall, August 9, 1982, 2–3, Select Committee on Indian Affairs, 97th Congress, Legislative Files, box 97–2, Records of the United States Senate, RG 46, National Archives, Washington, DC.

34. The difference between the Senate and House versions of the bill related largely to the retroactive authorization of past alternative contracts and did not

affect the general thrust of the legislation to recognize tribal authority to negotiate alternative agreements. See Association on American Indian Affairs, Inc., "Memorandum No. 82-20, S. 1894 Status Report," July 30, 1982, folder "Legislative and Administrative Memoranda, 1976–1982," box 293, no. 1–6 (reel 3), Native America: A Primary Record, series 3: Assn. on American Indian Affairs Archives, Publications, Programs and Organizational Files, 1851–1983; Council of Energy Resource Tribes, "'Alternative Agreements' Bill Passes Both Houses, Awaits Final Actions"; and John Melcher to Morris Udall, September 23, 1982, Select Committee on Indian Affairs, 97th Congress, Legislative Files, box 97–2, Records of the United States Senate, RG 46, National Archives, Washington, DC. For Udall's and Bereuter's explanation of the need for an updated law, see *Indian Mineral Development Act of 1982*, S. 1894, 97th Cong., 2d sess., *Congressional Record* (August 17, 1982): H6044–46; and Council of Energy Resource Tribes, "'Alternative Agreements' Bill Passes Both Houses, Awaits Final Actions." Melcher's quote is at *Indian Mineral Development Act of 1982*, S. 1894, 97th Cong., 2d sess., *Congressional Record* (December 8, 1982): S14196. Bereuter's is at *Permitting Tribal Agreements to Dispose of Mineral Resources*, S. 1894, 97th Cong., 2d sess., *Congressional Record* (December 10, 1982): H9440. Also, the House Committee on Interior and Insular Affairs held abbreviated, and largely redundant, hearings in July 1982. No transcript of these hearings was published, but according to staff notes from the National Congress of American Indians, only representatives of the Department of the Interior, the Ute Mountain Utes, the Northern Cheyenne, and Peabody Coal testified. All supported the legislation. Naomi Iizuka, "Notes on House Interior and Insular Affairs Cmte Hearing on Tribal Indian Mineral Resources Agreements," July 27, 1982, series 6: NCAI Committees and Special Issues, Box 238, "Mineral Resources—S. 1894," NCAI Collection.

35. Melcher's quote is in "Sen. Melcher Explains New Indian Mineral Bill," *Williston Basin Report*, January 19, 1983. Reagan's quotes are at Reagan, "Statement on Indian Policy," January 24, 1983, The American Presidency Project, ed. Gerhard Peters and John T. Woolley, 2 and 3–4, at http://www.presidency.ucsb.edu.

EPILOGUE

1. Marjane Ambler, *Breaking the Iron Bonds: Indian Control of Energy Development* (Lawrence: University Press of Kansas, 1990), 107. CERT officials labeled the 1982 annual conference "Indian Energy Development in the New Economic and Legislative Environment" to reflect the major legislative changes working their way through Congress and the altered energy economics caused by a rising glut of global oil supplies. In addition to the impending passage of the 1982 Indian Mineral Development Act, Congress had established a new Minerals Management Service to better track tribal oil and gas production and to ensure tribes received their share of royalties. Ed Gabriel, "Open Letter from Ed Gabriel," October 1982, series 5: Records of Indian Interest Organizations, box 149, "Council of Energy Resource Tribes (CERT)," National Congress of American Indians Collection, National Museum of American Indians Archive Center, Suitland, MD.

2. Council of Energy Resource Tribes, "David Lester Becomes New Executive Director of the Council of Energy Resource Tribes," November 17, 1982, box 43, folder 10, LaDonna Harris Papers and Americans for Indian Opportunity Records, 1953–2010, University of New Mexico, Center for Southwest Research; Marjane Ambler, "New CERT Director Has Made Career Out of Indian Economic Development," *Denver Post,* December 16, 1982. Marjane Ambler argues Reagan's budget cuts greatly influenced CERT's decision to close its DC offices, forcing the organization to prioritize tribal technical assistance over federal lobbying. Ambler, *Breaking the Iron Bonds,* 109–11.

3. Daniel Yergin, *The Prize: The Epic Quest for Oil, Money, and Power* (New York: Simon and Schuster, 1991), 717–22.

4. The Shell decision is at R. M. Rice to Crow Coal Commission, 30 1985, Eloise Whitebear Pease Collection, 17:13, Little Bighorn College Archives, Crow Agency, MT (hereafter LBC Archives). Shell officials also noted that the "continuing uncertainty regarding the application of Montana's severance tax to Crow coal" was another factor inhibiting their ability to proceed. The Supreme Court later clarified that states have the right to impose additional state taxes on Indian resources so long as the tax is not so high as to unfairly damage the marketability of tribal minerals. *Cotton Petroleum v. New Mexico,* 490 U.S. 163 (1989). As to Westmoreland's release, see C. J. Presley to Forest Horn, March 16, 1981, Eloise Whitebear Pease Collection, 16:49, LBC Archives.

5. Ambler, *Breaking the Iron Bonds,* 241–43; see also Garrit Voggesser, "The Evolution of Federal Energy Policy for Tribal Lands and the Renewable Energy Future," in Sherry L. Smith and Brian Frehner, eds., *Indians and Energy: Exploitation and Opportunity in the American Southwest* (Santa Fe: SAR Press, 2010), 69. Voggesser reports the 1982 peak of tribal oil and gas revenues to be $198 million but then notes the drastic fall over the next four years.

6. As to the attempted removal of David Stewart (1972–74), see Pauline Small, "Crow Tribal Council Minutes, January 13, 1973," January 13, 1973, Eloise Whitebear Pease Collection, 22c:3:1, LBC Archives. In chapter 4, I cover in detail the impeachment of Patrick Stands Over Bull (1972–77). For Forrest Horn (1977–82), see "Article of Impeachment against Crow Tribal Chairman Forest Horn," April 1979, Eloise Whitebear Pease Collection, LBC Archives. For Donald Stewart (1982–86), the removal of his executive powers, and a helpful summary of previous impeachment proceedings see Roger Clawson, "Crow Council Deposes Chairman," *Billings Gazette,* April 16, 1985.

7. For energy firms' appeal to the Department of the Interior for clarity, see Joan Davenport to John Bookout, November 15, 1977, Eloise Whitebear Pease Collection, LBC Archives; Joan Davenport to Lowry Blackburn, November 15, 1977, Eloise Whitebear Pease Collection, LBC Archives; and James Joseph to Cale Crowley, November 15, 1977, Eloise Whitebear Pease Collection, LBC Archives. Interior's almost identical response to the energy firms is found at Joan M. Davenport, Department of the Interior acting secretary, to Lowry Blackburn, AMAX Coal Company president, November 15, 1977; Joan M. Davenport, Department of the Interior acting secretary, to John F. Bookout, Shell Oil Company president, November 15, 1977; and Joan M. Davenport, Department of the Interior acting

secretary, to Cale Crowley, attorney for Gulf Oil Corporation and Peabody Coal Company, November 15, 1977, Eloise Whitebear Pease Collection, LBC Archives. The Westmoreland Company continued its mining on the Ceded Strip but supported efforts to have the Department of Energy restructure the Crow's apparatus for dealing with energy companies. Charles Brinley to James Joseph, November 17, 1977, Eloise Whitebear Pease Collection, 7b, LBC Archives. In the Crow's petition to the Energy Department for assistance in amending its government, the tribal attorney actually derided the federal government's reluctance to get involved with internal tribal politics: "The doctrine and the policy of the Congress is to grant 'self-determination' to the Indian people, which quite frankly, is a policy of saying 'go paddle your own canoe.' The canoe won't float with so many holes in it." Harold G. Stanton, Crow attorney, to James Furse, Department of Energy, November 17, 1977, Eloise Whitebear Pease Collection, 7b, LBC Archives.

8. For the disbandment of the Coal Authority, see Forest Horn, "Resolution No. 80–16: A Resolution Pertaining to Coal Negotiations with Shell Oil Company and to Clarify Which Committee and Entity within the Tribe Has the Authority to Continue Negotiations with the Shell Oil Company," January 24, 1980, Apsaalooke Nation Council and District Records, Crow Tribal Government Building, Crow Agency, MT. For passage of the 2001 constitution and the new governing structure, see "Takeover Marks Crow 'New Beginning,'" *Billings Gazette,* January 11, 2001; and "New Crow Constitution Wins Federal Approval," *Helena Independent Record,* December 2, 2001.

9. For Westmoreland's expansion onto the reservation proper, see Shelley Beaumont, "Absaloka Mine South Extension Approved," *Big Horn County News,* October 23, 2008; and Susan Gallagher, Associated Press, "Proposal Would Move Mining onto Crow Reservation," *Helena Independent Record,* April 4, 2008. Old Coyote's quote and revenue figures from the Absaloka Mine are at Darrin Old Coyote, "Testimony of Crow Nation Tribal Chairman Darrin Old Coyote," 3, in House Committee on Natural Resources, Subcommittee on Energy and Mineral Resources, *Oversight Hearing on "Mining in America: Powder River Basin Coal Mining the Benefits and Challenges,"* 113th Cong., 1st sess., July 9, 2013, available at http://docs.house.gov/meetings/II/II06/20130709/101096/HHRG-113-II06-Wstate-OldCoyoteD-20130709.pdf.

10. The Crow Reservation economic figures come from the Harvard Project on American Indian Economic Development, "On Improving Tribal-Corporate Relations in the Mining Sector: A White Paper on Strategies for Both Sides of the Table," April 2014, 87, available at http://hpaied.org/images/resources/general/miningrelations.pdf. In 2013, the Crow granted Westmoreland another lease for an additional 145 million tons of coal adjacent to the company's existing mine in the Ceded Strip. Susan Olp, "Crow Tribe Leases 145 Million Tons of Coal," *Billings Gazette,* April 11, 2013. In 2008, the Crow announced a partnership with the Australian-American Energy Co. to build a coal-to-liquids plant on the reservation that would extract 38,000 tons of Crow coal per day. Fluctuating global oil prices, however, once again caused that project to be restructured to reduce its scale, and as of February 2013, it is unclear whether the tribe will pursue the liquefication project. Erica Gies, "Rich in Coal, a Tribe Struggles to Overcome Poverty," *New*

York Times, October 25, 2011. In January 2013, the Crow announced an agreement with Cloud Peak Energy that would authorize the Wyoming mining company to excavate 1.4 billion tons of coal from the reservation. This coal, which is more than the United States consumes in a year, is earmarked for export to Asian markets, pending approval and construction of coal export ports in the Pacific Northwest. Sue Olp, "Crow Tribe Signs 1.4B Ton Coal Deal with Cloud Peak Energy," *Billings Gazette,* January 24, 2013. Finally, in March 2013, the Crow reached another agreement with Signal Peak Energy to prospect 400 million more tons on the reservation. Associated Press, "Signal Peak Energy Eyes Coal on Crow Reservation," *Billings Gazette,* March 19, 2013.

11. For the uranium moratorium and closures of Black Mesa Mine and Mohave Generating Station, see Dana E. Powell and Dáilan J. Long, "Landscapes of Power: Renewable Energy Activism in Diné Bikéyah," in Sherry L. Smith and Brian Frehner, eds., *Indians and Energy: Exploitation and Opportunity in the American Southwest* (Santa Fe: SAR Press, 2010), 235; and Enei Begaye. "The Black Mesa Controversy," *Cultural Survival Quarterly* 29, no. 4 (Winter 2005). For the failed Desert Rock Energy Project and Navajo Transmission Project, see Powell and Long, "Landscapes of Power," 236–43; Laura Paskus, "The Life and Death of Desert Rock," *High Country News,* August 16, 2010; and Sierra Crane-Murdoch, "On Navajo Nation, Power Authority Slips Away," *High Country News,* April 7, 2011.

12. Winona LaDuke, "Monster Slayers: Can the Navajo Nation Kick the Coal Habit?," *Indian Country Today,* July 31, 2013; Noel Lyn Smith, "Navajo Nation Enters the Coal Mining Business," *Daily Times,* November 2, 2013; Emily Guerin, "Navajo Nation's Purchase of a New Mexico Coalmine Is a Mixed Bag," *High Country News,* January 7, 2014; and Rebecca Fairfax Clay, "Tribe at a Crossroads: The Navajo Nation Purchases a Coal Mine," *Environmental Health Perspectives* 122, no. 4 (April 2014): A104–A107.

13. For ARCO's abandonment of the project and the impact to the tribal economy, see Jim Bruggers, "Energy Slump, Isolation and Turmoil: The Plight of the Northern Cheyenne," *Great Falls Tribune,* November 16, 1986. Tribal President Llevando Fisher recently testified to Congress that Northern Cheyenne unemployment remains above 60 percent. Llevando Fisher, "Statement of Llevando 'Cowboy' Fisher, President, Northern Cheyenne Tribe," 6, in House Committee on Natural Resources, Subcommittee on Indian and Alaska Native Affairs, *Hearing on H.R. 4350: The Northern Cheyenne Lands Act,* 113th Cong., 2d sess., May 7, 2014, available at://naturalresources.house.gov/uploadedfiles/fishertestimony5-7-14.pdf. The 2010 census figures are provided on the tribal government-endorsed blog "A Cheyenne Voice," available at http://acheyennevoice.com/northern-cheyenne.

14. Fisher, "Statement of Llevando 'Cowboy' Fisher," at 5–6.

15. United States Surface Transportation Board, "Section 106 Consultation Meeting for the Tongue River Railroad Construction Project: Transcript of Proceedings," February 13, 2014, 74–75, available at http://www.tongueivereis.com/documents/021314_section_106_transcript.pdf. In this meeting, Llevando Fisher discusses the tribe's 2006 referendum, in which tribal members were asked whether they would rather pursue traditional coal mining or coal bed methane

development. The tribe chose the former. See also David Melmer, "Northern Chey-enne to Vote on Resource Extraction," *Indian Country Today,* November 1, 2006, available at http://indiancountrytodaymedianetwork.com/2006/11/01/northern-cheyenne-vote-resource-extraction-128945. For additional coverage of the impending referendum, see Clara Caufield, "Northern Cheyenne Tribe to Vote on Coal Project," *Indianz.com,* February 24, 2014, available at http://www.indianz.com/News/2014/012639.asp; and Clara Caufield, "Northern Cheyenne Tribe Remains Split on Coal," *Indianz.com,* April 1, 2014, available at http://www.indianz.com/News/2014/013086.asp.

16. Passions over the new constitution ran so high that opponents forcibly, though temporarily, took over tribal offices to prevent its implementation. "Take-over Marks Crow 'New Beginning,'" *Billings Gazette,* January 11, 2001. To those opposed to reservation mining during the 1970s, the biggest concern with the new constitution was that it stifled public participation, preventing tribal members from raising concerns about energy projects negotiated by their leaders. In fact, members of the opposition group that orchestrated Patrick Stands Over Bull's 1977 impeachment claim that had the 2001 constitution been in place during the 1970s, the Crow "would be nonexistent now" because their faction would not have been able to "inform the people" of the dangers of development. John Doyle, Urban Bear Don't Walk, Larry Kindness, Dale Kindness, Dewitt Dillon, interview by the author, August 17, 2009, Crow Agency, MT, in author's possession.

17. Peter Iverson, *Diné: A History of the Navajos* (Albuquerque: University of New Mexico Press, 2002), 250–52; Peter Iverson, *The Navajo Nation* (Westport, CT: Greenwood Press, 1981), 187; and Ambler, *Breaking the Iron Bonds,* 102, 111–12.

18. Ambler, *Breaking the Iron Bonds,* 109–11.

19. Ibid., 113–16.

20. Voggesser, "The Evolution of Federal Energy Policy for Tribal Lands and the Renewable Energy Future," in Smith and Frehner, *Indians and Energy,* 69–72; see also the Harvard Project on American Indian Economic Development, *The State of the Native Nations: Conditions under U.S. Policies of Self-Determination* (New York: Oxford University Press, 2008), 165.

21. Peter MacDonald, "Remarks by Chairman Peter MacDonald, 1983 Annual CERT Meeting," November 18, 1982, 3–5, folder "Council of Energy Resource Tribes," box 85, no. 11 (reel 26), Native America: A Primary Record, series 2: Assn. on American Indian Affairs Archives, General and Tribal Files, 1851–1983.

22. Ibid., 12–13 (emphasis in original).

Index